TRAVERSA

TRAVERSA

Fran Sandham

Duckworth Overlook

London • New York • Woodstock

First published in 2007 by
Duckworth Overlook

LONDON
90-93 Cowcross Street, London EC1M 6BF
Tel: 020 7490 7300
Fax: 020 7490 0080
info@duckworth-publishers.co.uk
www.ducknet.co.uk

NEW YORK
141 Wooster Street, New York, NY 10012

WOODSTOCK
One Overlook Drive, Woodstock, NY 12498
www.overlookpress.com
[for individual orders and bulk sales in the United States,
please contact our Woodstock office]

A catalogue record for this book is available
from the British Library

ISBN 978-0-7156-3702-9 (UK)
ISBN 978-1-59020-036-0 (US)

Typeset by Ray Davies
Printed and bound in Great Britain by
Cromwell Press Ltd, Trowbridge, Wiltshire

Contents

(Illustrations between pages 118 and 119)

Acknowledgements

Thanks to all at Duckworth Overlook. for doing such a good job on the book, especially Caroline McArthur, Suzannah Rich, Ray Davies, Andrew Miller, David Marshall, Nick Webb and Peter Mayer.

Special thanks to the following people for all kinds of help, support and encouragement (grovelling apologies to anyone I've missed out): Adam Deacon; Alex Sullivan; Ali Kane; Becky Goodyear; Daniel May; David (Walvis Bay); David Atkinson (Hand Made Maps, London); Elsa Fuster; Emma Gregg; Eugene Hugo; Geoff Rogers; Guy Pickering and family; Hagen Nordbruch; Harry (Walvis Bay); Jamie Morcan; Jennifer Barclay; Jo Hodder; Katy Follain; Kokkie and Sinta Labuschagne; Louise Beecher; Mark Rogers; Matt McClements; Michelle Bhatia; Mike Brown; Neil Wilson; Niall McGowan; Nick Brealey; Pau Sandham; Peter Taylor; Phil Roscoe; Richard Carmichael; Sadie Mayne; Samuel Wehrli; Sanna Lindstrom; Sharon Martins; Simon Thorogood; Stuart Morton; Suzannah Redshaw; Sylvia Sandham; Wendy Toole; Wynand and Valerie Peypers.

Finally, a big thank-you to all the unnamed individuals in Africa who were kind and hospitable along the way.

Prologue: Swakopmund, Namibia

'But these hats look stupid.'

'It's a stupid walk – you need a stupid hat,' says Hagen.

We're standing in front of a shop window in the Namibian coastal town of Swakopmund, the sixth shop we've visited this afternoon. I need a hat, as tomorrow I start walking across Africa. Unfortunately the only men's hats for sale here are of the large and ridiculous floppy felt variety worn by village idiots back in Hardy's Wessex.

A further hour of searching leads us to the tackiest souvenir kiosk, somewhere I'd pointedly ignored earlier. Here I find a sensible bush hat buried under a mound of objects bearing the legend *I* ♥ *Namibia*. The great African explorers never had to go through this charade – Stanley and Livingstone didn't blaze a trail across the continent wearing *I* ♥ *Darkest Africa* baseball caps.

Hagen, a young German I met only two days ago at Windhoek Airport, has offered to drive me to the Skeleton Coast tomorrow, to the point where I start my journey. By way of mental preparation we spend my last night of freedom getting drunk in a German bar, the jukebox belting out UK chart hits from the late Seventies. Most of the beer in Swakopmund is brewed to German standards so it's not entirely our fault we get sloshed.

'I'll tell you what you need,' says Hagen, draining his glass and looking serious.

'Tell me what I need.' I match his earnest expression as the next round arrives: my walk across Africa is no laughing matter.

'*Gimme, gimme, gimme a man after midnight …*' says the jukebox.

'You need a trolley to carry all your gear.'

I'd already toyed briefly with the idea of some form of trolley, before rejecting it as likely to prove more trouble than it was worth – anyway, people would laugh. But sitting half-pissed in a comfortable bar, far from the desert heat and witty bystanders along the road, a trolley seems worthy of further consideration. The beer flows freely and Hagen warms to his subject: 'If the going gets tough you can sell things from your trolley. Cold drinks, ice cream, hamburgers, souvenirs: whatever you like!' The more I drink, the better the idea sounds. I take another hefty slug of Windhoek Lager and start thinking aloud. A trolley would also mean far less wear and tear on my rucksack, and surely I can find a decent one for less than I paid for my enormous army Bergen.

'So it will cost you nothing!' says Hagen, clearly sold on the idea.

I get another round in, although by this stage I can hardly think straight. We've been here drinking all evening, and the bar is lurching into a kaleidoscopic swirl of trolleys, deserts and overweight rucksacks – so many things to consider now the deal has been struck and it's too late for me to back out.

The following morning, despite our hangovers, we visit the shops again, only to discover that Swakopmund has no trolleys designed for anything more ambitious than white Afrikaners carrying groceries to the boot of their family car. I shelve the project for now, unaware that owing to harsh circumstances looming on the immediate horizon I'm to return to the trolley idea within a fortnight. And my attempts to find one lead me unsuspectingly into months of grief with donkeys, mules and some of the strangest individuals outside the walls of an institution.

Hagen drives us 200 kilometres north to the Skeleton Coast Park, the coast road shimmering in the midday heat with great pools of liquid sunlight glistening on its surface. I see my first desert mirage, huge inlets of water stretching from the sea right up to the road ahead. As we draw near they vanish like phantoms.

The spell is broken by a loud thump on the windscreen.

'Shit!' mutters Hagen. 'I just smashed a bird.'

I haven't even started walking yet, and already we're slaughtering the wildlife. I try to be philosophical; the low-flying seagull knew the risks. 'Yes,' agrees Hagen, 'flying is dangerous.' Back in Germany he's an amateur pilot himself, so he should know about these things; I feel better already.

We reach the gates to the Skeleton Coast Park, shaped like two enormous skull and crossbones: a melodramatic touch, but visually striking. And this is where the journey begins for me. I start walking down from the park gates to the sea, about three kilometres away, while Hagen drives on ahead with my rucksack. Walking without the weight of a big pack feels wonderful; I enjoy it while I still can, the ocean breeze cool and pleasant.

Twenty minutes later I catch up with Hagen, who is lying in the sun beside his car in the middle of nowhere. Prior to the trip he's been dosing himself with special 'sun vitamin' tablets, insisting they provide total protection against sunburn and remove all need for protective creams. His face by this stage resembles a beetroot, though I resist pointing this out as he's been kind giving me a lift this far.

We start chatting about trivialities; I realize I'm trying to delay the moment Hagen drives away, and to his credit he appears reluctant to leave me on this deserted coastline. I ask him to pin my handkerchief around the back of my neck in the style of the Foreign Legion.

'I feel like a condemned criminal being prepared for execution,' I tell him.

'I know what you mean,' he replies, fastening the last safety pin from my emergency sewing kit. I'd rather he hadn't said that.

Hagen still seems unable to understand why anyone should want to walk across Africa when they don't absolutely have to. He lifts my rucksack to test its weight, currently around thirty kilos, the weight of a small wardrobe. 'No!' he exclaims, putting it down again quickly. Unfortunately yes, and this is only the gear I've brought to last me the first week on the coast. Admittedly a lot of this weight is water; within a day or two my pack will get lighter. Already I've had to drink like a camel, to offset the effects of the previous evening's binge; I'm sweating a mixture of fear and pure alcohol.

But if I stand here panicking any longer I'll get straight back in the car and abandon the whole trip in favour of the Swakopmund bars. I shake hands with Hagen, and set off alone into the Namib Desert.

1. Darkest Wimbledon
(London, England)

> Now that I am face to face with inhospitable Africa there is something, it seems to me, which grinds out all hope of return.
>
> Henry Morton Stanley, 1874

My fascination with the explorers brought me to Africa.

I'd been spellbound by Africa from the moment I read my first Tarzan comic as a six- year-old in hospital, when I spent two months on traction with some virtually unidentifiable problem with my left hip joint (which has caused me grief ever since, particularly when lugging a heavy pack across Africa). Years later I grew out of Tarzan when I realized he was a complete waste of space, the white lord of the jungle in black Africa who swings through the trees and talks to apes when he's not murdering the natives. Instead I became intrigued by the Victorian explorers, legendary characters like Stanley and Livingstone, Grogan and Galton, the real figures who – according to Western-written history books – opened up the so-called 'Dark Continent' to European eyes.

Over the centuries Westerners have based their perceptions of Africa largely on myth. Even so, it's almost impossible today to appreciate fully the degree of venturing into the unknown involved in the early African expeditions. Until the second half of the nineteenth century the British public knew more about the surface of the moon than they did about the African interior. Hundreds of years earlier, explorers had already charted many famously remote areas of the globe such as the Amazon; but until the great explorations of the 1850s onwards central Africa remained a blank in the Victorian atlas, a vast wilderness of burning desert and dripping jungle, a fabled land of monsters and unicorns, of dwarves and cannibals, teeming with dangerous beasts, poisonous snakes and bloodthirsty savages.

Inevitably, the most successful explorers of Africa gained great kudos. Some paid a high price for their fame by dying long before their time, or at least wrecking their health completely. While many Victorian explorers became obsessed with the notion of being the first white man to set foot in some particular place, a few individuals came to regard crossing Africa overland from coast to coast as a goal to rival the discovery of the source of the Nile.

This overland crossing of Africa became known as 'the Traversa'.

By my late twenties I'd been on a few backpacking trips to exotic places, but I'd never done anything I could describe as truly adventurous. Instead, I was spending far too much of my time working in a West End bookshop. And merely reading books about travel and exploration on the 8.23 to Waterloo each morning somehow lacked the adventure of crossing high Tibetan passes by yak caravan or exploring the tropical African rainforest.

Looking around the train carriage each morning, it struck me that the books people read often say a great deal about what they'd really like to be doing, if they dared. I realized I was developing an obsessive urge to see for myself if anything still remained of the Africa of the Victorian explorers. I convinced myself that I could best find this out not through academic analysis of their achievements, but by sharing at least some of their hardships on my own modern-day traversa. This dubious notion finally crystallized into the decision to go when I was at a dreadful New Year's Eve party, at least as drunk as everyone around me.

The image of crossing Africa on foot seemed already firmly established in many people's minds as some exceptionally difficult feat. But how many people had actually done it? The idea held immediate and obvious appeal, the effects of eight pints of lager at the party banishing any logistical concerns. I decided to walk every step of the way from one coast of Africa to the other, completely alone: no back-up, no support team, no one to make arrangements for me, no one to carry my gear, no sponsors, no funding, no film crew, no journalists, no fuss, no cheering crowds and no strings attached; above all, it had to be on a one-way ticket, with no safety nets, no get-out clauses and nothing to fall back on. After all that, I couldn't think of anything else to exclude on what was turning into rather a Zen expedition.

The following morning, despite the hangover, I hadn't conveniently forgotten the whole idea, and still wanted to walk across Africa. The more I thought about, it the more I wanted to do it. Africa seemed the complete opposite of the life I was leading in London, to such a dazzling extent that even trying and failing was well worth the gamble.

But I had to make sure this was what I wanted, as the risks demanded sober consideration. At this stage I was not excessively worried about being eaten by lions or getting trodden on by an elephant, or even having my throat cut by bandits – every adventure worthy of the name must surely bring its share of danger. I was more troubled by the fact that if I walked across Africa I'd have to give up my flat and my job and then return to England penniless, probably ill and certainly exhausted, with no job and nowhere to live. Which would be enough to dishearten most reasonable folks.

Yet the whole equation was beautiful in its simplicity: all or nothing.

It was no easy thing to get to Africa in the first place. Lacking a magic wand, it took me over a year to get there, a year of the most undignified and soul-destroying scrimping and saving to squirrel away barely enough money to enable me to live like a tramp when I finally got there. I had no savings, no property, nothing to sell; the pay in the bookshop would barely support a fasting saint, let alone finance an African expedition. So it was goodbye to smoking and drinking and chocolate biscuits and half-decent coffee and buying books, and just about anything else that over the years had made life worth living. My rent was high, my draughty flat cost a fortune to keep even tolerably warm in winter; overnight my life had been reduced to a wonderfully simple choice: either walking across Africa or staying put in a London bedsit, huddled over an ancient electric fire with both bars on.

But in all that time of living on toast, porridge and raw carrots, wearing a coat in the flat to keep warm and walking miles to save pennies in bus fares, the idea of crossing Africa on foot lost none of its appeal. It was only when I had finally set out from the Atlantic coast of Africa that I realized what I'd let myself in for. By that time I was in the middle of the Namib Desert, carrying an enormous pack, panting like an elderly dog in the midday heat and feeling decidedly foolish.

Before I walked across Africa I first had to decide on a feasible route, which meant days of poring over maps of central and southern Africa. Although I wanted to visit some of the areas passed through by the great explorers, I decided from the outset to avoid following in the footsteps of any particular individual. Instead, there seemed enormous appeal in the idea of doing something no one had ever done before, even if this meant splitting the finest hairs of definition and pedantic quibbles about the *exact* route taken on previous African crossings.

The man usually associated with the first traversa is the Scottish missionary Dr David Livingstone, one of the most celebrated figures in the history of exploration. In November 1853 Livingstone set out on an extraordinary journey from Linyanti (northern Botswana) to the Atlantic coast at Luanda, accompanied throughout by a party of Makololo tribesmen sent by their chief to open a trade route from the interior to the coast. On reaching the Atlantic Livingstone realized that the path they had opened was far too difficult ever to function as a viable trade route. Bitterly disappointed at having failed in his main objective, Livingstone thought he might have better luck in the opposite direction – so after he'd led his party back to Linyanti they simply carried on east right across the continent, finally arriving at Quelimane in Mozambique in May 1856, having opened a new route to the interior. Livingstone completed much of this epic journey on foot; he also travelled by canoe or mounted on a foul-tempered ox called Sindbad.

On his triumphant return to Europe, Livingstone received a hero's welcome. The Victorian public hailed him as the first man to cross Africa overland, an idea vigorously supported by the great doctor himself, who found himself mobbed by adoring crowds almost everywhere he went. But in fact he was not the first. Two black Portuguese-African traders, Pedro João Baptista and Amaro José, had completed the first traversa over forty years earlier, taking five years to do so, crossing from Cassange in Angola to Tete in Mozambique. However, their achievement went almost unnoticed – inevitably, the heroic missionary-explorer travelling with only a handful of African companions appealed more to Victorian sensibilities than did a pair of native traders, so Livingstone received all the plaudits.

Livingstone's motives for undertaking the traversa were complex. In his own way he genuinely sought to bring good to Africa – unlike so many of the Europeans who followed him in what was to became the imperialist 'Scramble for Africa'. Largely driven by altruism, he dreamed of opening up the 'Dark Continent' to Christianity and commerce, and his life's work became the destruction of the vast African slave trade. Other explorers, however, were to cross Africa for very different reasons – including, in Stanley's case, the opportunity to exorcize his bitter resentment against the world, the legacy of a nightmare childhood.

Henry Morton Stanley, the brash Welsh-American journalist who became the greatest of the African explorers, is today best remembered not for his real achievements but instead for uttering the most famous greeting in history: 'Dr Livingstone, I presume?'* The hostile reception he received in Europe after 'finding' Livingstone did not go down well with the highly strung Stanley, who spent most of his action-packed life masking intense insecurity and emotional pain behind a web of lies and a thoroughly convincing façade of belligerence. His toughness was legendary – his name became synonymous with brutal determination and the will to succeed at literally any cost, and the Africans christened him *Bula Matari*, 'The Smasher of Rocks'. But the hurt child always lurked beneath the surface of Stanley's achievements; the stigma of illegitimacy and a Dickensian upbringing in a Denbigh workhouse had left him seething with anger against the world, a state of mind that drove him to extraordinary feats as an explorer – including the greatest African journey in history.

The death of Livingstone in 1873 gave Stanley the chance to turn his smouldering rage into positive action: he resolved to lead an African expedition of such stupendous scope that even his bitterest critics must concede he had assumed Livingstone's mantle as the foremost African explorer – either that or he would die in the attempt. Although today largely forgotten, Stanley's spectacular 999-day traversa from Zanzibar to the mouth of the Congo (1874–77) was at the time the biggest, most difficult and dangerous expedition yet mounted in Africa. But success came at a dreadful price: Stanley's expedition cost well over half its

---

*The gauche yet immortal 'Doctor Livingstone, I presume?' was coined at their meeting at Ujiji on the shores of Lake Tanganyika in November 1871. Stanley had finally tracked down the old explorer, who had vanished into the African interior years before and was widely presumed dead. Finding Livingstone in this way proved the journalistic scoop of the century and catapulted Stanley to worldwide fame, but only after a storm of controversy and resentment had greeted him on his return to Europe – as well as widespread public ridicule for uttering such a fatuous greeting. Many dismissed him as a fraud and a scoundrel, suggesting he'd never even met Livingstone at all, although Stanley was finally vindicated.

original 228 members their lives, and all three white men who accompanied him perished in the interior.[1] Finally emerging white-haired and emaciated at the mouth of the Congo (he was still only thirty-six), Stanley found himself this time the hero of the day, fêted by royalty and commoner alike back in Europe and America. But strong criticism emerged from certain quarters. In many ways the opposite of the peaceful Livingstone, Stanley preferred to blaze a trail, smashing through any obstacle, natural or human; numerous battles with hostile natives during the journey led to widespread accusations of gratuitous force.

Yet in 1887–89 Stanley led a second traversa, this time to relieve the beleaguered Emin Pasha, governor of the tiny province of Equatoria, which after the death of General Gordon in Khartoum stood alone in the path of the Mahdi's conquering dervish army. The Emin Pasha Relief Expedition, crossing Africa this time from west to east, from the mouth of the Congo to Zanzibar, proved a violent and highly controversial venture. Stanley did indeed appear to pluck Emin Pasha from the Mahdi's clutches; but after the initial furore of his triumphant return to the coast with Emin Pasha in tow as a virtual prisoner, grim details of the realities of the expedition began to filter back to Europe, causing public outcry. Accusations ranged from crass incompetence on the part of some of Stanley's officers to conduct unthinkable for Englishmen, whispered tales of sickening brutality and cannibalism. At the time of the expedition the writer Joseph Conrad commanded a ship at the mouth of the Congo, and he based his classic *Heart of Darkness* on some of its actual events – on Stanley's last traversa, the unspeakable horror of the Congo jungle was no invention.

While Stanley's expeditions remained the most sensational of trans-African epics, many Europeans with a taste for adventure flocked to follow his example. A few of the explorers who attempted the traversa were outright madmen. In 1878 the unlikeliest character of all set out into the 'Dark Continent': the Abbé Michel-Alexandre Debaize, an eccentric French priest, intended to cross Africa overland from east to west, his object to enhance 'the glory of God and the glory of France'. He left Zanzibar accompanied by 800 porters, carrying an extraordinary amount of useless equipment, including popguns, fireworks, bells, a hurdy-gurdy and two suits of armour. Even though he'd come better prepared for an eBay auction than a serious African expedition, Debaize lacked sense but not courage. Lost in the interior for over a year, his erratic progress across Africa finally petered out. Blind and delirious, he died of malaria on the shores of Lake Tanganyika.[2]

Some individuals made impressive journeys across Africa for reasons completely unconnected to exploration. For me the idea of leaving England to cross Africa had to be on some level an escape, unashamedly so, and yet at least one individual's African journey was quite literally a bid for freedom. In 1908 a tough convict called Creswell undertook a spectacular trek across southern Africa, his aim merely to gain his liberty. After escaping from the prison train carrying him to Salisbury (Harare) in Rhodesia (Zimbabwe), Creswell started his journey without food or money and still wearing handcuffs. After friendly natives helped him out of his manacles, Creswell walked from Rhodesia to the mouth of the Congo at Boma, throwing himself on the hospitality of local people as he went. From Boma he worked his passage to England, but the freedom he craved could not save his life. Penniless and critically ill with malaria, Creswell finally staggered into Mile End Police Station to give himself up. A prisoner once more, he was sent back to Africa but died before he could stand trial again in Bulawayo; the rigours and deprivations of his epic walk finally claimed another victim for the 'Dark Continent'.

One of the most famous crossings of Africa (1898–1900) was undertaken for a romantic pledge, with something of the fairy-tale quest about it, like those undertaken by suitors vying for the princess's hand in marriage. Ewart Grogan, a young man of wealthy Anglo-Irish background, is still regarded as the first person to 'walk' from the Cape to Cairo – even though he didn't actually walk all the way, having made significant parts of his journey by steamer or railway, and he started not from Cape Town but from Beira in Mozambique. Even so, it still remains an epic journey.

The idea came about when the unsalaried Grogan proposed marriage to an heiress; the girl's wealthy father was unenthusiastic about the match. At this time Grogan's prospects were poor; his sole academic achievement had been to get himself rusticated from Cambridge for locking a small flock of sheep in an unpopular don's study. However, the young man's sheer persistence proved difficult to deflect when Grogan hit upon an unlikely compromise, a trial to prove his worth: if he managed to cross Africa from the Cape to Cairo, would his intended father-in-law agree to the match? The latter agreed, assuming Grogan's chances of reaching Cairo alive were virtually nil. But after two years of fighting starvation and malaria, cannibals and countless other perils straight out of *Boy's Own* magazine, Grogan finally arrived in Cairo – whereupon he caught the next available boat home to his future wife.

When planning my own route across Africa, I first intended to cross the Congo. However, the civil war there resumed with renewed viciousness, making it virtually impossible even to enter the country, let alone leave it in one piece. After racking my brains over every alternative, I decided to start the journey from Namibia's Skeleton Coast – and in hindsight how could I not, with a name like that? Running along the western edge of the Namib Desert, the Skeleton Coast derives its name from the countless people who have died there over the centuries through thirst and shipwreck. Assuming I didn't add to their number, from there I planned to walk to Zanzibar, the island of exotic spice and Arab legend lying just off the Tanzanian coast near the Equator.

In principle it all seemed positively straightforward: from A to B with a minimum of fuss. But the distance between the Atlantic and the East African coast was such that I felt I could only decide on my exact route when I was on the road in Africa. Anything was possible, good and bad, since clearly I'd set myself the task of walking several thousand miles.

Decisions on equipment took longer, leading to weeks of procrastination. I wanted some advice from the explorers themselves, so Francis Galton's *The Art of Travel** became something of a bible on the journey, especially as Galton based much of this book on his experiences exploring the interior of Namibia in the early 1850s.

Unfortunately, by the time I decided to trek across Africa earlier problems were catching up with me. The previous summer I'd slipped on wet grass during a softball match and badly injured my knee, resulting in a couple of uncomfortable operations to remove the torn cartilage. Soon afterwards I realized my knee would never be completely sound again. For years I'd run marathons, but obviously this was out of the question now; I tried to take up running again, but after only a few miles

*Galton's *The Art of Travel* (1855) proved an extremely popular teach-yourself manual for budding Victorian explorers. A cousin of Charles Darwin, Galton was also a notable scientist and inventor.

my knee would start screaming for me to stop. And by this time my plans to walk across Africa with a heavy rucksack were already firmly fixed. Walking would be less punishing than running, but even so I began to wonder if I could actually walk such a distance, and my knee could give way at any time. Apart from anything else I'd look an idiot if my grandiose plans turned pear-shaped before I even left England.

There had to be something I could do to help myself. I visited a physiotherapist, a dour Scotsman who examined my joints with a great deal of tut-tutting: 'There's a fair amount of *wear and tear* here,' he concluded, shaking his head in a most discouraging manner. Foolishly I confessed that my joints had become alarmingly creaky whenever I moved suddenly: occasional mild popping sounds had recently turned into loud cracks that would frighten a burglar. 'Aye, that'll be the *exploding gas* in your joints,' he explained cheerfully.

Exploding gas aside, by this stage of my life, without a single noteworthy expedition to my credit, I'd still acquired a reputation as someone who enjoyed long walks, especially home from London parties. I'd think nothing of walking ten miles home from a good party, or even less of walking fifteen miles home from a really dreadful one – in the latter case the long walk became a therapeutic exercise. Yet I never felt the slightest interest in organized walks or runs, especially long and difficult ones.

Many people assumed I'd secured sponsorship for the trek across Africa, but I never even gave this serious consideration. I'd worked in charity fundraising for years, and knew full well how hard you have to work to squeeze a single penny out of anyone. Even if you're successful and raise the necessary funds, the sponsors understandably want their money's worth one way or another. That kind of deal would make my African trip no longer my own: I'd have to justify everything I did, everywhere I went, which was the last thing I wanted. I'd rather manage with very little money – if that meant living like a tramp in Africa, so be it. And the way things went in the early stages of the journey, I thanked my lucky stars I wasn't answerable to anyone. If sponsors had held me accountable for my actions or progress, I would have had to disappear quietly off the face of the earth.

And what if I failed?

If I failed, I failed.

I'd rather burnt my boats with this trip. If I made a dreadful mess of things I might die, or at least have to come straight back to London, which seemed part of the same process. Because of these gnawing doubts, before leaving England I even threw the I Ching, an exercise that produced the following advice: travelling would be difficult and exhausting, and often I would be friendless and lonely; sometimes I would find shelter and friends, but more often troubles and misfortune. This seemed plausible, if a little too clear-cut – I've always been suspicious of getting things handed to me on a plate. A second throw predicted an initial setback, but ultimately success and riches.

It didn't happen quite like that.

2. The Skeleton Coast
(Namibia: Windhoek to Swakopmund)

When a heavy sea-fog rests on these uncouth and rugged surfaces –
and it does so very often – a place fitter to represent the infernal
regions could scarcely, in searching the world around, be found. A
shudder, amounting almost to fear, came over me when its frightful
desolation first suddenly broke upon my view. 'Death,' I exclaimed,
'would be preferable to banishment in such a country.'

> Charles J Andersson, an early explorer
> on the Skeleton Coast

I leave London on a tidal wave of relief, the aircraft playing only an
incidental role. Despite the euphoria and the knowledge that whatever
I've forgotten to pack I can probably well do without, I've still brought
far too much gear. I'm worried I'll run into problems with weight the
moment I start walking. Even before that I'll almost certainly fall foul of
excess baggage restrictions at Johannesburg Airport, as I'm not even
within hailing distance of the twenty-kilo limit, despite having jettisoned
a whole heap of things at the last minute. After getting drunk on cheap
red wine with my friend Niall at Heathrow, I nearly miss the plane
altogether. Breaking into an undignified run, I find my great clodhop-
ping walking boots aren't built for speed; drenched in sweat, I'm the last
to board the plane.

But at last I've escaped.

The flight stops in Lisbon for four hours, but the delay seems as
nothing to me. In the airport toilets I wash my face to sober up; as the
liquid soap dispenser squirts cold snot into my hands, I catch my
reflection in the mirror and can hardly stop beaming. Already I look
healthier and happier than I did in London, and I only left three hours
ago.

At Johannesburg Airport I have to wait another eighteen hours for the
connecting flight to Namibia. Most people would consider this an awful

connection, and only days before it would have stressed me out totally – but now I'm in no hurry at all. I spend the best part of this time quaffing cheap South African wine while devising cunning schemes to avoid paying excess baggage by taking as much weight into the cabin as possible. As a last resort I'll wear every single item of clothing I possess, claiming I've always been on the large side when I board the plane looking like the Michelin Man.

For the first time in months I feel almost childishly pleased with myself. Then I realize I'm just pissed. I don't even mind getting evicted from the departure lounge, and even this proves a blessing in disguise when I spend a comfortable night for free in the plush lobby of the airport hotel. The following morning I share the bathroom with a group of well-dressed Asian businessmen, all of us coughing and hawking in an orgy of expectoration. To my delight the guy behind the South African Airways desk lets me on the flight without charging a penny for excess baggage. 'It's your lucky day,' he tells me. I agree with him totally.

Descending over hills of dry scrub savannah, the plane finally reaches the Namibian capital Windhoek. It's midsummer in this part of the world so I'm expecting a great blast of desert heat as soon as I set foot on the tarmac. This notion stems from my only previous visit to Africa seven years earlier; alighting from the plane in tropical Mombasa was like stepping into the steam room of a sauna. But Windhoek lies in the highlands, in a valley bordered by mountains to the north and south, and a long way from the Skeleton Coast. As a result the midday weather here is warm and bright and far from stiflingly hot, not so different from a pleasant summer's day in England. This serves my immediate purposes well, but does nothing to prepare me for the conditions awaiting me in the middle of the Namib Desert.

I pass through immigration without a hitch, even though I don't have the required onward air ticket; this is a one-way flight. Immediately I notice the large numbers of creepy-crawlies in Africa: a gang of beetles makes straight for my rucksack, mistaking it for a new home. I scrounge a cigarette from a young German guy called Hagen; we arrange to meet up later in Swakopmund for a drinking session.

I still have to get to the Skeleton Coast where I start the walk. The train from Windhoek to the coast doesn't leave until the evening, so I spend the afternoon wandering around the modern city. Once the capital of the German colony of Southwest Africa, Windhoek today is very Westernized by African standards. Half-timbered German buildings line the main road of this rather curious African capital, but they're upstaged in sheer incongruity by the towers and battlements of three German mock-castles looming above the town, fun-sized versions of those on the Rhine.

But I'm not here for sightseeing; the immediate practicalities of getting my journey underway take precedence. I'm woefully overburdened, carrying a ridiculous weight of just under forty kilos (horrified at how difficult it is to lug along, I weighed my rucksack before leaving the airport). I can't remember what half these things are for; I'm sure my rucksack didn't weigh nearly this much when I left London. I even wonder if the airport baggage handlers have smuggled a few bricks into my pack to relieve the tedium of their work.

After less than a mile I'm worn out, pouring with sweat and my bad knee is playing up. Maybe I'm overdoing it before I've acclimatized; as Livingstone observed, an Englishman 'must never forget that in the tropics, he is an exotic plant'.[1] To complicate matters, without any conscious decision I've started smoking again; I'd thought in Africa there would be little temptation in that department. Already my twin obsessions of the journey – weight and smoking – have started in earnest. Within days I've revised my ideas on weight; the problem of cigarettes proves more difficult to resolve.

After nearly an hour of walking around the city centre my hips hurt from carrying all this weight. Something is cutting into me; I'm praying it's my money belt and not the hip belt of my rucksack – I could fix any problems with a money belt much faster than finding a new rucksack at short notice. Suddenly paranoid about the rest of my gear, I test my water purifier in the toilet sink at Windhoek Station. Thankfully it works well; at this stage I'm still scrupulous about the water I drink – another attitude soon to change.

The evening turns pleasantly cool, and waiting for the train I find myself in high spirits again. It all seems a good idea once more – I can really *do something* with this trip. Everything is new and exciting, or at least radically different from London, which is just as good. Unless something truly extraordinary happens on this journey I won't reach any places no one has ever been before, if such places even exist today outside

13

the Sahara and the vast Congo rainforest. But wherever I go now will be new to me. I'm *here*, and nothing else matters – the knowledge I can go literally anywhere on my own two feet delights me. And there is something about Africa that makes my spirits soar.

I reach Swakopmund before dawn, the streets deserted and the town colder than anything I'd imagined possible in Africa. I wander around lost in the fog with my teeth chattering, wondering if my expensive compass has gone hopelessly wrong. After half an hour of inadvertently circling the *Alte Gefängis*, the old German prison, I realize the map in my guidebook is out of date – the colonial station building has been converted into a hotel and the railway station itself has moved. I didn't even consider that as a possibility, which doesn't bode well for navigating my way across Africa.

Namibia's second biggest town, Swakopmund is a pleasant if rather touristy resort of around thirty thousand people; it's certainly not what I'd expected on an African desert coast. As in Windhoek, the strong Germanic feel here stems from Namibia's years as a German colony, when the whole supply for Southwest Africa came through this harbour. Today many of Swakopmund's shops, stately colonial buildings and Bavarian spires would look perfectly in place back in Germany. The bakeries and butchers' shops here ply their customers with *Brot* and *Bockwurst*, and even the palm-lined streets have German names, as do many of the local black guys; I wouldn't have noticed if they had English names, but it feels strange to meet young Ovambos with names like Gerhard and Heinrich.

The morning mist is finally starting to clear when I check into a cheap, rather decrepit hotel near the beach. The white middle-aged landlady clearly needs an urgent shot of laughing gas, while her cadaverous mother is even worse; the latter's morose and wrinkled features remind me of an old and partially deflated balloon a week after the Christmas party. Between them they go a long way towards souring the breakfast-table ambience, glowering at me in a team effort over the stale toast. A constant fug of Peter Stuyvesant smoke billows from both of their mouths simultaneously; in the gloomy half-light of the breakfast room they look like a couple of devils. But I don't mind at all, I'm not taking them with me. All I need now is to find a way of getting up to the Skeleton Coast and then I can start walking across Africa.

The Namib Desert is the oldest in the world, stretching the entire length of the coast from South Africa as far north as Angola. It derives its name from the Nama word for 'waterless land'; the coast on average receives less than half an inch of rainfall annually. Offshore the cold Benguela Current chills the air, so clouds form out to sea and the resulting rain falls far from land. If the sea temperature here were to increase by only a few degrees, clouds would instead form over the land; the rain from these would then transform this whole region from desert to lush swamp. But conditions here won't change overnight: the area has been a desert for around a hundred million years.

This harsh landscape once proved a blessing in disguise to the people of Namibia; the desert effectively kept the slave trade away from the country, so Namibia avoided the vast human calamity that overtook so much of Africa. Undeniably beautiful, the Skeleton Coast is also extraordinarily bleak; in places it resembles the surface of the moon, and the sixteenth-century Portuguese sailors first arriving here called it *As Areias do Inferno* ('The Sands of Hell'). Dangerous cross-currents and impenetrable fogs combine with treacherous sandbanks, shoals and reefs to create a graveyard for ships. Some early visitors to the Skeleton Coast never left; after scrambling ashore, shipwreck survivors found their relief at reaching dry land short-lived, and many had cause to wish they had drowned at sea rather than face the horrors of a long-drawn-out death from thirst on the loneliest coast in the world.

'Here for nothing in the world is there even the smallest gain for our masters … there is only sand, rock, storm,' wrote the captain of a passing Dutch ship, the Bode.[2] In this he was mistaken; Namibia is now the world's largest producer of diamonds, providing nearly a third of the world's output. The country also has large deposits of high-grade semi-precious stones, to me their very names exotic: aquamarine, silver topaz, green tourmaline, blue lace agate, indigolite, amazonite, rose quartz and amethyst.[3] Sailors shipwrecked on the Skeleton Coast often stumbled across alluvial diamonds lying at their feet; then they died of thirst, carrying unimaginable wealth in their pockets.

I plan to start the journey at the southern tip of the Skeleton Coast, trekking down the coast back to Swakopmund before heading inland across the Namib Naukluft Game Park. While the entire Namibian coast is known loosely as the Skeleton Coast, technically the Skeleton Coast extends only as far south as the mouth of the Ugab River, some 200 kilometres north of Swakopmund. Since I'm planning to walk so far, I can't take the slightest chance of getting it wrong – and starting from 'The National West Coast Recreational Area' hardly has the same ring to it. The great African explorers didn't trouble themselves with 'recreational areas'; within my own humbler parameters neither should I.

I spend my first day in Swakopmund trying to organize a lift the 200 kilometres up the coast to my starting point. This proves impossible; apparently no one wants to travel up the coast this week. In desperation I remember the Namibian coast is one of the best fishing spots in the whole of Africa, so I check with an angling club. The secretary tells me that I've picked a week when the fishing is poor, and as far as she knows none of their members is going anywhere near the Skeleton Coast. So it looks as if I'll have to walk for days up the coast before plodding all the way back down again. Apart from the extra work involved, I risk problems finding water even before I reach my official starting point; as a demoralizing start this would be hard to beat.

I go and sulk on the beach while planning my next move. Here I bump into Hagen, the German guy I met at the airport; I tell him of my plans to get up the coast and later cross the Namib Naukluft Park. He offers me a lift in his hire car up the coast to the Skeleton Coast Park; even better, he offers first to drive down to the Namib Naukluft Park to check the feasibility of my intended route inland.

We drive into the Namib Desert, and only a few kilometres inland the temperature just *rockets*. The road through the Namib Naukluft Park looks designed to kill pedestrians, crossing endless dirty-white gravel plains, the landscape interspersed only by the occasional tiny rocky hill or *inselberg*. Despite the claims of nature documentaries, nothing seems to live here – or if it does it's hiding from the midday heat, buried somewhere under the parched earth. The thought of crossing this part of the desert on foot appals me. If I walk this way, I must either carry enough water to last five or six days or else gamble on someone driving past. Six days' water means carrying at least an extra thirty kilos on top of my existing load, if that's physically possible for me, and even that would be cutting it extremely fine. The distances involved aren't small, either: at 50,000 square kilometres the Namib Naukluft is one of the largest game reserve in Africa, and bigger than Denmark.

I change plans: instead of crossing the Namib Naukluft I'll walk inland along the main road from Swakopmund. Without the coastal breeze to compensate for the scorching desert heat, this new route will prove tough enough in itself. But if there's tarmac to walk on, I'll walk on it – I'm not proud.

After I've bought my sensible bush hat and spent two nights in Swakopmund drinking with Hagen, he gives me a lift to the gates of the Skeleton Coast Park. As he drives away, heading back towards Swakopmund, I think of all the reasons why I should be accompanying him and of all the unpleasant things that might happen to me if I don't. It's like a mental video fast-forwarding to all the really nasty bits.

For a few moments I consider chasing after his car; in the soft sand I could catch up with him before he picks up speed, then pretend I've forgotten something important back in town. But as soon as he's gone I become more philosophical. Here I am, and here I'll stay unless I do something about it. I set out alone into the Namib Desert.

I see no one for the rest of the first day on the coast. I follow a dry riverbed down to the ocean, where I take off my boots and cool my feet in the Atlantic. The water is remarkably cold considering it's lapping against hot desert sand. I climb over the wire fence into the Skeleton Coast Park then walk some distance north up the beach; I have to make absolutely sure I'm starting on the Skeleton Coast, not from some point 200 metres south of it. On this trip drunken despair might fit perfectly into the scheme of things, but not cheating.

I start south down the coast towards Swakopmund, the best part of a week's trek away if all goes well – the equivalent of walking from London to Bristol.

A couple of hours of hard work bring another huge surge of relief, equal almost to the euphoria I felt on boarding the plane in London. So I can actually do this. Until now I didn't know if I could get along at all, hour after hour, carrying this weight across a soft and sloping beach. But it's possible, even if lugging a bloody great rucksack across crumbling sand is a far cry from carrying the shopping home from Sainsbury's.

17

Thank God I invested in some trekking poles – after I've used them for less than an hour on the Namibian coast they become indispensable for the rest of the journey, and I feel almost naked on the few occasions I try walking without them.

I take things fairly easy for the first day. I couldn't go fast even if I wanted to; this mode of travel doesn't lend itself to sudden bursts of speed. At the same time I can't drag my heels, as my water supply won't last much beyond two days in the desert. And if I break an ankle I'm in serious trouble. But at least I'm unlikely to get lost, with the ocean right next to me.

Two jackals appear, less than a hundred metres away. They look friendly enough, gambolling like lambs and obviously the best of pals. The black-backed jackals on the Namib coast are timid creatures, feeding mainly on insects. I see the first of many snakes on the trip; unlike the more animated varieties I later encounter inland, this small fellow is as dead and dry as biltong, and even the hyenas have turned up their snouts at it.

I continue down the beach for the rest of the afternoon, the coastline desolate and the ocean dazzling with reflected sunlight. I stop and gaze out into the Atlantic. There is something almost scary about watching the sea like this when you're in a desert and the only person for miles around. While some people insist canned music has no place out in nature, I'm already glad I brought a Walkman and won't lose any sleep if it is one of the more overt trappings of civilization. Some of the explorers took a musical instrument with them, even if they couldn't play it properly themselves, and one or two even took wind-up phonographs. I listen to 'Eleanor Rigby' from the *Beatles Anthology*, just the strings arrangement, cold and unsettling, and watch the sea as though hypnotized. Out across the South Atlantic there is no land for thousands of miles; the Benguela Current races inland, cold and urgent, all the way from Tristan da Cunha and South Georgia. If I searched for months I could find no music more suited to this moment and this empty place, not even 'Fingal's Cave'.

Evening approaches with surprising suddenness. The ocean is very beautiful as the sun dies, the Benguela Current sweeping ashore like molten silver. In twilight it's easy to picture shipwrecked sailors struggling ashore, clutching at sludgy wet sand, retching salt water, convinced

18

they're almost safe – then leaving their bones to bleach forever under the burning desert sun.

There seems little point in pitching my tent: the evening is mild and I can't be bothered. Although tired, I feel fine physically and mentally, and tonight I could sleep on the proverbial clothesline. I unroll my sleeping mat and hide my boots inside my rucksack, in case the hyenas mistake them for food. The clouds inland look almost English, straight out of H.E. Bates; those out to sea are more spectacular, the kind favoured by artists depicting momentous biblical events or illustrating the covers of Wilbur Smith books. The clouds only a short distance inland have travelled right across Africa to get here, all the way from the Indian Ocean, which seems like an omen – I am, after all, heading in that general direction. Thousands of miles and long exhausting months away, if I ever get that far.

Then true darkness falls. The horizon far inland leaps closer as lightning flickers across the desert sky; the heavens plunge into blackness again, and the night stirs with the low growl of thunder. This could form the perfect setting for a western, the scene where the cattle start thinking along the lines of a good stampede. There's something delightful about the sound of a distant electrical storm when you know it won't reach you. After all, people in Swakopmund assured me it hardly ever rains on the coast. Even so, this thunder is *loud*, considering it's many miles away.

I wake in the middle of the night to find myself getting splattered by big drops of water falling from the sky. This bears every resemblance to rain. If technically it's not rain then it's near enough to make no bloody difference – I'm English, for God's sake, I should know. Whatever it is, after being drenched for half an hour I've had enough and start to pack my gear; I may as well carry on walking in the dark rather than sit here miserable, getting soaked to the skin. As soon as I've crammed all my soggy gear back in my rucksack this ersatz rain stops abruptly, as though some invisible hand has turned off a giant water sprinkler in the sky directly above my head. Sceptical, I go back to sleep.

Later, back in Swakopmund, people still insist this phenomenon is not rain, but condensed spray from the sea. I'm not entirely convinced; a month later it does rain briefly in Walvis Bay, real rain, universally acknowledged as such by coastal residents and meteorologists alike, an occurrence that even makes the front pages of the local papers (nothing much else happened that week). So why not here as well?

In the morning I find myself surrounded by hyena prints. Surely they were here when I stopped last night in the dark? If not, these creatures are less timid than people think. But at least my boots are still present and correct, with no obvious teeth marks.

Halfway through the second day I begin to see signs of human life – a handful of white guys fishing on the beach. At this point I'm about a kilometre inland and well supplied with water, so I don't bother approaching them. An hour later I return to the shore, and a South African family in a caravan appears. The guy behind the wheel, a modern-day motorized *Voortrekker*, does most of the talking. He looks in his early fifties, with a beard like a hedge; his enormous eyebrows not only join in the middle but also merge seamlessly with his sideburns, so his face is entirely surrounded by thick black hair. This lends him a slightly startling appearance, like one of the monsters from *The Muppets*.

Without warning his friendly manner evaporates, to be replaced by a fierce growl:

'Do you like the fuck-alls?'

'I beg your pardon?'

'Man, I said: "Do you like the fuck-alls?"'

I've no idea what he's talking about, but this is clearly no rhetorical question; he wants a definite answer, with no beating about the bush. The suspicion dawns on me that this question forms the Namibian preamble to fisticuffs. Good manners in these situations back in England require the belligerent party to make a similar enquiry, such as: 'Did you spill my pint?' or 'Are you staring at my bird?' But this knowledge doesn't help much here, and the guy's providing no clues as to what I've done to offend him. Maybe I've trespassed on some small stretch of coastline he considers his exclusive fishing preserve – these fuck-alls might be some kind of fish, and he's accusing me of poaching. In his vehicle he looks a large fellow, so I'm alarmed when he starts to climb out. Fortunately when his feet touch the sand he reaches no higher than my shoulder – he just has a big head.

'The fuck-alls, man!' he cries, his eyes bulging in their sockets while he points furiously to the empty desert behind me.

So they're not fish then; at least we're a bit further on. But I still can't see a thing where he's pointing; there's nothing but sand as far as the horizon. I'm not enjoying this – we're not on the same page here, the guy's rushing me. I feel a mild panic attack approaching, like those I experience back at home at busy supermarket checkouts when I can't open the plastic carrier bags quickly enough and there's an angry queue breathing down my neck. If this bloke's going to thump me anyway, I almost wish he'd get on with it; perhaps I should regain the initiative by giving him a smart clip round the ear with one of my trekking poles, then take to my heels into the desert. I abandon this plan immediately – my heavy pack would slow me down to a plod, and I could hardly outdistance his family if they gave chase in their vehicle. The caravan is crammed with burly sons and nephews, and even the hefty grandchildren look as if they know how to mix it. And it would be unfortunate to get beaten up by the very first group of people I meet on my walk across Africa.

Then the man throws his head back and gives a great bellow of mirth: *'FUCK-ALL GROWS AROUND HERE!'*

His family inside the vehicle joins in the laughter, and tears are actually streaming into the guy's beard before he finally calms himself down. Relieved that the situation is a peaceful one, I change the subject to safer ground and explain the nature of my journey. He seems interested, and gives me half a packet of Chesterfields. I'm sorry to say that cigarettes right now are more welcome than all the encouraging words in the world – for a good smoke I'd happily stand admiring fuck-all for the rest of the afternoon.

Then another thought strikes him: 'Man, you need a girl with you, eh?' For a moment I think he's about to produce one, or at least ask his family for volunteers. But finally he climbs back into his vehicle and drives off along the beach, pausing only to stick his head out of the window and roar back in my direction: *'THE FUCK-ALLS, MAN!'*

His parting guffaw floats dreamily across the desert, before vanishing as though it had never been. I half-expected it to remain long after he'd gone, like the grin of the Cheshire Cat.

My first human encounter on the Namibian coast is by no means typical, and after several days of plodding along the beach I start to acquire the status of a minor celebrity. The same people pass me day after day – and

so much for unadventurous folks back in Swakopmund telling me no
one is going anywhere near the coast this week. Most of the people
fishing along the coast are kind and friendly; many stop to offer me a
cold drink, food, a cigarette or a joke. Sometimes their good intentions
outstrip their means: 'Man, I'd give you a bottle of wine if I had one!'
declares one guy called Paul. 'But if I did, you probably wouldn't get
where you're going.'

Who cares? I'm in no rush.

A family stops to offer me a cold Coca-Cola and some sandwiches.

'Are you doing this for Jesus?' asks the mother.

'Actually I'm not.'

'Did you hear about that young man a few years ago, who walked
across South Africa for Jesus?' No one seems entirely sure how Jesus
benefited from this arrangement, but apparently all parties concerned
came out smelling of roses.

Two elderly and extremely camp Germans offer me a brandy and
Coke with real ice in it, along with a knowing smile. Most people I meet
are ready with advice, often revolving around the supposed drawbacks
of my solitary mode of travel. While much of this advice is sensible, a
few suggestions are unfit for my delicate ears. But when people stop and
offer food and water, or even just words of encouragement, it raises my
spirits tremendously. It also changes my views on accepting charity. I
realize I'm entertaining the folks who stop for me, making their day
slightly more interesting, like a busker or street performer plying his
trade along a desolate African coastline. And I reckon that's worth a cold
drink or a sandwich.

I'm not the first person to benefit from this ploy – on Livingstone's
traversa his Makololo companions often persuaded local women to feed
them by dancing: 'The young women were especially pleased with the
new steps they had to show, though I suspect many of them were
invented for the occasion.'[4] To capitalize further I memorize some good
jokes for when the next vehicle stops – though I'll give the one about the
fuck-alls a miss, not wishing to get thrown headfirst into the sea.

Partly owing to these mercenary attitudes, I abandon walking on the
beach itself and move instead to the coast road. The relief is immediate:
I realize how exhausting it was plodding along a gentle slope of crum-

bling sand. Although the road consists almost entirely of gravel and salt, it provides a much better walking surface and I speed up noticeably.

'Are you doing penance?' asks the mother of one family who stops for me. 'What's the name of that song, the one about mad dogs and Englishmen?'

'Listen,' interrupts her husband with a conspiratorial wink. 'No one would know if we gave you a lift!'

'But I'd know,' I say, trying not to sound self-righteous.

'Then I'll sign a form saying you walked the whole way.'

'But think what would happen to your good name, sir, if people found out ...'

'Then I'll sign it in my brother's name.'

Later on the third day I reach Cape Cross, the spot where the Portuguese arrived in the late fifteenth century, the first Europeans to set foot in Namibia. And it took all their skill and courage to get here – apart from anything else their tiny caravels measured scarcely more than twenty metres long. Back at home I'd think twice about setting out on Regent's Park boating lake in a vessel that small.

Although brave and intrepid sailors, the Portuguese had for many years feared venturing south of the Canary Islands, thinking strong currents would prevent their ships from ever returning home. They imagined the sea along the African coast was so shallow it boiled in the sun; others insisted it had the consistency of treacle, and Christian ships would surely stick fast, easy prey for the huge sea serpents flourishing along the waterless coast. And as the clearest sign of all of God's displeasure in this blighted land, the fierce African sun would surely turn white skins black – for how else had negroes acquired their colour? South of Cape Bojador on the Saharan coast lay the Ocean of Darkness, a seething black hell of fire, storm, whirlpool and mountainous waves, teeming with monsters and where Satan's foulest hosts ran riot. Beyond this lay the Sea of Obscurity, a lost half-world of mist and slime at the ends of the earth, a place from which no one had ever returned.[5]

Despite this catalogue of terrors lurking out in the Atlantic, commercial interest entered the equation when the Portuguese sought to discover a sea route around Africa to the rich spice markets of the East. Reaching the Gulf of Guinea, they were appalled to find the coast turned south again for thousands of miles – the vast African continent was very much larger than they had ever imagined. But in 1485, on his second attempt to circumnavigate Africa, the brilliant Portuguese navigator Diego Cão reached the coast of Namibia.

He was horrified at the inhospitable land he had discovered.

Here on the rocky headland now known as Cape Cross, Cão planted a *padrão* (stone cross) bearing the following inscription: 'In the year 6685 of the creation of the earth and 1485 after the birth of Christ the most excellent and most serene King Dom João II of Portugal ordered this land to be discovered and this *padrão* to be placed by Diego Cão, gentleman of his house.' But his expedition could go no further without proper supplies and was forced to sail for home. In despair at failing a second time, Cão died here on the coast and was buried on a rock outcrop nearby.*

Cão's stone cross remained standing here on the bleak desert headland, forgotten for centuries. Eventually in 1893 the captain of a German warship transported the cross back to Germany, and it now rests in a Berlin museum. Today, two replicas of Cão's *padrão* (one German, one Namibian) still stand watch on this lonely headland, now with a quarter of a million seals for company. Even from the road the smell is powerful, so I keep moving.

But before I leave Cape Cross I can't help thinking that, of all the cruel deaths on this coast, one episode strikes me as particularly poignant, partly due to the complete mystery surrounding the human tragedy. In 1943 a slate was found buried in the sand here beside twelve headless adult skeletons and that of a young child. Scratched on the slate was the date 1860 and the following message: 'I am proceeding to a river sixty miles north, and should anyone find this and follow me, God will help him.' I assume he must have been trying to reach the Ugab River – exactly where I started my own journey. If he ever got that far, almost certainly he would have found the river bed completely dry, as it was when I saw it three days ago.

---

*Two years later another Portuguese navigator, Bartolomeu Diaz, sailed around the Cape of Good Hope and entered the southern Indian Ocean before being forced to turn back. The great explorer Vasco da Gama finally completed the work of Cão and Diaz, reaching Calcutta in 1498.

By the evening I'm worn out, and call a halt for the day before I fall over. Then a family stops to present me with some particularly scrummy food, the best yet, everything from steak sandwiches and home-baked cookies to a couple of cans of South African lager. I feel so much better I continue walking for another two hours.

I follow the road south in darkness, the slight ocean breeze cool and refreshing, the moon on my left, the muted roar of the Benguela Current to my right; dead ahead, the Southern Cross hangs lopsided in a sky the colour of Indian ink. The stars tonight are extraordinarily clear; the Bushmen call the Milky Way 'The Backbone of the Night'. An aeroplane in the night sky floats past, a lonely firefly exiled to outer space because of its abnormal size.

I sleep in a curiously shaped depression in the sand, a low mound at one end lending it all the appearance of a freshly filled grave. After unpacking my gear I find some particularly large hyena prints around me. I don't wish to wake to find such a creature sinking its teeth into my arse. Such things can and do happen; enough people over the centuries have lost feet and ears and elbow joints in this way. Livingstone once met a local tribesman whose upper lip had been bitten off by a hyena, leaving his teeth exposed in a permanent snarl. On another Victorian safari a hyena bit the nose off a sleeping Swahili porter. In the ensuing uproar the animal beat a hasty retreat and the porter somehow managed to retrieve his chewed appendage. His friend tied it back on for him, although the string slipped during the healing process and the poor fellow's nose grew back askew.[6]

Despite such behaviour, hyenas always get such a bad press that I'm sure a lot of it must be unfair. Rather than cowardly scavengers, in many parts of Africa the better-known spotted variety are often brave and resourceful hunters, bringing down large game. The hyenas along Namibia's coastline are known as the *strandwolf* ('beachwolf'). Smaller than their East African counterparts, their thick hairy coats actually make them look bigger; shy and rarely aggressive, they still possess immensely powerful jaws capable of crunching large bones like Japanese rice crackers. They don't normally hunt big animals, preferring instead to feast on insects and birds and the occasional putrid seal; they've also developed the ability to survive for long periods without water, and can cover fifty kilometres a night scavenging for food.

25

Ernest Hemingway revealed a cruel streak when it came to hyenas, taking great pleasure in blasting them to pieces with a high-velocity hunting rifle, even though they made poor trophies and even worse food. Once he recorded his delight watching a hyena he'd just shot, the wounded animal frantically biting its stomach and dragging out its own intestines in its agony. But hunters should make well sure of their aim; Herero folk tales describe how a wounded hyena searches furiously for the arrow or shot lodged in its flesh, if necessary killing itself in the process. If the hyena finds the missile before it dies its ghost will follow the hunter forever, bringing disaster to his entire family. In African legend the luminous eyes of a hyena at night are the glowing spirits of the dead.[7]

Out in the open desert at night like this, the last thing I want to see is a pair of malevolent headlamps eyeballing me from a few metres away, accompanied by growls and an overpowering waft of carrion-induced halitosis. But stretched full-length in my grave-like depression in the sand, hunger takes precedence over tiredness or worrying about wild animals. I lie under the stars chewing the last piece of steak donated by that kind family, hoping the hyenas don't smell it. God, it tastes good. Afterwards I brush my teeth in beer. Right now I don't care if they all fall out, provided they do it quietly and without pain. I had enough dental problems immediately before leaving England, with the removal of a back tooth determined to stay put. After half an hour of dreadful struggling, a piece of my jaw splintered while the dentist wrestled with the roots, more or less with his foot on my chest. My mouth still hurts, and I keep spitting out tiny slivers of bone that have worked their way to the surface. For the moment I can't bite on the left side of my mouth, and elegant eating is out of the question; but who needs table manners in the middle of the desert? There's no one here to object if these days I have to eat like the Elephant Man.

In spite of the problems it caused, I'm still glad I had the tooth taken out before I left home. A dentist in any city or big town in Africa would be fine, but I'm reluctant to visit some remote village practitioner, however eagerly he might welcome new patients. The African explorers used to stop the bleeding following tooth extraction with a red-hot ramrod; but then some of them were slightly crazy.[8]

By day the desert provides ample opportunities for studying sand. You can conduct research on a continuous basis; after another week in the desert, what I don't know about sand won't be worth knowing. Here you can appreciate sand more or less with all five senses. Although I'm too far south to experience the strange 'roaring dunes' of the northern Skeleton Coast, I've consumed enough sand in my diet lately from sand soup and sand on the rocks to sand taken neat; I've also revised my views on how sandwiches originally got their name. But there's one un-expected advantage. Back in Swakopmund I was appalled to find the supermarket had completely sold out of crunchy peanut butter, with only the smooth variety remaining. Why they even stock such a product I've no idea – everyone knows smooth peanut butter is strictly for wimps, a vile unctuous paste that has no part to play in tough African expedi-tions. But after several days in the desert my nauseatingly smooth peanut butter has turned crunchy enough to satisfy the most demanding con-noisseur. And by now I'm well past being snooty about food of any kind.

Another of my staple foods along the coast is the dried rusk. This South African delicacy is a cross between a sweet biscuit and a chunk of sandstone. The idea is to dunk them in coffee or tea; as I have neither, and regard dunking in the same light as smooth peanut butter, I'm forced to eat them dry. While there's every chance of cracking your teeth on a well-baked rusk, you can acquire a taste for them if your teeth are either false or fundamentally sound. This is just as well, as when you're constantly hungry they're more addictive than crack.

An ongoing problem around this time is blisters, something I'd badly underestimated. On previous trips I'd never walked day after day; I'd always given my feet a chance to recover, which makes all the difference – a couple of days spent resting and complaining will solve most problems of this nature. But blistered feet when you can stop and rest are not the same thing as blistered feet when you have to walk another five days on them. Even so, you can get used to most things; my blisters may be agony, but in the desert there's no one to take offence at my foul language.

Seeking diversion from the constant pain of squelching blisters, I turn to the soothing power of music. The only radio station I can pick up here on my Walkman is the local white religious channel, which plays nothing except third-rate white Gospel music. So much black Gospel music is excellent, full of spirit and joy – why do they have to play this depressing stuff? We are, after all, in Africa. The words to most of the songs on this station are so mind-numbingly predictable that I can sing along even when I've never heard a particular song before. I try this for a while, before deciding it's less painful to keep my mind on the blisters.

The radio station is merely a sign of the times. So far along the Namibian coast I've found it almost impossible to feel I'm in black Africa; most of the people I meet are white, and the only black people are family servants. Even so, there's still a wide variety of people fishing here, ranging from intellectual types to flatulent beer-boys, the latter arriving in back-up trucks creaking under stupendous loads of Windhoek Lager. One such group have obviously tired of fishing, and seize on my appearance as the ideal excuse for a beer break, despite the fact that they've clearly been sousing themselves in lager for hours already. The most vociferous of the group, a stockily built fellow with a slight aura of the leader of the pack about him, shoves a beer in my hand and insists I allow him to pose for a photograph carrying my rucksack. 'By all means,' I tell him. Unfortunately, within the last hour I've refilled all my water bottles and my rucksack weighs as much as ever. The guy seizes its straps enthusiastically, attempts to lift it, gives me a quizzical look and quickly sets it down in the sand again, followed by a tremendous beer belch right in my face that practically parts my hair. His friends immediately accept his failure as a challenge and take photos of each other staggering around with my pack, each giving vent to great boozy guffaws at the weight of it. I'm tempted to bet them they can't each in turn carry it one kilometre down the beach in the direction I'm going, though decide I'd better not push my luck. But they're nice guys really; as I leave, one of them presents me with a can of ice-cold Sprite and a couple of bollock-warm toffees from the depths of his shorts pocket. I tell him I'll look forward to enjoying the toffees later, and press on south.

Halfway to Swakopmund I reach the outskirts of Henties Bay, a small fishing resort. I sit beside the road like a tramp, watching a poor old local man on his way home. He carries a home-made rod and a little bag of fish he's caught, hurrying past the holiday homes rented by comparatively well-off white folks. I feel sorry for him, at the same time wondering if my sympathy is vaguely patronizing. Scurrying or not, he's literally the first black guy I've seen fishing here.

Then a caravan stops and a white family offers me a lift.

'Thanks, I have to walk – but could I possibly buy some bread or something from you?'

'Bread? Haven't got any bread, man – why don't you come round for dinner?' says the man at the wheel, whose name is Lionel. 'We have a chalet in town; you can stay the night and carry on tomorrow.'

I've made more difficult decisions than this. Lionel's a pleasant guy, enthusiastic about everything and always joking. His family have come up from South Africa for a week's fishing, which he insists is far superior here to anything South Africa can offer. He tells me they live in the Free State.

'Is that the Orange Free State?'

'Man, the same! But now there's no oranges, nothing's free and it's in a hell of a state.'

The meal is enjoyable, and would have been so even if I wasn't ravenously hungry. Lionel's father Gert has his arm in a huge bandage. The previous day he caught a ray, and tried to throw it back into the sea. Mistaking his intentions, the ungrateful creature attacked him, sinking its barb into his arm before swimming off, no doubt congratulating itself on teaching Gert a lesson, which indeed it had.

On the sixth day, I pass the biggest salt works in Africa, busy churning out 180,000 tonnes a year, extracted from seawater in huge evaporation ponds. I'm delighted to see this – not through any particular interest in salt, but because it means I'm nearly in Swakopmund, where I can rest for a couple of days.

I reach the outskirts of town skinny and exhausted with a nose like a sun-dried tomato. It feels like I'm carrying half the Namib Desert in my bag.

Crossing the poorer part of town, I head straight to the nearest service station where I stuff my face with dreadful rubbish – anything unhealthy and immediately satisfying. Crisps, chocolate and biscuits do just fine, followed by three or four cigarettes, lighting each from the previous. I notice that a lot of Namibians like to smoke at petrol stations while actually filling their tanks; my journey across Africa could still end prematurely in a huge explosion, like a Steven Seagal movie.

It's already late afternoon, and tonight I plan to sleep in the desert somewhere on the southern edge of town, near the Swakop River. To cut expenses to the absolute minimum I've resolved for the whole journey to take a room only if I can have it for the entire day and night. So when I'm not camping and I arrive somewhere late in the day, the cheapest option is to sleep rough somewhere just outside town and find a room the following morning. Disreputable, certainly, but it does save money.

I sit in the desert still stuffing my face with junk. I get the strangest sensation that I could continue eating forever like this, sitting here munching steadily until eventually I keeled over and died – but perhaps this is a normal reaction to trekking for days in the desert. A microlight buzzes overhead, circling slowly. I wonder if these machines are as fragile as they look; every slight movement of the pilot's body makes the whole structure tremble and shake, and he looks too heavy for the contraption, as though he's eaten all the pies before taking to the air.

When twilight approaches the microlight disappears, and I move on to find a suitable patch of sand for the night. I'm trudging through the desert around the back of town, looking decidedly shifty, when a white guy hails me from one of the outlying houses. I curse under my breath; the man's only trying to help, but I just want people to leave me alone so I can crash out discreetly. But there's little point in even trying to explain to strangers why I actually want to sleep in the desert, so I go and speak with him; I don't want anyone setting their dogs on me.

The man introduces me to his neighbour, Frenus, who runs an idiosyncratic backpackers' hostel called The Alternative Space. I don't usually like hostels, never having cared much for sleeping in a room full of strangers, half of them bonking. But this particular one proves very agreeable, and even the bonking remains at civilized levels, with only one or two amorous couples going at it hammer and tongs.

Frenus is a white guy in early middle age, a genuinely interesting and entertaining fellow, and something of a natural raconteur. An architect by trade, he designed and built The Alternative Space himself; an unusual building, its white exterior is almost Moorish or Greek in style, and the whole place is filled with local sculpture and painting. It's comfortable here, especially after the trek down the coast, and I stay at The Alternative Space for four days.

During this time a young Turkish guest reveals himself as a practising naturist; he's also phenomenally well endowed, so the other guests are understandably taken aback. Even Theo, a gigantic German biker and hardly the most shockable person in the world, wonders what's going on when one lunchtime we find the guy lying naked in the yard with his legs spread. While no one feels especially drawn towards the goods on display, it proves difficult not to look – he sort of fills your vision, even when you just want to chat about some completely unrelated topic like the price of vegetables. Eventually people start laughing at him; to his credit, the Turkish guy can take a joke and puts his tackle away for the next hostel on his itinerary.

Late one night a drunken couple from London keeps everyone in the room awake by arguing loudly, the guy making most of the noise. After nearly an hour of listening to the complex history of their marital problems, I've heard enough for one night and ask him politely to shut the fuck up.

'We're trying to sort out a domestic dispute here, pal!' he yells back.

As he's been making this point rather well for the last hour, I become cross and a shouting match ensues. Our heated exchange fails to reach any resolution, despite my reasonable suggestion that they both piss off into the desert for a romantic argument under the stars. Eventually I go off to the kitchen for a drink and stay up till dawn, becoming obscenely drunk with the German biker Theo, who starts every sentence: 'Oh, my English!' The next day the guy from London apologizes, promising not to argue loudly in the middle of the night again for the rest of my stay. He's as good as his word on this – instead of arguing for the next few nights he and his girlfriend engage on some marathon bonking sessions, going at it like a couple of feral cats.

Domestic squabbles aside, the atmosphere here is one of peace and normality. Yet this does little to reflect the political turmoil Namibia – Africa's newest nation – has gone through in recent memory. The country only gained its independence from South Africa in 1990, after tens of thousands of Namibians had lost their lives in thirty years of guerrilla warfare, one of the longest conflicts in African history.

I find it difficult to leave places where I've been more or less happy, especially leaving to carry on walking alone like this. I'm half-tempted to abandon the whole idea of trekking across Africa. Instead I could spend a few months in Swakopmund as drunk as a lord. Sooner or later I'd meet some gorgeous woman, if only by the law of averages – and even if I didn't, several months of boozing it up sounds more fun than a year of trekking across a continent carrying a heavy rucksack.

I have to leave before these thoughts get out of hand. The desert is waiting, and my pack suddenly seems bigger and heavier than ever before. I realize this is going to be hell: away from the coastal breeze, the surface sand temperature in the Namib at midday can reach seventy degrees centigrade. As it turns out, 'hell' proves something of an understatement – if I'd had any idea just how bad the next three days would prove, my walk across Africa would indeed have ended in the nearest bar in Swakopmund.

3. Into the Desert
(Namibia: Swakopmund to Arandis)

When dying of thirst in the desert ... the supply to be found in the stomach of the camel should not be overlooked or forgotten ... People dying of thirst are not very nice.

Thomas Baines, artist and explorer

As I leave The Alternative Space several people express horror at the weight of my rucksack. Theo the German biker is the only other person here who can lift it, let alone carry the bloody thing any distance. With all this water sloshing around in various containers it now weighs in at about forty kilos, which is far too much to lug across a scorching desert.

I remind myself that the porters on the great African safaris often carried a similar weight, at least at the start of their journeys. This may be hard going, but I'm no worse off than they were – apart from the fact that I'm completely alone, and I'll have to cover ground much more quickly than they did, at least across the desert. And carrying a lot of weight was something the great explorers didn't usually have to do for themselves, whatever else they had to put up with; and when ill or incapacitated they could usually persuade someone to carry *them*. During their almost impossible journeys involving great hardship and danger, even the weight of crushing responsibility must at times have paled beside the backbreaking work of their native porters, largely the unsung heroes of the great safaris.

The porters' loads were usually bulkier and more awkward to carry than a well-designed rucksack today. Each man would carry a cylindrical bale of trade cloth (the main currency in the African interior) weighing around thirty kilos, or other trade goods wrapped in the same cloth. In addition the porters carried a sleeping mat and cooking gear, their gun and personal belongings. Inevitably, the start of every safari became a free-for-all as the loads were weighed and apportioned. The stronger

33

porters usually succeeded in bullying the weaker into taking the heaviest or most awkward loads, such as the boxes of ammunition, while they themselves seized favourite loads entitling them to a more prestigious position in the caravan. As a small consolation, the weight gradually reduced throughout the journey: the trade goods such as cloth, wire and beads were bartered for food en route, or used to pay *hongo*, the toll levied on travellers passing through tribal lands – a foretaste of modern tourist visas.[1]

Less than four kilometres out of Swakopmund I have to stop and perform running repairs on my feet; that first stretch along the coast was tough hiking, and despite resting for several days my blisters are far from healed. Then I remember I've left my book with someone at The Alternative Space. Back outside the hostel for the second time, I lose the rubber tip of one of my trekking poles then spend twenty minutes fruitlessly searching for it in the sand. Eventually I give up. While hoisting up my rucksack once again, its weight suddenly pulls me over flat on my back. At this precise moment a few guests from the hostel appear, to find me sprawling around in the sand like an overturned tortoise, cursing fluently as I disentangle myself.

My inauspicious start inland across Africa maintains tradition perfectly. Even in the heyday of African exploration, the first day of any safari invariably turned into farce; caravans leaving the east coast at Bagamoyo usually consisted of porters so drunk they could barely stand, let alone march in a straight line. Some explorers hoped the use of wheeled transport would make for an easier start, as did Major Cornwallis Harris, setting out on a hunting expedition from Graaff-Reinet in 1836. After hiring a group of Nama ex-convicts at bargain rates, on the day of his departure Harris discovered that his new employees had different priorities from his own. Having pawned their muskets en route to the nearest gin shop, the Namas threw themselves wholeheartedly into an orgy of drunkenness and debauchery; by the time Harris finally managed to drag his men away from the shebeens, they were so drunk they had to be 'loaded like pigs into the wagons they had been hired to drive'. Still under the influence of Cape Smoke brandy, one of the Namas then drove his wagon straight into the side of the nearest house.[2]

At least I have only myself to worry about – although even this is to change shortly.

Just out of Swakopmund I pass a group of camera-clicking Japanese tourists clustered around a fourteen-tonne steam tractor. Known as the *Martin Luther*, this is one of the unluckiest machines in African history. Imported from Germany in 1896 to carry goods into the interior, it arrived at Swakopmund but proved too heavy to unload, so had to be brought ashore at the deep-water port at Walvis Bay further south. Then the tractor's owners discovered that the only engineer who knew how to operate it had gone home to Germany. Eventually an American gold prospector managed to get it running, only to find its water consumption so astronomic that a team of labourers had to carry water all week merely to use the machine at weekends. The tractor took three months to clunk and grind its way the thirty kilometres up the coast to Swakopmund. After only a handful of short transport journeys inland it broke down permanently, and all further plans for it were scrapped, its owners abandoning the machine at the exact spot where it last juddered to a halt. Then some local wag remembered the words of Martin Luther, speaking out at the Reichstag of Worms: 'Here I stand, God help me, I cannot do otherwise.' The name stuck, and in 1975 the tractor was made a national monument

Anxious to get inland as quickly as possible, I spend little time admiring *Martin Luther*. This proves a mistake; within days this unlucky contraption has come to symbolize utterly my fortunes in this part of Africa.

The first day out of Swakopmund I cover only twelve kilometres. As expected, the climate changes dramatically; without the coastal breeze the temperature *soars*, and walking along the coast now seems a picnic by comparison. Merely imagining the change in climate was one thing, when the difficulties and hardship ahead seemed part of a great adventure – but the actual experience of carrying a forty-kilo pack through this murderous heat is quite another. My head is thumping and my vision distorting; sweat stings my eyes constantly while the distant rocks shimmer in the heat like nightmare figures dancing on water.

I jettison some more gear.

By late afternoon I'm completely done in. I sit beside the road, slumped like a sack of potatoes against my rucksack, so weary I can't imagine ever wanting to move again. But I move quickly enough only

35

moments later when a scorpion crawls out from underneath me. This fellow is about ten centimetres long, completely black and strangely *confident*; it doesn't scuttle but trundles along with almost a swagger, taking its time and exuding a calm authority. There's nothing furtive about this one, even though it's just been sat on. Common sense suggests I could do far more harm to this creature than it can do to me; I'd rather enter the battle armed with a big flat foot than a scorpion's admittedly excruciating sting. But I still feel a strong and childish urge to kill it, to stamp it into the ground, to teach it a lesson. Fortunately I don't do anything so wicked; I'm equally glad it doesn't come back. African medicine in history advocated cauterizing a scorpion sting with a hot iron – if this failed to make the patient feel better they should instead crush the offending scorpion and bind its squashed body to the affected area.[3]

As soon as the sun sets the awful heat of the day vanishes. Walking inland at night soon becomes a nightmare of a different sort, on the road at least; vehicles pass only sporadically, but their headlights are shockingly powerful, ruining my night vision for several minutes. This is particularly unsafe when I'm so tired; caught in their glare like a petrified rabbit, I can't even tell if I'm standing in the road or not.

I've had enough for one day. I lie down in the sand, keeping close to the road so I'll be able to find it in the morning. Sleeping under the desert stars along the coast was wonderful, but did nothing to prepare me for the conditions here. I'm expecting the night to turn cool rather than cold, which proves naïve in the extreme. The coastal fog in the Namib can stretch over sixty kilometres inland, and tonight it soon sweeps over me. Without any insulating clouds the temperature plummets and an icy breeze picks up, its biting quality out of all proportion to its strength.

I really, *really* should have pitched my tent.

By the middle of the night I'm wearing every item of clothing I possess. Sleep is totally out of the question; the noise of my chattering teeth alone would keep an army awake. But however uncomfortable I might be, the thought of having to get up and faff around in the dark trying to pitch my tent is even worse. Later on in the journey I could put my tent up blindfold in a force ten gale, but not yet.

At five in the morning, I'm so frozen I abandon all thoughts of sleep and get up in the dark to start walking for the day. The cold by now is even worse, the fog thicker. Fog can be so atmospheric, carrying every suggestion of lurking horrors – but in these temperatures it loses all its spookiness; all I can think of is the cold. Fog is the only reliable source of moisture for most of the Namib Desert, and many species of plants, insects and animals have adapted to take advantage of it. There's even a beetle that performs headstands during foggy winds; the broad surface this presents allows the fog to condense, and tiny drops of water run down the creature's body into its mouth.

Wonders of nature aside, all I want to do is escape from this horrible bloody fog and never experience it again. Eventually a pale and watery sun rises like an apparition over the desert. Right now I'd prefer the furnace-like midday sun to this ghostly poor relation. It takes hours for the fog to clear completely and the sun to give off any real heat; the night has chilled me so utterly, I'm still wearing my coat at ten o'clock.

The second day in the desert I cover about twenty-five kilometres. While the day proves hard going, the night is a vast improvement on the last, although the sun sets so quickly here that I find myself putting up my tent in the dark. The ground is full of sharp stones so I don't bother with the inner tent. But even with just the flysheet covering me I feel comfortable and secure; there is something so *homely* about a tent. Now I have my own private space, the day ends on an almost optimistic note and at least I'm cosy. Even so, I'm short of water, and I know the following day will be tough.

The following day isn't tough, it's a complete bloody nightmare.

Without the usual heavy fog, the morning chill quickly evaporates from the face of the desert. By nine-thirty in the morning the heat is appalling, without even a hint of cooling breeze; by midday the sand is burning to the touch. I work like a fiend to keep walking at a reasonable pace and in a straight line. Drenched in sweat and panting in the motionless desert air, it takes me until mid-afternoon to reach the small town of Arandis. By this time I'm a complete wreck, dizzy and de-hydrated and exhausted beyond expression.

I can't carry on like this.

This is sheer murder. It will kill me, perhaps literally – and even if it doesn't, the thought of spending the next year like this is heartbreaking. I'll have to give this up, make some other plan, do something else, something *bearable*. Carrying this weight in such heat is nearly impossible for me, and so far removed from anything remotely enjoyable that only an idiot would continue.

But what else can I do, now I'm here?

Maybe I could go to South Africa, travel though Zululand, make this a different journey altogether. Whatever I do, I'll have to stay in Africa – it's where I've chosen to be, and I worked so bloody hard for so long to get here. But it seems absurd to spend over a year working like a one-armed paperhanger merely to finance this journey, then as soon as I get here to start another job ten times harder than the one I've just left.

This can't be what I wanted.

Back in London it seemed all very well in theory to look forward to the totally different climate I'd encounter in Africa. On a cold winter's night huddled over an electric fire, deserts and jungles sounded just what I needed. I think of the Gary Larson *Far Side* cartoon, in which Pinocchio's wish to become a real boy is unexpectedly granted during a safari vacation. This happens without warning when he's surrounded by lions, whose indifference to a wooden boy snapping happily away with a camera in their midst suddenly turns to real interest.

As of this moment I've lost all desire to become a real boy.

Deep down I know I can still do this. I can reach the other side of Africa on foot, even if things get no better than this. But it simply *isn't worth* enduring this hardship to walk across a continent. Surely I'm entitled to make a decision, to choose not to do it? At least by avoiding sponsorship for the journey I've effectively bought myself the right to say 'sod it' to the entire project if I so choose. It's no one else's bloody business if I decide to quit. After all, I am here of my own free will; I could always go back to England and carry on as I was before – I didn't leave home one step ahead of the buckshot ...

Still in a mood of defeatism I find a mini-supermarket in the main street in Arandis, and gulp down two litres of cold milkshake, spilling half of it down my shirt in my eagerness. I find a secluded shady wall and sit there dazed and depressed, staring at nothing while the afternoon heat bounces off the dusty street in front of me.

Mentally the restorative effects of water when you're truly thirsty are remarkable. After the first hour of resting in the shade I feel more able to ponder my immediate future. The horizon both real and figurative looks bleak. To avoid the complete awfulness of my current situation I start thinking back to London again, of what I've left behind and what I've come here to escape. Already it seems a long time ago, but it's clear I might have to return to it sooner than expected, to that awful last year again, that whole saga of fanatical scrimping and saving like some Dickensian miser, of knee operations, of working every hour God sends for hardly any money, that whole year of general London unpleasantness, and all that time with no chocolate biscuits.

By the time I'd left London I'd reached the point where I couldn't wait any longer. For the entire year I'd seen the world through tunnel vision, with Africa almost as my salvation. Now I'm in Africa I can see London with a clarity I never managed at the time, shuffling along in rush-hour crowds with invisible chains around my ankles, surrounded by hundreds of thousands of people hurrying to work and then hurrying home again, and to what? How I'd wanted to be in Africa and *not here*. How I'd wanted to escape from all the pathetic problems back at home, which seem so important at the time but which as a way of life grind you down and make you ill and ugly. How much better to face problems of real immediacy, like hunger or thirst or having to get out of the sun urgently before you collapse from heatstroke. Please, I'd prayed silently, let me swap this London awfulness for steaming jungles and burning deserts, vast distances, danger, fierce heat, sickness, exhaustion, wild animals, snakes, the villainous itch of mosquito bites, cockroaches the size of Dinky toys, the clatter of tropical rain on a tin roof, a riot of African colour ...

A load of romantic shit, of course – and yet how much better than a load of unromantic shit, back in London, stuck where I simply didn't want to be. Having got to Africa I'd somehow escaped from missed opportunities, from all the time I'd wasted throwing mud against a wall or at least searching for a sticky piece of mud. By my late twenties I could hardly bear to wait another day in London; I didn't even mind if I had to come back later, provided I went soon, very soon. Even if most of my plans had no more substance than a child's fantasy of running away from home and thinking they'll find nothing but adventure if they do.

And now I'm here.

In Arandis.

Christ.

In Arandis, mid-afternoon in the middle of the Namib Bloody Desert. This dusty town, this desert, this bloody journey, lugging this bloody great rucksack in this ridiculous heat … This is more than an oasis for me, it's the last refuge of the scoundrel. I haven't even been ill yet, for God's sake, and I'm supposed to be quitting.

To hell with it. I can't give up this easily.

I've walked about 270 kilometres already. I'm exhausted, dehydrated, pissed off and extremely doubtful of my chances of actually walking across Africa in quite this absurd manner. But I must find another way to make this journey. Some lateral thinking is required.

Thankfully a long rest in the shade makes an unbelievable difference. Insurmountable obstacles gradually appear less threatening, water and shade bringing optimism flooding back. Water, blessed water, lovely water. Water is *brilliant*, definitely my favourite thing in the whole world, I just never realized it until this moment. And water feels a thousand times better sloshing around inside my stomach than when I'm lugging it around on my back. When you're truly thirsty all you can think of is the thirst; nothing else has the slightest relevance.

But now I've slaked my thirst my brain can work again. I *make a plan*, as Afrikaners say. If I can push or pull my gear instead of carrying it on my back, I can continue on foot. I'll hitch a ride to Windhoek and there try to get my hands on some kind of trolley; then I'll find a way of transporting the trolley back here to Arandis to carry on walking where I left off, this time with my gear in the trolley. I should have listened to Hagen that first night back in the bar in Swakopmund.

I return to the supermarket for another two litres of milkshake, leaning heavily on the shop-counter. This time I feel capable of un-demanding conversation with the owner, a middle-aged Austrian whose Bobby Charlton comb-over only draws attention to his hair situation.

'Turned out warm again, hasn't it?' Three days in the desert heat has left me scraping the conversational barrel, with nothing else to say that makes any sense to me at all.

'You think it's hot now? My God! You should have been here last week.' But people always say that sort of thing to strangers. He offers me a seat next to his counter; as I sit down, I'm so tired I nearly miss the chair entirely. While I revel in the draught from the shop's fan, the guy recognizes a captive audience when he sees one and starts telling me his life story: 'I've lived in Namibia now for seventeen years – but now I'm sick and tired and I want to go home to Austria …'

After a while I go back outside to the street and sit in the shade. In my mood of new-found optimism I even feel able to take a slight interest in my surroundings. Nondescript Arandis is a very small town, dusty and shabby, with few white residents; it's financed by the world's largest opencast uranium mine, nearby at Rössing. I'm more worried about heatstroke than radiation; even in the shade the heat is staggering.

A friendly crowd of children gathers around me, demanding to know what I'm doing, where I'm going and what all my gear is for. I've asked myself the same questions many times since setting out from the coast. This attention can sometimes be enjoyable, but right now all I want is peace and quiet. Still, I try to take it all in good part. To entertain the crowd a kid starts playing a length of plastic tubing like a didgeridoo, producing some quite professional sounds.

'I'm coming with you!' announces one young woman, who displays an alarming level of interest in my travel plans, among other things. 'But first you must invite me.'

'You talk just like the English people on TV!' says a teenage kid.

'Where are you going?' asks his brother.

I tell him I'm walking to Zanzibar. 'English people are funny people …' he says, shaking his head, while his friends nod sagely. I've never met these children before, and will never see them again; but it dawns on me that the attitude of others towards what I'm doing is more important to me than I'd care to admit. But at least my journey across Africa is still an ongoing project.

In the early evening I start back towards the main road, followed by a large crowd of kids and a slightly crazy-looking dog. Everybody wants to guide me, although in all honesty I just want people to leave me in peace so I can struggle along with my heavy pack. But they're only being friendly, and they're not asking for money. When the children eventually have to leave, I shake hands with the entire party except the dog. Unfortunately the route they've shown me has taken me several kilometres out of my way, but it also means I camp on the side of a beautiful *inselberg*, complete with a picture-postcard sunset. I'm glad I came here, even if it was by accident.

Once again I've underestimated how quickly darkness falls in Africa.

I put my tent up in the dark for a second time, trying to avoid the evil-looking black spiky plants scattered around: the larger ones resemble mating tarantulas. While they're unlikely to win any prizes at the Chelsea Flower Show, the vegetation in the Namib has to be tough. Many plants here carry sharp thorns, to prevent hungry animals making their lives even more difficult. Bushman legend tells how the god Thora tended the garden of Paradise, and one day discovered some ugly trees and plants in the garden. As he pulled them out, they scratched him with their thorns; furious, he threw them out of Paradise and they fell to earth. Most landed upside down in Namibia, and here they remain, their branches sunk into the sand and their roots pointing skywards.

The next morning I hitch a ride to Windhoek. A trailer van stops for me, driven by a white guy in his late thirties called Kees. He works in the salt production plant at Walvis Bay; today he has a day off, so he's taking his ten-year-old daughter Karlene to Windhoek to see the dentist. She has such short hair that at first I think she's a boy. Kees proves extremely helpful; on reaching Windhoek we look into the trolley situation while Karlene gets her teeth filed. But after visiting an engineer who could build a suitable trolley, Kees tells me some of his friends back in Walvis Bay could do the job for less. And getting a trolley built in Walvis Bay would mean I wouldn't have to transport the bloody thing 400 kilometres back to the coast.

'Maybe you should get a donkey!' he jokes. At first I laugh with him; but the more I think about it, the more the idea of a donkey begins to appeal. Involving any animal would surely create its share of headaches; but every other option I've tried so far has brought me more than enough grief. Kees grows enthusiastic about the idea: 'You could buy a donkey from the Topnaar people,' he tells me. 'They live near Walvis Bay. They're the only people who use donkeys in that part of the country.'

So I travel with Kees back to Walvis Bay, the long drive punctuated every few minutes when a big moth comes into contact with the windscreen with a loud SPLAT! We reach town around ten, and I go to his house for a coffee. His family are nice, particularly his shy two-year-old daughter. He also has a tiny dog, like no other breed I've ever seen; at first I think it's a little woolly lamb. I've never understood the strange attraction human feet seem to hold for dogs; this one comes to sniff my socks, which I've had on for three days in the desert, then runs off yelping.

I don't stay long. Kees tells me a backpacker hostel has just opened on the other side of the street, which looks reasonable. But I need to save even small amounts of money, and it's impossible to explain to people why I need to sleep rough without them getting the wrong idea – or the right idea, depending on which way you look at it. I tell Kees I want to go for a walk by the sea before I crash out at the hostel, then spend the next hour looking for some quiet spot to sleep for the night.

Walvis Bay*, Namibia's only deep-water harbour, lies on a huge natural lagoon. Tonight the town is cloaked in spooky mist rolling in from the sea like something out of *Scooby Doo*. It reminds me of an old sailing port, the kind where drunken mariners usually ended the evening shanghaied or murdered. Later I discover that Walvis Bay looks more prosaic by daylight, but my priority now is to find somewhere discreet to sleep.

The waterfront by the lagoon looks far from promising; although there's not a soul around, the prosperous-looking houses are too close together, the streets too well lit. Every house has a resident dog, and I set every single one barking; a few charge down to the gates to do battle. Mercifully only one creature, an objectionable breed of spaniel, is small enough to squeeze between the bars of its owner's gate. Standing in front of me it has second thoughts – I think we understand each other. It seems to realize that if my boot came into contact with its backside with a fair amount of kinetic energy involved, it would sail right over the rooftops into the lagoon. So the stupid creature just stands there yapping in an embarrassed no-man's-land, halfway between full-scale attack and full-scale retreat. But I'm not here to make enemies; I tell the dog to piss off, then move on with the entire canine population of Walvis Bay voicing its opinion from all points of the compass.

Eventually I find a patch of wasteland. One drawback to sleeping in such places is the likelihood of lying in dogshit: dogs are very much out of favour with me tonight on every level. But I don't have much choice if I want to avoid spending any money. And people back in England

*Pronounced 'Vahl-fis Bay', and originally named after the large population of whales offshore (*walvis* is Dutch for whale). The whales here were hunted almost to extinction as early as the 1830s.

43

think I'm living the fancy life out here, pampering myself on some kind of posh safari. Already I'm getting fed up with lurking in the shadows on the outskirts of human settlements, like Grendel on holiday. Thankfully I don't realize at this stage I'll be doing a great deal of this before the year is over.

Despite the tramp-like associations of my sleeping arrangements, I get a good night's rest. This is just as well, because it's my last for the foreseeable future. On leaving Swakopmund only four days earlier I could not have imagined how bad things would turn in the desert. Here in Walvis Bay more or less the same thing happens, but for completely different reasons. If I'd had any idea of just how long I'd be stuck here, any inkling of the problems gathering like storm clouds on my immediate horizon, I would have wished myself almost anywhere else in the world. Even back in the freezing desert, with a ridiculously heavy rucksack lying inert in the cold sand beside me, a silent witness to its owner's folly.

4. Where You Get Stuck
(Namibia: Walvis Bay)

My heart was still as cold as a potato towards my beast of burden.

Robert Louis Stevenson

I wake to the kind of daylight that suggests it's already been light for some time. Three black children in school uniform are watching me from about fifty metres away, whispering and pointing. I sit up, wide awake now. The moment the kids realize they've been spotted they perform a rapid disappearing act so smooth it looks rehearsed. Instantly camouflaged, they stand silent and motionless among the trees like human stick insects. It's time to move on.

I check in at the hostel opposite Kees's house, called The Spawning Ground, named after a graphic novel. Brightly painted in orange and startling primary colours, it stands out from the surrounding streets. It's literally just opened, and I'm the first guest. A young Ovambo called Foster looks after the place and takes the money. Talking to Foster proves something of a lesson in the different ways Africans and Europeans communicate. His English is excellent, so at first I'm unaware any problem exists. Although Foster has encountered many white Afrikaners, I'm the first European he's met and certainly the first person who speaks English with an English accent. This means he barely understands a word I say, although this only becomes evident after days of mutual confusion. The misunderstanding between us doesn't stop with accent. Europeans, especially the English, tend to draw out information by suggestion, fully expecting to be contradicted if they're wrong. An English person might ask: 'How far is Brighton – twenty miles?' and hear in reply: 'No mate, it's more like thirty.' But many Africans prefer not to contradict the speaker, considering it more polite to agree it's twenty miles to Brighton rather than give an answer likely to disappoint.

'I'm looking for a donkey,' I tell Foster.

'Ah yes ... a donkey,' says Foster, no more fazed than if I'd asked where I can get a packet of fags and a newspaper

'I need to get to the Kuiseb Valley, to see if the Topnaar people can sell me one of their donkeys.'

Foster tells me he knows a white guy called Eugene who, by an extraordinary coincidence, travels daily from The Spawning Ground to the Kuiseb Valley, specifically to visit the Topnaar people and their donkeys. 'So maybe he can take you!' Foster beams. Encouraged by my enthusiastic response, he tells me Eugene is a farmer, and extremely religious, always talking about the Bible. From these lurid descriptions I'm expecting some monstrously bearded middle-aged Boer from the history books to arrive in a creaking ox-drawn wagon, brandishing a bullwhip in one hand and a huge hide-bound Calvinist family Bible in the other. Foster's embellishments prove somewhat wide of the mark when Eugene himself suddenly appears; he's a likeable guy in his late twenties, boyishly enthusiastic about everything. He doesn't work as a farmer; he owns the hostel, and he proves about as religious as I am. He's keen on the donkey idea, and the following day arranges for a Topnaar called Hermann to take me down to the Kuiseb Valley to buy a donkey. So far, so good.

Hermann drives through the Namib Naukluft Park towards the Kuiseb Valley. The heat inland is fierce, the desert stark and silent, its vast gravel plains broken only by intense orange dunes. Some kilometres from the coast thin grass finally starts to appear, a result of recent rainfall, and the desert now resembles an endless prairie. A lone ostrich runs away from the road as we pass; later when we return it races off in the opposite direction. 'That guy's always on the run,' laughs Hermann. On the outward journey a donkey stands motionless on the far side of the valley, staring into space; when we return in the afternoon it hasn't moved an inch, still staring at nothing. They're not the brightest of creatures.

Despite their lack of brains, donkeys are essential to the Topnaars, who rely on them to harvest the !nara* an unusual edible fruit that grows in profusion here and nowhere else in the world. !nara plants use their long probing roots to trap the scant underground water, sometimes nearly fifteen metres below the surface, and then retain the life-giving

*! indicates a click.

moisture through the simple expedient of having no leaves. Hyenas and jackals love to eat them off the bush, while the Topnaars use them in more adventurous ways, often baking them into !nara cake or even pressing them to make sugar beer. The fruit is about the size of a big orange, with a spiky rind and yellow-orange flesh; on reaching the first settlement I try one. The flavour is pleasant, though slightly tart; when you're not used to them the acid burns your mouth, and for the next hour my tongue and lips are on fire, as though I've been eating chilli powder straight from the jar.

As well as harvesting the !nara, donkeys here are used to transport just about everything the Topnaars possess, which in most cases is not much. Hermann tells me how he recently joined some Topnaars on a hunting expedition, and they were lucky enough to shoot an oryx; when they tried to load the butchered carcass the smell of fresh blood sent the donkeys berserk. So for the long journey home the Topnaars had to divide the oryx between themselves, Hermann carrying most of the oryx's back and flanks, bent double with the creature's head peering over his shoulder: 'And it was heavy, man!' he declares with feeling.

The human population along the Kuiseb seldom exceeds one thousand; most of the Topnaars here are extremely poor, living in corrugated iron shacks along the riverbank. The people here are friendly, although few speak English. They seem to like the idea of a white guy crossing Africa with a donkey. Eventually we reach a little settlement near the Kuiseb River, called Hoameb. There's even a small campsite here, surrounded by acacia trees, and owing to the recent rains the river for once has some water in it. It's not every day you can paddle in the middle of a desert, and with ample shade around you while you're doing it; I waste no time in cooling my feet.

Despite this pleasant diversion I'm here to buy a donkey, and things are not going well in that direction. By early evening we've got precisely nowhere: all the donkeys are out for the day harvesting the !nara. We reach the last settlement as darkness is falling. Here, finally, someone wants to sell a donkey, an old guy called Solomon, in dreadlocks. Despite his years he has that curious ageless quality some Africans possess. From appearances alone he could be any age between thirty and ninety, his eyes as bright as berries; he dresses and moves like a trendy teenager, and would raise few eyebrows in a Brixton nightclub.

47

We get down to business, with Hermann translating. At first Solomon tells us he can't spare any donkeys, then suddenly changes his mind: if we come back the next day he can sell me a donkey called 'Bullet'. I guess I should be relieved, but somehow I'm not. In hindsight, I'd like to regard this as a premonition.

On the way back to Walvis Bay we pass a school in darkness, and Hermann nearly crashes the car into a wall – the pupils have left a pile of boulders right in the middle of the road. I follow Hermann into the schoolyard while the teacher assembles the class, then Hermann gives them a terrific bollocking. To their credit the kids do listen, and some of them shamefacedly go to retrieve the rocks. To my embarrassment they're all very interested in me.

Back at The Spawning Ground Hermann names a stiff figure for his services for the day. 'If you can't manage it you can give me less,' he adds magnanimously. At least I've sorted out a donkey, so I hand him the sum named. Unfortunately this sets the tone for our subsequent dealings. Already this donkey project is costing me a lot of money – if today was a lesson for me in the art of bargaining in Africa, I've failed miserably. But without Hermann's help in finding a donkey I'd have got precisely nowhere.

Like the Topnaars, most of the white people I meet seem to like the idea of me travelling with a donkey. 'It will be so cool if you manage to take the monkey right across Africa!' says Hans, a young Dutch guy staying at The Spawning Ground. When his error is explained, Hans grows even more enthusiastic: 'Yes, you should get yourself a big chimp; they are powerful creatures. Every morning you can put your rucksack on this chimp, give it a bunch of bananas and a kick in the ass, and you will make a great team ...'

Chimpist remarks aside, other suggestions involve getting a camel; but I intend to spend only a comparatively short time in the desert, and a camel wouldn't take kindly to the climate in the tropical northeast of the country. Another option would be an ox; I'd certainly have no worries about it being strong enough for the job, although they can be dreadful creatures to manage. Livingstone crossed much of Africa mounted on his cantankerous ox Sindbad. Delirious with malaria, he'd often fall from his mount; Sindbad would then kick him as he lay on the ground, and once pitched him headfirst into a river. Galton's experience with oxen on his Namibian travels was more rewarding. Near Otjimbingwe he ran into the Namas on the warpath, led by their legendary chief Jan Jonker Afrikaner. Galton managed to restore the peace, partly by making bombastic threats of reprisals from the Cape, but mostly owing to his extraordinary appearance, wearing a bright red hunting coat and jack-boots and mounted on Ceylon, a gigantic ox that 'snuffed the air like a war-horse'.[1]

In theory a donkey should pose fewer problems than an ox or camel; yet throughout history they've proved themselves at best a mixed blessing as pack animals. Joseph Thomson, who explored East Africa in the 1880s, discovered that while his donkeys could carry twice as much as a man, they wasted so much time that the expedition moved twice as fast without them. It took ten men to load each donkey every morning, the animals fighting like devils the whole time, and for the rest of the day they did everything they could to dislodge or scatter their loads. When the last donkey died Thomson felt only relief.[2]

But while a donkey will almost certainly cause me problems, I've expended so much effort already to find one that I'll see how far this takes me before changing plans again.

At the appointed time I return to the Kuiseb Valley with Hermann, and three donkeys are waiting in Solomon's little corral. I'm hoping one of the bigger animals is the one for sale, but it's not to be; apparently 'Bullet' couldn't come. Hermann loses no time in assuring me that size doesn't matter (that old chestnut), and that it's no reliable indication of strength or endurance.

The donkey on offer is a small, light-brown creature, mournful in demeanour even for a donkey. When I approach him he shows no interest in meeting me, instead keeping his nose buried in his bowl in the corner of the corral. He's called Tsondab, named after the Tsondab River further east – in the Nama language this means 'The Place Where You Get Stuck' (this river is particularly muddy and donkeys often get bogged down there). At this stage I still know next to nothing about donkeys, which partly explains why I've just bought one called 'Where You Get Stuck'. While Tsondab shows little interest in the plans underway for his future, the Topnaars appear distinctly unmoved about his imminent departure. I'm soon to discover why.

As a trial run, I plan to spend the night in the desert near Swakopmund with Tsondab before walking him the thirty kilometres back to The Spawning Ground the next day. The walk home should take less than a day, and I don't envisage any major problems with water supplies. After dark I head out with Hermann to the desert a kilometre or so out of Swakopmund; we unload Tsondab and tether him to a convenient telegraph pole. On Hermann's departure I bed down in the sand beside Tsondab; at this stage he's calm enough, completely absorbed in the tray of lucerne pellets set before him. He's a surprisingly dainty eater, and I drift off to sleep to the sound of gentle crunching.

Unfortunately I've completely forgotten the railway line only a couple of hundred metres away. The first train passes around midnight with all lights blazing, making a noise fit to wake the dead. Tsondab, I realize too late, has never seen a train, or even imagined such a thing could exist; meeting one for the first time in the middle of the night, he obviously feels it has all the charm of a monster from hell. He goes berserk, charging round the telegraph pole in a frantic attempt to escape, in the process knocking over his dinner, which even in the heat of the moment I find rather poignant.

Finally I manage to calm him, but I'm dreading the arrival of the next train. To my intense relief he remains fairly calm when the second one passes in the early hours, presumably having realized that despite their dreadful noise trains don't actually eat donkeys. His earlier panic is understandable; at Wadi Halfa, the first time Grogan's Watonka companions saw a train one of the bravest of them reached automatically for Grogan's heavy-bore hunting rifle.[3]

In the morning Tsondab looks comparatively relaxed, and we set off south for Walvis Bay. To avoid traffic we take the route across the gravel plains behind the dunes running along the coast. I'm worried Tsondab will prove true to his name and get stuck in the mud crossing the dry Swakop River. Swakopmund's original Nama name 'Tsoaxous' – a reference to the river's deep muddy colour when it floods laden with desert sand – translates roughly as 'shit'. And we'd certainly be right in it if we burst through the thin crust and found ourselves up to our thighs in glutinous mud. With no one else around we could be stuck for a long time, if not forever. Or maybe Tsondab will refuse to cross the river at all. Grogan had enough problems with his donkeys when crossing large streams: his men usually had to take them bodily by all four legs and throw them in – a tall order on my own. As it turns out, at this stage Tsondab is on his best behaviour and we cross the Swakop without the slightest hitch, then head south across the gravel flats.

For a couple of hours we make good progress. In hindsight this is obviously because Tsondab assumed I was taking him back home to the Kuiseb, as we're heading in that general direction. But this can't last, and it doesn't. Towards midday I'm virtually dragging Tsondab along, which is exhausting work. I try being particularly nice to him, calling him a good donkey and every variation on that theme. When I start calling him rude names he speeds up slightly. Naïvely, I take this as a good sign. He then switches from brisk trot to full gallop and takes off like a racehorse.

Even as this unwelcome scene unfolds before my eyes, I'm amazed that such a small donkey can run so fast – it's just as well I didn't buy that other donkey called 'Bullet'. For a short distance I manage to run along behind him at about a hundred miles an hour. But I can't hold him – the rope starts running through my hands, and if this were a cartoon I'd have smoke coming off my palms. I have to let go of the rope, but not before it takes a big chunk out of my finger; I'm left standing alone in the desert with jewels of bright blood dripping into the thirsty sand.

Wrapping my finger in my handkerchief, I spend the next three hours trying to catch Tsondab. He chooses to loiter at the scene of the crime, but always at a safe distance from me. I try every conceivable ploy, starting with a no-nonsense approach, marching up sternly like a sergeant major, barking: 'Now then, that's enough of all this nonsense!' When this falls flat I try creeping up slowly, but Tsondab merely trots away easily whenever I approach too close. When I stop he stops, and just stands there, always about twenty metres away. I try acting Mr Nice Guy, but my forced affability won't even fool a donkey. I try to look as pathetic as possible in the hope that he might feel sorry for me – by now I don't have to pretend too hard. Nothing works, not even holding up my injured finger for him to see what he's done to me. To rub it all in he's very obviously daydreaming about lady donkeys, unless he's getting some kind of sexual thrill out of outwitting his new boss – and it's true what they say about male donkeys.

Eventually I accept the inevitable and abandon the chase. I start back towards The Spawning Ground, where I can decide what to do about this unfortunate turn of events.

I'd imagined only a couple of rows of dunes lay between the inland road and the ocean – no distance at all, really. So it seems reasonable to cut straight across the dunes to the coast road, and from there hitch a ride back to Walvis Bay. The reality proves very different. The dunes go on forever, and climbing up and down them is exhausting; after half an hour of this my legs have turned to jelly, with no more strength in them than two strands of cooked spaghetti. Looking westwards, where the ocean is supposed to lie, an endless sea of dunes awaits me. It's like walking on the surface of the moon. Dunes, dunes, then more bloody dunes, their ridges as sharp as knives; some are rippled like damp sand on a beach, some as smooth as a board. As well as big, they're also very beautiful – the colour of light apricot, composed of a surprising variety of sand, some firm, some so loose I sink up to my ankles at every step.

Before long I'm so tired I begin to wonder if I can reach the sea by nightfall. I've no remaining water, and the thought of spending the night here is very unappealing. There's no one in sight, nothing except sand, sky and burning sun. The silence is overwhelming, and God only knows where Tsondab has cleared off to by now. But however harsh the climate, there's something almost spiritual in a desert, something pure in its sheer harshness: no comforts, no distractions, only a strange beauty. Completely unexpectedly, it starts to have a calming effect on me. So my donkey has abandoned me; it's not the end of the world, and could even be part of the grand scheme of things.

I'm determined not to stop, and I reach the sea before nightfall. Finally back at The Spawning Ground, I ring Hermann with the news that my newly purchased donkey has gone AWOL.

'Wow!' says Hermann. 'Sorry, man – I never heard anything like that before!'

Neither have I, but that doesn't solve the immediate problem. Hermann says he'll ring up his crew, to go and look for the donkey 'before it gets too dark'. As it's already dark, I don't see how it can get much darker. I'm sceptical about their chances of finding Tsondab – even at midday when he was no more than 200 metres away he looked completely black against the desert. I have serious doubts our paths will cross again.

Yet a couple of hours later Hermann and his crew appear with Tsondab in a *bakkie* (back-up truck), the younger guys in predictably good spirits. 'We nearly lost him!' declares Hermann. 'He was heading back home to the Kuiseb, and he was clever at avoiding the van.'

I'm genuinely impressed. Hermann attributes their success to what he calls his 'donkey sense'. They've also done a spot of crime scene investigation, having found my tracks where I'd tried to catch Tsondab, gradually becoming more and more disheartened with the whole business: 'At first you were walking *very strongly* ... but soon your steps were getting closer and closer together ...'

To his credit, Tsondab does look slightly ashamed of himself. More likely he's just fed up because his bid for freedom ended in failure, and I can't entirely blame him.

I spend the following day feeding Tsondab in the back garden of The Spawning Ground. He soon becomes popular with the guests here, everyone making a fuss over him. To make him feel at home I try to make handfuls of grass look as realistic as possible, but he's interested only in grass he pulls out of the ground himself. And he absolutely refuses to eat carrots. Despite the reputation of farmyard animals, in some ways he has better manners than many humans; he's an amazingly dainty drinker, and without splashing or slurping the water level in his bucket lowers silently.

Unfortunately one of the neighbours doesn't care much for donkeys and complains to the council that they don't wish to live next door to one. The council in turn informs Eugene that Tsondab must go, with immediate effect. So I now have to take him to the stables in Walvis Bay, which requires Hermann's services again. Hermann turns up several hours after he said he would, this time accompanied by a young Topnaar called Petrus. Hermann makes some inflammatory – if understandable – remarks about white middle-class folks complaining to councils about donkeys. 'This always happens!' he insists. 'Always!'

Despite Tsondab's reluctance to come to The Spawning Ground in the first place, he's even more unwilling to leave now, and it takes nearly half an hour of determined struggling to get him into the vehicle. When finally we set off, the streets of Walvis Bay are practically deserted, so Hermann decides to drive like Michael Schumacher. I'm in the back with Petrus, sitting on top of Tsondab to prevent him standing up; whenever Hermann hits a bump at speed we're literally thrown in the air. Each time this happens Tsondab, recognizing a pattern, redoubles his attempts to stand up, nearly pitching us into the road. By some miracle we arrive safely, and leave Tsondab in the corral.

I need to get some saddlebags made for Tsondab to carry my gear in when we set out across Africa, so I take him round to a nice old black guy called David, who has an upholstery workshop in the industrial part of Walvis Bay. I have a hell of a job getting Tsondab across town – he's frightened by the cars and the unfamiliar sights and noises from every direction, and his ears start rotating like slow-motion propellers. The worst part is taking him down the cul-de-sac to the workshop; he seems convinced we're heading for the knacker's yard, and I have no way of convincing him otherwise – after all, he doesn't entirely trust me. But eventually we reach David's workshop.

After being measured like a rich gentleman at his Savile Row tailor, Tsondab waits outside the upholstery shop while David makes the panniers. At this point a caravan stops outside the workshop and a very affable local fellow climbs out. He bears a strong resemblance to the boxing promoter Don King, lacking only the latter's electric-shock hairstyle.

'My friend, I wish to borrow your donkey!' he declares beaming, clearly confident I'll agree. 'My church is performing a religious play this Easter, and the Lord Jesus has to ride through the gates of Jerusalem on the back of a donkey.'

'I'm sorry, sir, but I don't think he'd be much good on stage.'

'I am playing Jesus Christ, of course.'

Even this fails to tip the balance. I manage to persuade him that Tsondab isn't cut out for such a pivotal role, never having shown the slightest interest in the performing arts. Instead of transporting the Lord Jesus as planned, he'd be more likely to bring the gates of Jerusalem crashing down on the audience's heads, like the blind Samson dragging the roof down on top of his Philistine tormentors. A couple of guys dressed up as a pantomime horse would do a much better job. Fortunately the man accepts my refusal in good spirits, and he seems genuinely interested in the idea of me travelling across Africa with a donkey. He drives off, then returns a few minutes later to present me with a tape of Gospel music, promising me 'This will give you extra strength when you need it.'

The bags are completed by late afternoon. Tsondab makes much better progress on our way back to the stables, fairly trotting along. I can almost feel vague stirrings of optimism.

A daily routine sets in over the next two weeks, while I try to prepare Tsondab for his big adventure. Each day I get back from the stables knackered, frustrated and covered in shit; soon I'll be as fed up as my donkey. Around this time a photo of Tsondab and me makes the front page of the *Namib Times*, under the headline: 'Tsondab is a Naughty Boy!' Immediately I acquire a degree of mild notoriety in Walvis Bay, with children shouting: 'Donkey!' after me in the street. But I'd rather get on with training Tsondab in peace, without local guys stifling their smirks as I pass. Even the lady who runs the haberdashery shop in Walvis Bay shows me a poster she made during a period of slack trade, bearing the legend: *'Tsondab – Where You Get Stuck!'* 'I got the idea when I saw your donkey in the paper,' she tells me. 'It reminded me of the far corner in my shop – the old folks get stuck there for hours gossiping.'

Being stuck in Walvis Bay myself does give me the chance to get to know this small, quiet town better. Without Swakopmund's pretty colonial architecture, it's laid out in a grid of characterless modern buildings; the gardens look a little world-weary, as the groundwater only three metres below the surface contains over four times as much salt as seawater, so only shallow-rooted or salt-resistant plants like casuarina can grow here. The town is something of a dog lover's paradise; as I noticed on my first night here, every breed of evil mutt is represented, and I'm fed up with them barking at me outside every house I pass, even in daylight. But the dogs pale into insignificance beside the town's bird population: at one end of town the huge tidal lagoon is home to an extraordinary number of seabirds, well over 120,000 – a figure that triples each year if you include migratory birds. Almost half of southern Africa's entire flamingo population lives here.

One evening instead of the usual backpacker crowd six black South African sailors arrive at The Spawning Ground. They've jumped ship after one argument too many with the captain of a Portuguese merchant vessel, a man they all utterly detest. I'd always imagined that sailors after jumping ship would go on a massive binge, wreck several bars and then retire drunk in the early hours with a couple of prostitutes each – but these guys couldn't be more different. After cooking a communal meal and quietly discussing their immediate future, they give the whole kitchen an extraordinarily thorough clean, bringing out the buckets and mops, the full works. I've never seen anything like it before from paying guests.

I need information on the laws surrounding taking a donkey across the Namibian border. I consult the State Vet at Walvis Bay, a nice German lady called Mrs Braun. 'The authorities want proof your animal's not infected with dourine,' she tells me (dourine being a serious venereal disease affecting donkeys and horses). 'But you probably don't need to worry – it's unlikely your donkey has it.' To make sure she takes a blood sample, promising the results in a week or two.

Back at the corral I find Tsondab has cut his nose and chest. At first I wonder if local kids have been throwing stones at him; but it's more likely he cut himself trying to escape from the enclosure, the poor boy. I borrow some antiseptic from the friendly young black stable hands who always behave kindly towards me. Some of the white folks seem less well disposed; I suspect they think I intend to work my donkey to death. Tsondab was skinny when I acquired him, so obviously I'm starving him into the bargain. When the white stable owners see his cuts, they become convinced I beat him as well, so relations in this direction are less than cordial.

The overall picture is not good. It's becoming obvious I'm in totally the wrong situation to try to establish good relations with my donkey. In Africa you often find a curious attitude towards loading a vehicle or pack animal. Many people regard it as no great disaster if the vehicle or animal collapses and the journey takes twice as long as anticipated, or even if they never get there at all. African donkeys expect their masters to behave in a stern manner, and Tsondab regarding me as a soft touch only makes both our lives more difficult. Despite his lack of enthusiasm for our big

56

adventure, I've no wish to act unkindly towards him, and I don't want to trek across Africa with a donkey if it's going to die en route. But without help it's impossible to determine exactly how much he can carry, and how much is pure laziness on his part.

Neither of us is having the best of times, and we haven't even set off yet. I can't adjust quickly enough to this stressful scenario; the new situation of owning an animal feels like the responsibility of looking after a child suddenly thrust upon me. I know I've brought about this bizarre state of affairs, but we both need more time to get used to it. In my innocence I'd been looking forward to the time when Tsondab and I would think as a team. I can't draw on any useful previous experience with animals, either; the only pet I had as a child was a goldfish called Neptune, and even that ended badly when Neptune decided he'd had enough one night and committed suicide by leaping out of his bowl.

From the moment I decided to get a donkey, the problems have massively outweighed any benefits, real or anticipated. It's still possible I might be able to travel with Tsondab, but only just. And such moments of optimism are evaporating as quickly as the morning fog over the Namib Desert. Tsondab has not passed his training with flying colours – he's failed in practically every department. In other circumstances he'd make a nice pet, and we'd get along fine if being a pet were the only thing expected of him. But as a working animal he's a lost cause. Should I simply accept that we can never cover more than four or five kilometres a day? I can picture myself staggering back to Walvis Bay out of the desert, carrying the donkey on my shoulders.

By now, any attempt on my part to make light of my situation is more like gallows humour. The truth is that my imminent departure with Tsondab fills me with quiet dread.

5. Devil Mule
(Namibia: Walvis Bay to Usakos)

Mules require men who know their habits; they are powerful beasts, and can only be mastered with skill and address … They have odd secret ways, strange fancies, and lurking vice.

Francis Galton, *The Art of Travel*

The day of reckoning arrives, and all my worst fears come true.

Merely loading Tsondab is a terrible job, taking several hours. We set out, covering no more than one kilometre across the bird sanctuary on the edge of the desert. Then we simply have to stop.

I literally don't know what to do. Tsondab is obviously distressed; he can't do the job, it's as simple as that. If we go on, he'll die in the desert. We can't go back, either, as the white people at the stables in Walvis Bay are so unfriendly there's clearly no future there. And that self-righteous neighbour at The Spawning Ground complaining to the council has removed our only other option of returning. We're completely stuck, with nowhere to go – and we certainly can't stay put, standing beside a road on the edge of the Namib Desert.

Then a *bakkie* stops and a white man gets out, all hot and bothered; his florid complexion looks even more striking against his silver hair and beard. 'Your donkey's overloaded, man!' he cries, clearly expecting an argument.

'I think you're right,' I tell him quietly. At this he becomes more amenable, and starts giving the impression he'd like to help. I explain the situation.

'I have a small farm a few kilometres from here,' he tells me. 'You can take your donkey there.' This seems a wonderful idea, particularly as I have no other option.

This newcomer's name is Harry; he appears to be acting in good faith, even if he does seem of a volatile temperament. 'I have some materials at the farm,' he continues. 'You can use them to build a donkey cart.

And I know a chappie who builds donkey carts, perhaps he can help you.' I take up his offer. He tells me to put the donkey into his *bakkie* to get it to his farm. 'That's very kind of you, sir,' I tell him. 'But I have to walk him there; I promised him he wouldn't have to travel in any more vehicles for a while, and a promise is a promise.'

Predictably Tsondab is a complete hairy bastard all the way to the farm. At times he'll hardly move at all, even though he doesn't have to carry a thing now. I walk all this way to save him getting in a van and this is how he thanks me. I know I'm being unreasonable but by now I'm too furious to care. But eventually I get him along without thumping him, more or less in the right direction.

The farm itself is a dilapidated smallholding with pigs, goats, bullocks, geese, pigeons and now a donkey. Tsondab and the cows are initially suspicious of each other, the latter clearly unimpressed with the new arrival. I have a bizarre mental image of the toughest-looking bullock cornering Tsondab the moment my back is turned and showing him who the daddy is around here. But before long they're all munching along together contentedly enough from the huge pile of lucerne in the enclosure.

The farm's sole human occupant is a crazy old toothless Ovambo called Adolph. He talks as though he's permanently drunk or else has hit his head, both of which turn out to be the case. A few years previously he worked for a friend of Harry's, but proved so incompetent that the friend – in Harry's words – 'gave him' to Harry, who now 'has to look after him'. At least that's Harry's version of their curious association. In some ways Harry has indeed helped Adolph, having given him a job and somewhere to live, when otherwise he'd be living as a tramp. That's the positive side of their odd relationship; I'm soon to become acquainted with its negative aspects.

My room at the farm is spartan in the extreme, but it's free and I wasn't expecting the Hilton. I'm worn out after the day's excitement, but I sleep only fitfully thanks to Adolph; at regular intervals he produces the most extraordinary cough, a cross between a cowboy's whoop and a half-strangled scream, as though a desert snake has wrapped its coils around his neck. At first I think he's putting it on for a lark. I finally get to sleep, wondering what the hell I'm going to do with Tsondab and how I'm going to get back on the road as quickly as possible.

'Man, you need a mule for your journey,' Harry tells me the following morning. 'Mules are half-donkey and half-horse: they're much stronger than a donkey, and they shit like hell!' He indicates Tsondab with a dismissive sweep of his hand: 'This fucking donkey can't carry all your things!' Tsondab pointedly looks the other way.

I decide to follow Harry's advice and get myself a mule, which seems to offer a solution to my immediate problems. Tsondab definitely can't do the job, and a different donkey would almost certainly prove equally useless. If I can get a donkey cart and load it with all my gear, the mule should be able to pull the cart while I do the walking. Harry kindly gets in touch with some of his farming contacts inland, to see if anyone has a mule for sale, but without success. I decide to stay at the farm until I can find one for myself.

The next day I visit Harry's home in Walvis Bay. He takes me on a domestic tour while I make the appropriate polite murmurs of approval over every picture, ornament, sink, toilet and towel rack in the entire house. 'And look here!' he introduces each new item. I'm going cross-eyed by the time we reach the most interesting exhibit, a flattened Coke bottle that has literally melted under the Namib Desert's furnace-like sun.

It soon becomes obvious that Harry's in very poor health. Now in his early sixties, he's already had several heart attacks, a couple of strokes and a recent by-pass operation. Sometimes his concentration flags and he flits from topic to topic with little connection. He has a curious habit of one moment talking about a serious issue, then suddenly switching to something so banal I can't help bursting out laughing. At one point he starts telling me about his health problems: 'My brain is buggered, my body is broken – I'm at the end of my life and I will die soon … But look here, this is a tea towel with a nice picture of a desert pony on it …'

Always impeccable in his appearance, Harry can be charming, at least while things are going smoothly; when things aren't going smoothly he loses no time in working himself into a fine lather. 'It's the politics that get me going!' he tells me; in reality, the politics form only the tip of the iceberg. In his more reflective moments Harry's full of surprising theories, making long discourses in particular on his pet subject, the Ovambo nation. Although the Ovambos have the most privileged position of all the tribes in Namibia since independence, Harry seems to ignore the fact that many of them still live in poverty. 'They're the chosen race!' he declares, nudging me as though trying to draw me into some outrageous confidence. 'First it was the Jews, now it's the Ovambos. I tell you, man, I wish I was black!' But I doubt if he really means this.

While Harry's manner is largely one of sound and fury, his diminutive bête noir, Adolph, behaves a great deal more subtly. Almost everything about Adolph is slightly weird; a psychiatrist or anthropologist would find him fascinating. He's much cleverer than one might at first think, although his mental powers weren't enhanced by a recent heavy blow to the head when he fell off a roof. Allegedly still in his fifties, Adolph looks at least eighty, having spent the last forty years embalming himself in alcohol and smoking himself into the texture of biltong. Personal hygiene comes low on his list of priorities; he sleeps in his enormous rubber boots, still fully dressed in his overalls, which by now are partly cotton and mostly dirt. Harry is convinced Adolph's outfit would stand up by itself if he ever took it off, but it's unlikely anyone knows for certain, not even Adolph, who is usually deep in his cups long before bedtime.

Harry and Adolph are somehow made for each other, inexorably bound to drive each other crazy. One particular bone of contention between them surfaced a couple of years previously, when Harry was seriously ill in hospital following his first stroke. When it seemed likely that Harry would die, Adolph decided to help by selling off some of Harry's property at the farm. 'I tell you, man, he had a *fucking feast!*' declares Harry with long-pent-up feeling. Adolph's private enterprise on this occasion clearly remains a stumbling block in their fraught relationship, as does his fondness for alcohol. 'Adolph doesn't drink like a human being, he gets *paralytic*. He pours whole bottles straight down his throat without it even touching his lips – I tell you, man, it's like emptying a bottle down a sluice!'

Recently Harry's son needed his roof painting, and made the mistake of involving Adolph. The latter was provided with a paint pot and ladder; a large brush was placed in his hand and detailed instructions given. Despite Adolph's track record with alcohol, no one at this point realized he was drunk; but the thought of spending an entire afternoon actually working had filled Adolph with such dread that he'd spent the morning fortifying himself with cane spirit. To be on the safe side he also smuggled a fresh bottle on to the roof, to top himself up while he painted.

After a couple of hours Harry's son came to inspect the work, by which time Adolph had made such a dreadful mess he was ordered to stop immediately. Cursing himself for allowing Adolph anywhere near his property, Harry's son departed on other business. Instead of climbing down, Adolph stayed on the roof as drunk as a lord, covered in paint and forgotten by the rest of the world, while the afternoon floated by in a dreamlike haze. Towards evening he felt the time had come to return to earth and stretch his legs in search of another drink. Although the ladder had long since been tidied away, Adolph's imagination – together with the effects of two bottles of cane spirit – supplied all the missing details. Stepping out into empty space, a short and spirited battle with gravity followed, ending with Adolph hitting the ground headfirst, long before he'd even realized the ladder was gone.

'But fortunately he was drunk,' explains Harry. 'So no major bones were broken. My son gave him a lift home, because Adolph had fallen off the roof during working hours. And Adolph was so drunk he repaid my son's kindness by shitting himself ... I tell you, man, he shat in my son's car, and had to be thrown out into the desert! My own son's car! How could a man do such a thing?'

The following day I call round again at Harry's house and find him particularly ill, looking as though he's about to drop dead at any moment. I accompany him to the doctor in case he collapses en route. When Harry drives his *bakkie* his dog, a giant African whippet of a kind I've never seen anywhere else, usually travels in the back. A typical journey consists of a frenzy of barking from both parties, with Harry roaring at the dog: '*FUCKING SHUT UP, MAN! FUCK YOU, MAN!*' This only makes the dog more excited and she barks even more furiously. Harry always ties her lead in such a position that she barks right beside his ear, which only compounds the problem. But the dog obviously enjoys travelling in this way; whenever she realizes Harry is about to leave she takes a great joyful leap and sails like Pegasus into the back of his vehicle.

The doctor gives Harry an injection, which seems to calm him slightly, together with strict instructions to go home to bed and stay there or else call an undertaker. On the way back to Harry's house we call on one of his friends, who facially bears a strong resemblance to the actor Leo McKern. Harry thinks the man might be able to offer me a lift to a farm with mules for sale, but unfortunately he turns out to be the most bigoted racist I've met so far in Africa, despite some stiff competition. He's obviously well educated and intelligent, even a cultured man, but almost everything he says ends like the refrain of a ballad with the words: 'We're just giving the country to the kaffirs!' A local paper lies on his coffee table, the front page carrying details of a serious road accident. 'We should give a medal to Toyota,' he says, indicating the paper. 'They've killed more kaffirs than we ever did in the wars!' Next to the paper lies a book on Tamerlane, the fourteenth-century Scythian conqueror whose extraordinarily violent career devastated much of Central Asia and resulted in millions of deaths. 'He had the right idea when it came to niggers!' declares our host, seeing me looking at the book's cover. 'He just wiped the buggers out ...'

'Well, I'm not a racist,' says Harry, seeing my embarrassment and presumably by now wishing this stupid man would shut up as well. Does his friend imagine we want to hear all this crap? Since I've been in southern Africa I've found certain white people will throw the word 'kaffir' into the conversation with you – not merely because it's still a common expression, but also deliberately to test the water when talking to a foreigner, to see how you react. But this guy is so far off any scale of normality that he presumably doesn't care what anyone thinks. We stay only for about five minutes, until Harry's friend announces he can't help with a lift, which suits me fine – if he keeps on about kaffirs and niggers much longer I'll have to walk out anyway, or else shake him warmly by the lapels. When we leave I feel guilty for not telling the man what I thought of him. Already it's clear that if I'm going to get any help with finding a mule, somewhere down the line it will mean accepting help occasionally from people I'd rather not have lunch with.

Harry's friend is hardly alone in his views here. I visit one of the engineering workshops in the industrial part of Walvis Bay, to see if I can get a donkey cart built on the coast; here I talk to a middle-aged fellow from Manchester who has worked in Namibia for years. Like many Europeans who have lived in Africa for a long time, he's taken to local prejudices like a duck to water, regarding black people with a curious mixture of contempt and superstitious dread. He lectures me on the dangers facing a white man travelling through parts of southern Africa, insisting that if I'm not careful I'll certainly get killed by black people. 'Listen, mate, I'll tell you what you should do.' He tightens the chuck on his lathe with more force than seems strictly necessary and looks me right in the eye. 'If you're driving along at night and a black tries to stop you for a lift, just run the bastard over. Then report an accident at the next police station.'

I doubt if this guy would actually do such a thing, but you never know. He doesn't seem to quite understand the nature of my journey, and I leave without feeling any inclination to explain it further to him. He's right to claim that parts of southern Africa are dangerous, but often the real situation isn't nearly so bad as some of the more privileged and paranoid white folks suggest. Perhaps one day this idiot will return home to Manchester and tell his mates down the pub how for years in Namibia he braved the *swaart gevaar*, the black threat. Often in Africa it worries me when racist whites like this man are so friendly and well disposed towards me. In the meantime, countries like Namibia aren't going to change overnight.

While I'm trying to sort out a mule for the journey, I still have to look after Tsondab at Harry's farm. Every day I cut reeds for him near by; I've been warned about snakes living in the reeds, but I never see any.

This period drags on for a couple of weeks, during which time the prospect of spending an entire evening alone at the farm with Adolph is always rather scary; so I usually head back to The Spawning Ground in Walvis Bay, returning to the farm only to sleep. On several occasions I'm forced to spend well over an hour in the dark trying to find the farm at night; there's no electricity here, and when Adolph is blind drunk he has no need for any light, so the farm is in pitch blackness. I'd always imagined desert nights to be illuminated by brilliant stars, but this is not always so, especially when the coastal fog creeps inland. The low farm itself lies so close to the earth that at night it's visible only from within about a hundred metres, and even less in the fog. On pitch-black nights the difficulty lies in getting that close to the farm in the first place; in daylight it all looked so straightforward.

The first time this happens I find the farm only after a long and devious search. I try deliberately casting inland from where I know it must lie, my eyes just above ground level, rather like an anteater, hoping the farm's silhouette will momentarily blot out the distant lights of Walvis Bay. This in theory *must* work, yet when finally I stumble across the farm it's almost certainly down to pure luck.

A few nights later I find myself in exactly the same situation. Every ploy to find the accursed place comes to nothing, yet I know I must be close. This goes on for well over an hour, and it's bloody cold. It's pointless calling Adolph – there's no way he'd get out of bed on my account, and why should he? He'll almost certainly be paralytic by now. I start praying that Adolph will start coughing, so I can find him in the dark; he does it often enough in the middle of the night when it's the last thing I want to hear. Please, Adolph, one cough … just a little one … you can do it, Adolph … *ADOLPH, JUST COUGH, YOU FUCKER!*

No cough is forthcoming. I can't face the long hike back to town, so I try to sleep in the sand. It's so cold that five minutes later I'm back on the road to Walvis Bay anyway. By now I'm so tired my vision blurs; the distant town lights assume weird oval shapes, like endless rows of white Zulu shields. It's a long walk. The following day I lay out elaborate rock markers in the sand pointing towards the farm from the road. I also ensure that as a last resort I can find the bloody place on a compass bearing, and from now on even in daylight I never leave the farm without my compass.

Then the plot suddenly thickens regarding Tsondab. Mrs Braun from the State Vet's office tells me that Tsondab has tested positive for the venereal disease dourine. What a bloody shame – apart from the donkey being ill, this complicates matters immensely. It's against the law to treat dourine in Namibia; the only treatment allowed is to sterilize the infected animal, so that it can't spread the disease. After that it has to take its chances: around fifty per cent of animals infected make a full recovery, while the rest die. So at the very least Tsondab will have to be castrated, the poor boy. I don't want him to suffer; he's lazy, useless and has done me no favours whatsoever, but he never asked to come along on this trip. He never shared my enthusiasm for walking across Africa – he merely wants to go everywhere his balls go, and it's not to be.

Then Harry tells me he's learnt of a farmer called van Zyl on the other side of the country who can sell me a 'tame mule' for 700 rand. This sounds reasonable, but it would mean Harry driving hundreds of kilometres to fetch the creature and then back again. This seems a ridiculous amount of trouble for him to go to on my behalf; but Harry assures me he's also interested in buying some other animals from van Zyl. Even so, the precarious state of his health makes this journey a most unwise proposition. And when I speak to van Zyl on the phone it becomes clear he knows next to nothing about the animal he's trying to sell.

'How old is this mule?' I ask him. 'And what sort of work has it done?'

'I can't tell you,' growls van Zyl. He has a very deep voice.

'Well, is it male or female?'

'I tell you, man, I don't know! It belonged to a black who worked for me. I caught the bastard stealing from me; now he's in jail, and I'm selling the mule to cover my costs.'

This is getting worse by the minute. I tell van Zyl I'll consider his offer carefully, and I'll be sure to get back to him if I decide to go ahead with it. Later that day I wonder if this might have sounded ambiguous, a rather feeble English way of turning something down rather than a forthright Afrikaner 'No way, man!' So I phone him again to cancel the deal; he's out, so I leave a message on his answerphone.

I realize that waiting for Harry to organize a mule will do neither of us any good – after all, it's not his problem. I tell him not to buy the mule from van Zyl on my account as I'll try and sort one out elsewhere. 'That's fine,' says Harry, who at this stage seems completely reasonable about everything – which only makes his subsequent behaviour even more bizarre.

I decide to look for myself further inland, but the prospect is daunting: I don't know the country and I certainly don't know any farmers. However, my quest to find a mule goes much better than I expected, and in the little town of Usakos a white farmer called Kokkie Labuschagne helps me find a dark chestnut mule called Marieke. She's a beautiful creature, glowing with health and definitely strong enough to do the job. While we have no problems loading her on to Kokkie's trailer, I find it unnerving just how big and heavy mules are – several times the size of the diminutive Tsondab. They're stronger and much tougher than horses, so they can work longer and harder; on the other hand, they can also kill a grown man easily with a well-placed kick.

'This may sound unmanly,' I tell Kokkie, 'but I must admit I find mules scary.'

'Man, I've worked with mules all my life and they still frighten me!' he replies. I find this reassuring and worrying in equal measure.

Very kindly Kokkie and his wife Sinta let me keep the mule in their corral while I sort out all the problems with Tsondab back in Walvis Bay. I phone Harry and a strange story unfolds, worse than anything I could have imagined.

In order to get my expedition moving again I seem to have entered into some strange kind of Faustian pact with certain individuals – and I've still to hear the details of Harry's extraordinary journey. Despite the fact that he knew I'd cancelled the meeting with van Zyl, Harry now tells me he proceeded anyway to this ill-starred rendezvous. As a result, he's now the owner of a demented wild mule, and he's raging like a maniac himself.

I tell him I'll come round immediately.

Even after speaking to Harry on the phone I'm still unprepared for his apoplectic state when I arrive at his house. His towering rage is directed mainly towards his black workers; without speaking Afrikaans I can't determine the exact nature of his complaint, but it's clear he's accusing them of some form of treachery. By now his fury has reached such whirlwind proportions that I doubt even his employees can understand what he's shouting about. If this was the first time I'd met Harry I'd be tempted to call the authorities. Watching this ailing, elderly man charge around like an inmate from Bedlam, I'm waiting for his lips to turn blue and for him to keel over clutching his chest. Either that or his sheer intensity of wrath will produce a sonic boom.

After treating his workers to another volley of frightful oaths Harry rushes off again, his curses ringing across his newly laid patio like the howls of a banshee. I hear him on the rampage somewhere in the depths of his house, and half expect him to come storming back to bury a meat-cleaver in the head of one of his workers. Sure enough, he re-appears in another sudden blast of fury, this time staying long enough to make some inflammatory remarks about Ovambos before vanishing back into his house. I consider calling a coroner now, to save time later.

Eventually Harry manages to calm himself enough to sit down and tell me the details of his expedition to van Zyl's farm. 'I could write an entire book on this one trip!' he cries. 'No, three books – three, I tell you!'

The previous day had started badly for both parties. Van Zyl, despite his later denials, had obviously received the telephone message I'd left to cancel the deal. As a result he didn't turn up to meet Harry, who waited two hours at the arranged rendezvous before ringing him to find out what had happened. Strong words followed immediately. Harry then drove to the farm to meet van Zyl, a large and brawny fellow with a great black beard and forearms worthy of Popeye, who lost no time in making outrageous demands:

'I want 200 rand from you before we go any further.'

'200 rand! What the hell for, man?' demanded Harry.

'What the hell for? For compensation, man! We had an arrangement – I've been buggered about by you, and buggered about by this fucking Englishman!'

After this shaky start the negotiations go steadily downhill. I never find out the exact details of Harry's arrangement with van Zyl made earlier by phone, but it seems he planned to buy a couple of horses, a dog and a mule, with a view to keeping the mule for himself. What for he never tells me, and exactly how he expected to transport two horses, a mule and a dog back to the coast remains a mystery. Even I can see his *bakkie* is too small to transport anything larger than a donkey the size of Tsondab.

After calming himself somewhat, van Zyl started his sales pitch: 'Here, I'll show you two good, healthy horses. Man, I'm giving you a bargain, eh?' They approached the first animal, which immediately galloped off. 'It jumped over a big fence like a bloody kudu, then ran off into the bush,' Harry tells me. 'And that was the last we saw of it. "That's not a tame horse!" I said to van Zyl. "I know horses, and that creature is not a tame horse!"'

Van Zyl scowled ferociously at this unforeseen development, and quickly led Harry towards the next horse on offer, which greeted them by foaming at the mouth and rolling its eyes horribly. 'And this one's sick!' cried Harry. 'You can't expect me to buy a sick horse, man!'

Van Zyl's scowl grew even more ferocious as they moved on to the mule. 'This is a good tame mule,' he growled, 'a strong worker …'

'But it wasn't a mule!' Harry tells me. 'Not by a long way. It was a devil – a fucking devil, come to earth in the form of a mule … You'll see for yourself!'

By this stage Harry was reluctant to conduct any further business with his host. Sensing his sales patter wasn't working as well as he'd hoped, van Zyl adjourned the proceedings by bellowing for kudu meat, promptly served by a suitably cowed houseboy. Lunch at van Zyl's resembled a caveman feast, with great haunches of roast kudu and nothing else. Van Zyl set to with gusto.

'I can't eat kudu meat,' said Harry after an uncomfortable silence. 'I have a heart condition.'

'That's too bad, man!' said van Zyl, his mouth full of half-masticated kudu. 'Here, I'll help you out, eh?' Still only halfway through his own enormous hunk of meat, van Zyl seized Harry's kudu joint from under his nose and started on that too. 'Man, I've never seen anything like it!' Harry tells me. 'It was like watching a wolf eating.'

Van Zyl's immediate appetite for red meat sated, he returned to the mule negotiations with renewed zest. All this time the mule in question had been cruising the farm's corral like some monstrous creature from a gladiatorial arena. Seeing no other way out of the situation in which he found himself, Harry agreed to buy the creature. All things considered, and despite the events of the return journey, this was probably a wise move – had Harry tried to leave the farm without parting with any money, van Zyl might simply have shot him.

The deal concluded, the newly purchased mule still had to be loaded on Harry's *bakkie*, so a four-hour battle commenced. The mule put up a tremendous struggle, its capacity for violence impressive even in a continent well known for its large and powerful beasts. Only sheer exhaustion and weight of numbers finally won the day; even so, it's a miracle no one was killed or horribly maimed.

The creature finally loaded, Harry and his helpers prepared to leave. Further unpleasantness ensued when van Zyl calculated the total bill for goods and services rendered, taking the opportunity to sell Harry some old mule harnesses for twice the going rate, together with some crumbling timber to fortify Harry's *bakkie* against the mule's inevitable onslaught. Then he started up again about compensation for having been inconvenienced by my phone call, the very call he'd earlier insisted he never received.

'I'm going to shoot this fucking Englishman!' he shouted. 'He's unreliable! I tell you man, these English, they fucked us around during the Boer War and this Englishman is trying the same trick again! Man, he needs shooting!'

'But he hasn't done anything!' said Harry. 'He's innocent.'

'Bullshit, man! I'll shoot the bastard anyway – he needs a rifle bullet up his arse!'

Since van Zyl was clearly warming to the idea of bloodshed, Harry more or less gave him whatever he asked for, just so he could leave the farm in one piece. Mercifully his vehicle didn't break down while he was still on van Zyl's land – had it done so, I think none of his party would have left the place alive.

'Thank you, sir,' Harry shouted to van Zyl over the noise of his revving engine as he departed. 'It's been an honour and a pleasure to meet you and do business with you … may God bless you … *and I pray our fucking paths never cross again!*' Van Zyl opened his mouth to reply, which fortunately was drowned by the sound of Harry's accelerating vehicle and the mule's struggles.

If Harry's problems with van Zyl had ended, his problems with the mule were only beginning. Its performance at the farm was a mere foretaste of its true capacity for destruction, and it fought like a demon all the way back to the coast, pausing only to catch its breath before continuing with renewed fury. After covering less than fifteen kilometres it tangled itself in the harnesses, nearly strangling itself, and Harry had to stop several times to cut it loose.

Halfway back to the coast, Harry decided to phone his wife from a public phonebox; like Penelope, she's had to wait at home while her errant husband pursues his strange odyssey, so on the off-chance she might want to hear from him at two in the morning Harry started dialling. His call was rudely interrupted by sounds of dreadful violence from his *bakkie*, the crash of hooves on metal and splintering wood, interspersed with screams of panic from his helpers as the mule escaped again. With a great oath, Harry charged out of the phone box to find the mule standing on the roof of his *bakkie*, smashing the driver's cab with massive blows from its hooves.

Another long and spectacular struggle followed before the mule was restored to captivity. After being driven halfway across Namibia the mule didn't even wait to be unloaded at the farm; it was so pleased to have finished travelling that it leaped straight off the back of Harry's vehicle and charged off to the far end of the enclosure.

So now Harry's *bakkie* is more or less in pieces, as indeed is Harry after his apocalyptic drive back to the coast. I take a quick look at his vehicle – after the mule's assault it looks like James Dean's car after the crash. But at least everyone involved in the trip is still alive. Thankfully by the time I leave his house on this occasion Harry has calmed himself enough to laugh about the whole episode. I suspect he feels he may as well.

Back at the farm later I see the mule in question prowling the corral, and I realize Harry wasn't exaggerating. This Lizzie Borden of the animal world is a monstrous creature, black and evil-looking and obviously completely untamed. Even the weighty thump of her hooves in the sand as she cruises the enclosure suggests raw power and inspires dread. She'd scare the shit out of all Four Horsemen of the Apocalypse, or at least take them on as equals.

I can scarcely take in how quickly the problems of pack animals have multiplied. I'm still desperate to get moving across Africa as soon as possible, but first I must sort out this whole sorry mess with donkeys and mules. I need to get the mule at Kokkie's farm trained for the journey, and to find a cart so she can pull my gear. Before that I need to somehow extricate myself from this awkward situation at Harry's farm, and to decide what to do with Tsondab. My head is spinning with all these complications. Getting a pack animal was supposed to make my journey easier. But two mules and a donkey are too much for me – I came here to walk across Africa, not to re-enact *The Musicians of Bremen*.

After the drama of Harry's extraordinary journey, an uneasy calm returns to his farm. The crazy mule keeps itself to itself, refusing any overtures of friendship from the other animals, even though poor Tsondab makes it clear he'd like to become pals. I'm worried she might kill him; I daren't go anywhere near her, and Adolph wisely keeps well away, even when he's pissed.

Then Harry kindly offers Tsondab a home on his farm, which is certainly the best solution for the donkey. So that's one major headache removed. Harry then announces that he plans to ship the crazy mule out to Bolivia, insisting that mules are 'worth a lot of money out there'. It sounds like a wonderful opportunity for the mule – I just hope she's sedated for the entire voyage, or she'll take the whole ship down to the bottom of the sea with her. Harry also manages to get hold of a ready-made donkey cart on my behalf and at a reasonable price, so that's another problem solved. This cart needs some work on it, but will certainly do the job. All I need to do now is get the donkey cart up to Usakos, train the mule and then I'm back on the road, thank God.

But there's still one final moment of drama before I part company with Harry and Adolph. Another council official appears without warning at the farm, demanding to inspect Harry's pigsty. Sandboarders on the nearby dunes have complained about hordes of flies coming from the farm – specifically from Harry's pigsty. The official informs Harry that he must either line the pigsty with concrete so it can drain properly, or the pigs must go. Harry accepts this ruling with surprising equanimity, which smacks of the proverbial calm before the storm.

Loading the pigs for their last ride to the abattoir in Walvis Bay bears a striking similarity to loading the crazed mule at van Zyl's farm. Harry and his workers spend a whole morning building a ramp for the three enormous pigs to walk up, and then a pitched battle commences. The pigs neither understand nor sympathize with Harry's plans for their immediate future, and for most of the afternoon his volcanic temper ensures that internal relations in his workforce are strained. After an hour and a half of Harry's curses and inflammatory remarks, directed in turn at the pigs, his workers and the entire Ovambo nation, they finally get the first pig on the ramp. They need only to shut the trailer gate behind it, but by now the pig is suspicious and looking for a way out.

'Shut the gate!' shouts Harry.

'What gate?' says Adolph, scratching his head nervously.

'THAT FUCKING GATE!' roars Harry as the pig saunters back down the ramp the way it came.

Harry's response to this setback is to spend several minutes bellowing wordlessly in pure rage. A further hour of cajolery, threats and grunts sees the first animal loaded, the gate securely locked behind it. But the two remaining pigs show no inclination to follow the example of the first. After another great volley of oaths aimed at his workforce, Harry turns his wrath on the pigs themselves, explaining to them in the most intemperate language that whether they like it or not they must join the first pig on the trailer. But the struggle continues for the rest of the afternoon. The job is finally completed only when Harry stops roaring at the heavens and instead swears a solemn oath before Almighty God that if all three pigs aren't loaded in five minutes flat he'll smother Adolph in shit.

With the pigs safely loaded peace descends once more on this eventful corner of the Namib Desert. By now Harry is too exhausted to address his workers further, and they in turn are too exhausted to care. Adolph staggers off to his room mumbling, while Harry somehow manages to drive home to Walvis Bay for his usual low-cholesterol supper, probably seasoned with gunpowder.

The time has come for me to leave Harry's farm and transport the donkey cart by rail up to Usakos, where I can get the mule trained and then carry on across Africa. As I leave the farm Adolph gives me a look that could melt a heart of stone if you didn't know how crafty he is. 'So you are leaving me all alone?' he asks in a small and sad voice, looking so pathetic I do feel sorry for him, however much I want to get away.

I give Tsondab a hug and tell him I hope there are no hard feelings between us. I'd thought at times that our brief partnership had brought him nothing but unhappiness, and that he would have been much better off if we'd never met. But things have ultimately worked out in Tsondab's favour. Apart from his forthcoming uncomfortable operation the future looks reasonable for him, and he stands a much better chance of recovering from dourine here than he would if he'd remained in the Kuiseb Valley. He won't have to do a stroke of work now to earn his board and lodgings, and he'll have more than enough to eat. It's a pity I can't explain to him that he can more or less look forward to the fancy life from now on. But I expect it will gradually sink in.

I say goodbye to Harry back at his house in Walvis Bay. I find myself wondering not for the first time why Harry has done so much to help me, in his own inimitable way; for all his faults and unreasonableness, Harry has gone to a lot of trouble on my behalf. But I sense it would embarrass him to ask him for his real reasons. It's clear enough that he knows his time on earth is nearly up, this prematurely aged man at the end of his life; somehow he seems to regard me as a young adventurer, a young man off on his travels, someone who in some way can still *escape*.

While we're talking Harry's wife Eva enters the kitchen. 'If there's one person in the whole of Africa you won't forget, it's Harry.' She tells me. 'If he ever went to London it would burn down like the Great Fire of London – the very first taxi driver who gave him some cheek …'

She's quite right, and I leave with the feeling that my life can only get duller without Harry's violent eruptions.

Back again at Kokkie's farm in Usakos, I christen my new donkey cart *The Lady Alice*, after the portable boat Stanley used on his 1874–77 traversa. Stanley named it in honour of his American fiancée, the seventeen-year-old Alice Pike, who rewarded his unrealistic romantic expectations by marrying a rival suitor and having children even before Stanley finished his epic journey.

Kokkie's uncle Gert kindly gives up a Sunday to weld the donkey cart, and for a very reasonable price. He builds a disselboom out of heavy steel tubing, and also a tough wooden crash plate for the front of the cart in case the mule lashes out backwards with her hooves. With the donkey cart's basic structure in place, I spend two weeks giving it an intricate paint job, which includes some detailed African motifs, and even a panel painted in the style of an Ndebele house. At one stage I try to incorporate a stylized mule into the design, but abandon this idea when the mule's face starts looking more like Batman. Whenever I set my drink down behind me to assess my painting progress, the coffee keeps mysteriously disappearing from my cup; I attribute this to freak evaporation until I catch the Labuschagnes' little black dog in the act of drinking from my mug, her tail wagging furiously.

I reckon *The Lady Alice* is the best-painted donkey cart in Namibia, possibly all Africa. And Marieke, an attractive mule by anyone's standards, looks even more attractive in front of such a stylish cart. But it's obvious I'm concerning myself far too much with appearances. Deep down, I'm gradually starting to wonder if I'm in denial of some kind, and whether this is all a giant cop-out. I should be making more progress with trying to train the mule; instead, I'm literally putting the cart before the horse. I may score highly on artistic merit, but I'd swap all that gladly for distance covered. The longer all this drags on, the more my frustration mounts – after all this time, money and effort, both the mule and the donkey cart are becoming an expensive reproach to me.

Problems with the mule aside, my time in Usakos is characterized largely by the attentions of vast numbers of corn crickets. I assume the first one of these unlovely creatures I see in the sandy street is some gigantic freak of nature, but I soon realize these Schwarzeneggers of the insect world are all this big. Their bodies are about five centimetres long and armour plated, like matchbox-sized Sherman tanks; instead of caterpillar tracks they have six powerful legs, with long feelers in the place of radio antennae, and even the baby ones look scary. Their distinctive shade of puce adds to their general aura of unpleasantness. They also make a tremendous noise, a distinctive high-pitched chirrup; you can hear a solitary cricket from ten metres away. When there's a whole gang of them, as there usually is, the noise is amazing. By day thousands of corn crickets hang from the bushes like loathsome Christmas tree decorations. At night they're everywhere, trying to eat everything in their path, even curtains. And they're as tough as they look; one night when I stay in Kokkie's spare bedroom I have to whack one of them with my boot half a dozen times before it finally expires, its insides erupting in a yellow burst of viscous fluid like pus. Even after this treatment I'm still convinced it will come back to life like The Terminator. Throughout the evening I clobber several other unpleasant specimens, the last making its forlorn exit from this world via the sink, floating off towards the drain like poor Ophelia. This is enough for one day – if I see another horrible creepy-crawly tonight I'll run around the room screaming.

Each day I venture into corn cricket headquarters to cut hay for Marieke for several hours – rather more time in fact than I'm spending on trying to train her. But cutting grass and painting a donkey cart aren't getting me across Africa, and by now I'm seriously worried about the prospect of travelling alone in this manner. If I ever manage to get moving with the mule and donkey cart, I'll be a prime target for thieves. Throughout the country it will be difficult for a white guy with a gaily painted donkey cart to blend into the background. Travelling alone, I won't be able to leave the donkey cart even for a moment – and if I do get robbed there's no way I can chase the culprits without leaving the rest of my gear behind for their accomplices to steal. I consider carrying a big stick, such as a Zulu *kerrie*. A more likely scenario might run thus: 'What nice machetes you gentlemen have; I would like to make you a gift of this fine donkey cart and all its contents.'

There's also every chance the mule will simply run away – after all, I couldn't even hold on to Tsondab on that first day near Swakopmund, and he's a babe in arms compared to the massive Marieke. When tethering a mule to a tree you have to choose your tree carefully or the mule will run off with the tree, literally. If a mule strays it can cover immense distances, and it's almost impossible for a man on foot to overtake or catch it. Even when Marieke is already in captivity in Kokkie's corral I find it difficult to catch her each morning, let alone do anything towards training her. It takes three farmhands to head her off in the enclosure, but I can't keep poaching Kokkie's workers for this purpose as he's getting understandably grumpy on the subject. Even once she's been caught it's seldom long before she bolts with such sudden energy and strength that I'm left standing with a broken harness in my hands, feeling only relief that she hasn't taken my arm with her.

By now I've realized it will be a miracle if I ever reach the stage where I can manage my mule in one place, let alone cover any distance with her. She knows full well I'm a total novice, and when we're alone out in the bush she'll take the first opportunity of either going AWOL or murdering me, or both. It's proving impossible to train her by myself – she's too big and powerful, and I simply don't have the experience. I need a team on this project, at least initially; but I'm the only one involved, ironically how I planned it all along. So I've well and truly stitched myself up.

After another two weeks at Kokkie's farm and failing miserably in every department with Marieke, I realize that there's no way I can learn on my own with such a powerful beast. Finally I have to accept that I'm hopeless with animals, and always will be. From the moment I first took up with donkeys and mules the logistical problems of the trip have snowballed. I've been throwing good money after bad and wasting a huge amount of time I can ill afford if I want to reach the east coast before Christmas.

I accept the inevitable: this whole mule deal is not working out, and must end.

I'm here to walk across Africa. I've now been in Namibia for nearly three months, and so far I've covered only about 270 kilometres of the journey – and virtually all of that was in the first two weeks. Despite nearly collapsing in the desert near Arandis, I was making reasonable progress under my own steam. But in the ten weeks since I decided to make my life easier with a donkey and then a mule, the only part of the actual journey across Africa I've travelled is the single pitiful kilometre with Tsondab outside Walvis Bay before we ground to a halt. That's fourteen metres a day – at this rate it would take us around 800 years to reach Zanzibar, or even a couple of centuries longer if we were delayed for any unexpected reason.

I'll carry on alone, taking only what I can carry myself, which is how I'd originally planned things all along. To hell with it. Plan B has been such an unmitigated disaster that Plan A suddenly doesn't seem so bad after all. The walking itself was not so great a problem; it was carrying far too much weight that did for me in the desert. I'll jettison some more gear. And since I won't have a donkey or mule with me, I needn't worry so much about the tsetse fly – now I can head straight across Africa towards Zanzibar, directly through the tsetse belt.

Above all I'll be free again. Life will be worth living once more, as it was before all this self-inflicted grief with donkeys and mules descended on me like a sack of shit …

Before I can continue east I walk the stretch between Arandis and Usakos. This takes a day and a half, but it's literally the first time I've experienced any peace of mind in the last two and a half months of going round in circles with donkeys and mules and getting absolutely nowhere. The relief is palpable, and I feel like singing 'Morning has Broken'.

On leaving Usakos, I give away most of the extra equipment I accumulated when I planned to travel with the mule. I bequeath *The Lady Alice* to Kokkie's daughter Elizabeth, and a whole lot of other gear to his family and workers. So at least some people gain out of all this. Marieke has a good home here on Kokkie's farm, and he's welcome to sell her if he wants to. Secretly I'm convinced she never liked me – for all his faults, I much preferred Tsondab.

I'm ready to leave by midday. I sit under a shady tree just out of town, revelling in the knowledge of moving under my own steam again. I've made more progress in twenty minutes than in the last ten weeks. I'll head northeast, diagonally across the country to Bushmanland – if that proves impossible through lack of water in the Kalahari, I'll head instead through the Caprivi Strip towards Zambia and Victoria Falls. Either way I'll be moving in the right direction again, and that's all that matters to me now.

Thank God I've finished with animals. I'll never again involve myself with any beast of burden. From now on I carry or drag everything myself, however difficult it gets. And I'll even try to stop complaining.

6. The Waterberg Plateau
(Namibia: Usakos to Otjiwarongo)

Every Herero, whether armed or unarmed, with or without cattle, will be shot.

General Lothar von Trotha

The first evening out of Usakos feels remarkably peaceful as I head east, following a path beside the railway tracks. Now I'm finally on the move again I find myself reluctant to call a halt for the night. The air is warmer than in the desert, so I can't be bothered to pitch my tent; unfortunately this means I spend most of the night fighting off hordes of corn crickets, approaching in sinister formations like miniature panzers advancing across the Russian steppes. Every time I switch on my torch they've multiplied, until they're strewn across the dark landscape like the teeth of the Hydra. After I've given those within reach a good whacking with a trekking pole the survivors beat a hasty retreat, but they're brave and determined; regrouping constantly throughout the night, they return to crawl over my face and hair, every so often emitting a particularly piercing chirrup right in my ear to make sure I can't sleep. I've no idea what pleasure they could possibly derive from this exercise.

East of Karibib I leave the road and head across the wide-open thorn bush savannah in the direction of Omaruru. Intended as a short cut, this proves far more tiring than walking on a tarred road; apart from the uneven terrain underfoot, the grass is festooned with horrible little spiky balls that stick fast to clothes and skin. It's impossible to cover more than ten metres without having to stop and pull them off one by one; it takes real patience to dislodge them, but to leave them attached is torture. They're particularly painful sticking to your feet, or worse – my jogging pants are totally unsuitable for this kind of grass, and after half an hour they're full of spiky grass balls, inside and out. By this stage my bad language is so foul that even the corn crickets rein back in horror and disgust.

But it's a huge relief to be on the move once more, to be back on the journey across Africa. And it's wonderful to get away from people again, to return to open countryside. You don't have to go far to avoid human contact; Namibia has one of the lowest population densities in the world, less than two people per square kilometre. This part of Namibia is still very much white ranching country, and apart from the game lodges there's comparatively little human settlement between the towns – unlike the dense villages I encounter later in the northeast of the country, when I reach black Africa.

The main roads here are punctuated at regular intervals by picnic spots, usually consisting of a concrete table and benches with some form of shade, either a metal canopy or sometimes just a suitable tree. It's difficult to reconcile these picnic sites with the idea of a tough expedition, but they're bloody convenient. Some of the signs for picnic sites are riddled with bullet holes, a legacy from high-spirited beer-boys armed to the teeth. I stop at one such spot twenty kilometres out of Karibib, my evening meal enlivened by a large bat flapping around my head. I'm still so pleased to be making progress once again that I continue walking after eating, and this night is one of the very few on the entire journey when I actually enjoy walking in the dark. Since leaving Usakos I've grown accustomed to walking through flat treeless bushland, but the Khan River provides enough water for an abundance of trees. The surrounding hills in moonlight resemble those from an ancient Chinese painting, while the moon throws into relief the distant shadowy Erongo Mountains, famed for their ancient rock paintings and secret caves. After the Namib Desert and the broad featureless bush, the valley of the Khan River at night is like walking into an enchanted garden.

The following lunchtime I reach Omaruru. Surrounded by mountains, this small town is home to Namibia's only vineyard, an anomaly in such an arid country. The town's name derives from the Herero word for 'bitter thick milk' – any cattle grazing on the local bitterbush produce appropriately bitter milk. I play safe and settle for a litre of sterilized banana milkshake from the Spar supermarket. Looking for somewhere outside to sit and drink it, I notice a low wall outside the shop has been lined with a row of evil-looking spikes, obviously designed to discourage the idle; but if anyone was drunk or careless enough to sit on one of these spikes they'd remain stuck fast, which surely defeats the object. This is

80

mirrored in nature here; many of the bushes are covered in backwards-slanting thorns like fishhooks, and to extricate yourself you need the skill of Houdini. I thought vegetation was designed to keep animals away, not hold them in a horrible thorny embrace until they died.

The night after passing through Omaruru I sleep beside the railway track again. I'm still not bothering with my tent; in any case, the ground is as hard as slate, and by the end of each day I've barely the energy to hammer in my tent pegs. In the middle of the night a vehicle stops fifty metres past me, and a group of local black guys start conferring loudly. I find this most unsettling; when I stopped in pitch blackness I'd assumed I was in the middle of nowhere. I have to remind myself that genuine robbers tend to keep their voices down – even those learning the trade rarely go above a stage whisper. The following morning, when everything appears decidedly less spooky, I discover I've been sleeping near the entrance gate to a game lodge, some distance from the road and invisible in the darkness. At this stage it's still easy for me to camp undetected, even next to roads – it's only later on the journey when I'm crossing far more heavily populated areas that I start having real problems.

By far the most noticeable living creatures here are the corn crickets; east of Omaruru their numbers reach the proportions of an Egyptian plague. A tremendous insect noise issues from every bush; the crickets certainly have enough to shout about, as their short lives are filled with danger and drama. The roads here are covered with dried rhubarb-and-custard stains, all that remains of the millions of crickets squashed by passing vehicles. After the hatching season following rainfall, such vast numbers fill the roads that cars literally skid on their bodies. The crickets killed in this way are then eaten by their neighbours, who during their meal are themselves squashed by other cars and then eaten by the late arrivals, all in an endless gooey cycle of unpleasantness.

Corn crickets are aggressive creatures, usually spoiling for a fight. Merely approaching one usually makes it arch its back to look bigger and sound its battle cry, a particularly piercing chirrup, somewhat higher pitched than their normal call. Whatever their faults, they don't lack courage; even so, their fierce cannibalistic nature remains for me their least attractive quality. While humans might regularly do worse things to each other than any creepy-crawly could dream up, the average corn cricket doesn't even wait for an injured one to die before starting to eat it; the moment any cricket becomes *hors de combat*, one of its colleagues seizes it without ceremony and devours it alive, usually starting with its face.

I've never been much good at rationing food. Fortunately at this stage I still don't need to walk for more than a couple of days at a stretch without reaching some small town. I can go completely without food better than many people can, but going without altogether is often easier than rationing, and takes far less self-control. I've always thought that people who can eat half a chocolate bar and leave the rest for later simply don't know how to have a good time. On the road in Africa I've been eating really unhealthily so far, and it's becoming obvious how much soft drinks and junk snacks like crisps produce a raging unnatural thirst. I never noticed this back at home, where you can drink your fill whenever you choose – but it's a different story when you're carrying a heavy pack in the African heat, trying to ration your water. Although the weather here at the moment is not especially hot by local standards, and the nights are rather chill, carrying a heavy pack all day still means I lose a great deal of water through sweating.

Two nights past Omaruru another large bat keeps me from sleep, flapping enthusiastically around my head as I lie on the ground. I try everything to scare it off, shouting and waving my arms, throwing things and swearing, which only excites the creature's interest. Nothing works until I stumble across the magic words for banishing bats: 'BUGGER OFF!' Every time I shout this – and literally no other expression works, even far more explicit suggestions – the bat follows instructions and disappears for a short while, before returning to hassle me again. African folklore often depicts bats as the spirits of the dead, evil figures bringing disease and suffering to the living; but if people give them blood to drink, they can help find hidden treasure. Owing to the attentions of bats and corn crickets, as well as the falling temperatures as winter approaches, from now on I start pitching my tent every night, and reluctantly have to abandon sleeping under the stars.

If the bats here originate from the next world, they've come to the right place; the following morning I reach the small settlement of Kalkfeld, which feels like a tiny ghost town, decrepit and slightly depressing, its shops all closed and the houses falling to pieces. I see few people here, none of them white – this place seems well suited to the monotonous bushveldt stretching for miles around.

Around 160 million years ago this whole area was covered by an inland sea. A dinosaur left its footprints when it ran across wet sand that later turned to sandstone. Experts have concluded merely from studying the prints that this creature looked liked a kangaroo and ran like an ostrich. I'd like to see for myself, which involves making a long detour. Fortunately the countryside here at this time of year is beautiful and a real pleasure to walk through; the scrub savannah grass is greener than the semi-desert further west, the trees and bushes growing noticeably denser. Huge sand-coloured termite mounds are becoming more common beside the road, some of them tapering to several metres high, their shapes sometimes resembling exotic Khmer temples in Cambodia; I resist the temptation to sit leaning against them during rest breaks.

Unfortunately my map places the footprints on the wrong stretch of road, so by the end of the day I still haven't found them. There's little point asking for directions – I have enough trouble pronouncing short and simple Herero words, and the dinosaur tracks are located on a farm called 'Otjihaenamapareno'. After walking thirty kilometres in the wrong direction, I'm even more determined to see these footprints; but at nightfall I have to postpone finding them until the next day, and I crash out beside the road. I'm treated to another display of night-time manoeuvres from the corn crickets; throughout the night I keep waking to the approach of each new phalanx of crickets, advancing like robots in the eerie moonlight, the creations of some mad scientist. In the morning I find a fat black snake next to me, over half a metre long, like a hefty portion of *boerewors* and very dead. I can't tell exactly how it passed away, but I'm glad it did. I suspect it was already there, deceased, when I lay down in the dark.

Several hours later I find the dinosaur footprints; they're rather a let-down, and made by a small three-toed creature that today wouldn't scare a free-range chicken. After walking so far to get here I'd been hoping for Godzilla-sized depressions in the earth.

Around Kalkfeld I see baboons for the first time on the trip. They become a common sight for much of the journey, but I never grow to like them. The little ones are cute enough, but the adults always seem so greedy and aggressive. I start to worry that I'll wake one morning to find a stinky old baboon sitting on my face.

Despite the hard work of walking across Africa, the locals often seem friendlier towards me than they are towards foreigners zooming around the country in expensive vehicles. On the down side this can get exhausting when I'm surrounded by a large animated crowd, everyone discussing the possible contents of my rucksack. At the same time, why shouldn't local people show curiosity? Here I am, a white guy, plodding along with an enormous pack, my trekking poles giving me the appearance of skiing down the road, the bandanna wrapped round my head making me look like something from *The Pirates of Penzance*. Sometimes I forget I look rather *singular*, looming out of the twilight with ski sticks and tottering under the weight of a huge military pack.

I'm making good progress now, at least thirty kilometres a day. After all the delays with Tsondab and the mule it still feels good to be eating up the miles again – sometimes it's hard to bring myself to stop for the night and I carry on for an hour or so after sunset. But walking in the dark still poses problems, with vehicle headlights ruining my night vision. One solution is to shut one eye as the vehicle passes – but carrying a heavy pack over uneven ground I stand a good chance of falling over, possibly under the wheels of the passing car. And it's not such a good idea when one of the big trucks thunders past: the driver might think I'm winking at him, and stop to investigate.

Late one night a few kilometres before the farming town of Otji-warongo I encounter dozens of black policemen along the road. One group of officers stop for a chat, and to suggest that they 'take me along'; at first I'm not sure if they're offering a lift or a night in the cells for vagrancy. To be on the safe side, I wait for a couple of hours until all police presence has vanished before pitching my tent. It's against the law here to camp where you please, even though through necessity that's how I'm living these days.

I reach Otjiwarongo the following morning. It's taken me just over a week to get here since leaving Kokkie's farm at Usakos, covering around 220 kilometres; I want to rest here for a day or two. The town's name in Herero means 'the pleasant place', which sounds good enough for me. As I walk through the town a municipal dustcart strews the road with rubbish; trash flies like confetti from the back of the van, while a team of workers in front diligently pick up the fresh rubbish, presumably left by the same van on its previous circuit half an hour earlier. At least this exercise is keeping some people in a job.

I find the tourist office located in a German hotel. The pretty girl at the desk is very kind to me, letting me take a shower for free in one of the hotel rooms. By way of thanks I buy her a piece of expensive cake from a German bakery, but I have to assume she doesn't date vagrants. Quite apart from the nature of my journey, my personal appearance these days is doing little to make any amorous encounter more likely. I haven't seen a mirror for days; I'm actually forgetting what I look like. It strikes me just how often back at home you see your reflection: there are mirrors everywhere, and you can't help clocking yourself in shop fronts and car windows even when you genuinely don't mean to. Sometimes it's healthier not to even care what you look like.

Livingstone recorded the reaction of natives on first seeing themselves in a looking glass: '"Is that me?", "What ears I've got!", "What a big mouth", "I have no chin at all", "I would have been beautiful but for these high cheekbones", "See how my head shoots up in the middle", "My ears are like pumpkin leaves" – and laughing heartily all the while because the disparaging remarks are made by themselves.'[1]

Although officially the days of apartheid are over, such an all-encompassing system could hardly have sunk without trace in such a short time – especially when many white people here still regard it as not such a bad thing while it lasted. As a visitor you can easily distance yourself from blatantly racist views, but remaining symptoms of the old system can still take you by surprise. In the library at Otjiwarongo, where the librarian is black, I find the front page of a Tintin book stamped 'Administrasie vir blankes' ('Administration for whites'). A minor sign, perhaps, and though ugly it no longer applies. But I find it striking because it's so unexpected, in such an everyday setting. How genuinely weird, to place these obstacles in the way of black children who might want to read the books in their own country's library. As a white guy I feel almost guilty, as though I'm a part of the system that created such a situation – back at home I've never had to deal with laws preventing white middle-class readers from using a library system run by black people. This stamp in

85

the book feels almost like finding a Nazi slogan years after the event daubed on some hidden wall in Germany, or a number tattooed on an old-age pensioner's arm. But here in Namibia it's so recent – laws may change overnight, but not such deep-rooted attitudes.

I visit the Waterberg Plateau, scene of the climactic battle of the doomed Herero uprising* against the German colonial powers in the early twentieth century. The revolt was the cruellest and saddest episode in Namibia's history; in terms of sheer human suffering this struggle outweighed the atrocities of the recent and much longer war of independence. Germany's policies during the war caused outrage in much of the civilized world, but this came too late for the Hereros. By this time a pastoral people had been almost exterminated as a nation, with the survivors losing all their land and cattle.

The seeds of the tragedy had been sown many years before. Alarmed at the growing threat from the German colonial powers, in 1885 the Herero Chief Maherero attempted to avert hostilities by signing a protection treaty with the Germans. The Nama chief Hendrik Witbooi wrote to him: 'You will regret giving your land and rights up to the white people ... this thing will be for you as if you were carrying the sun on your back ...'[2] Witbooi's words were to prove prophetic, and a tragedy of biblical proportions loomed for the Hereros. In 1897 rinderpest wiped out large numbers of their cattle, leaving the Hereros on the brink of starvation. Plagues of locusts followed outbreaks of malaria and typhoid, driving them to desperation; to add to these natural disasters, they suffered much brutality at the hands of the German settlers, ranging from savage beatings and rapes to outright murder. Eventually the new chief Samuel Maherero realized that armed insurrection was inevitable, and in January 1904 the Hereros declared war on Germany. Maherero ordered that women, children and non-German Europeans were not to be harmed: although this was a struggle for the very survival of his people, he insisted the war was solely with German men, an extraordinary stance for someone in his impossible position.[3]

In the early days of the revolt over a hundred German soldiers and settlers were killed, often by their own servants, although their families

*The name 'Herero' is thought to be onomatopoeic, symbolizing the sound of a spear in flight. (See Adrian Room, *African Placenames*.)

were spared. The Hereros then laid siege to German garrison towns, including Windhoek and Omaruru, though ultimately without success. The German commander-in-chief, General Lothar von Trotha, then proceeded to crush the rebellion utterly, achieving his aims by a policy of genocide that even he himself described as 'sheer terrorism'.[4]

On 11 August 1904 the Herero combatants and their families gathered at Hamakari near the Waterberg Plateau; estimates for their numbers range widely, between 35,000 and 80,000. Here they faced a German force consisting of 1,488 men, 96 officers, 30 cannons and 12 machine guns. Though heavily outnumbering their enemy, the Hereros were no match for the better-armed and highly disciplined German forces. The Germans surrounded the Herero position, deliberately leaving an escape route towards the waterless Kalahari sandveldt in the east. Thousands of Hereros died in the ensuing battle, while the rest were driven into the Kalahari. The Germans took no prisoners. Instead, they formed a cordon stretching 250 kilometres to prevent the Hereros from returning; then they poisoned the water holes, shooting on sight any Hereros attempting to return. In this way the surviving Hereros were sealed off to their fate.[5]

'The Herero must be destroyed as a nation,' wrote von Trotha. On 2 October 1904 he issued a *Vernichtungsbefehl* (extermination order) against the entire Herero tribe, women and children included: 'I, the great general of the German troops, send this letter to the Herero people. Within the German borders, every Herero, whether armed or unarmed, with or without cattle, will be shot.' Between 25,000 and 40,000 Hereros were driven into the desert; of these, only about 5,000, including Maherero himself, managed to escape to Botswana and South Africa. The others died of thirst or by German bullets when they tried to break through the cordon to reach the wells; many staggered brokenly onto the German guns, preferring a swift and violent end to the long-drawn-out agony of dying of thirst.

The cordon drew a giant curtain over the horrors taking place way out of sight in the silence of the Kalahari. But during the next rainy season German patrols advanced into the sandveldt to see what they had done. Here they found armies that had died of thirst, and the bodies of men, women and children lying next to excavations they had dug in frantic final attempts to find water.[6]

Berlin finally realized this policy of extermination would destroy their resources of cheap labour and ruin the colony – already it had taken 17,000 troops and £20 million to crush the rebellion. So instead of shooting Hereros on sight the Germans now captured them alive, sending them as forced labour to concentration camps on the coast. Conditions in these camps proved so terrible that the genocide continued more or less unchecked: thousands more Hereros died here, while the survivors had their land and remaining cattle confiscated.

While the German forces engaged in the destruction of the Hereros, Hendrik Witbooi saw clearly that von Trotha planned a similar fate for the Namas. Accepting the inevitable, the Namas joined the rebellion and waged a skilful guerrilla warfare against overwhelming odds. But despite inflicting heavy losses on the Germans, defeat proved inevitable. Witbooi himself died aged eighty in battle in October 1905; his men buried him in secret where he fell, determined his body should never fall into German hands. The war reduced the Namas to fewer than 10,000; almost half the entire Nama population died in the struggle against Germany, and a further 2,000 Namas died of hunger, disease and exposure in the forced labour camps on the coast.

After the First World War the land taken from Germany was given to South African whites – the idea of returning it to its original owners seems scarcely to have occurred to any of the decision makers. Instead the Hereros were granted areas of semi-desert in the east – ironically the very region where so many Hereros died in their headlong flight from the Germans after their defeat at Waterberg.*

In 2004, to mark the centenary of the Herero revolt, the German ambassador to Namibia visited Hereroland and apologized on behalf of the German people, acknowledging that Germany's policy had been one of genocide and that today von Trotha would be prosecuted for crimes against humanity. This apology was not enough for the Hereros actively

---

*The new South African administration treated the native population little better than the German colonial powers had done. In the early 1920s a pass system and harsh vagrancy laws forced black Namibians into white employment, and whites gained police-like authority over their workers; a black person could be asked by any white person for their pass, and if the papers were not in order they could be arrested and punished. The South African regime eventually had to abolish parts of the pass laws – but only as recently as 1977. (See Nangolo Mbumba and Norbert H. Noisser, *Namibia in History*, London 1988.)

seeking $2 billion redress, who pointed out that much of their ancestral farmland is still in German hands.[7]

As I head towards the Waterberg Plateau I wonder if any young child involved in the Herero flight from the Germans or Witbooi's guerrilla war is still alive today. It's just possible.

By late afternoon I reach the Waterberg itself, a huge sandstone plateau 50 kilometres long, towering 150 metres above the surrounding plain. It derives its Afrikaans name from several fountains surfacing at the base of its cliffs. Beautiful and eerie as the sun sets, it looks for all the world like Conan Doyle's *The Lost World*. Dinosaurs have left their tracks in the rocks here, although after the last experience I won't be making any huge detours to see them.

Galton and the Swedish explorer Charles Andersson were the first Europeans to come to the Waterberg, and it probably doesn't look much different now – in fact for once there's actually more game today than in the 1850s. In lush contrast to the scrubby thorn savannah below, the plateau is largely covered in thick semi-tropical vegetation. Over 200 different species of birds live up here, and 25 species of game have been translocated to the plateau itself, from cheetahs and buffalo to black rhino. The conservation programme has been very successful in protecting animals from poachers and predators, although a short-sighted rhino died recently after stumbling over the edge.

In the Waterberg park's well-maintained campsite I get a good night's sleep on a decent patch of grass for once. A slight drizzle throughout the night feels surprisingly pleasant, the first rain I've encountered in over three months.

In the morning I climb up to the Waterberg. After wandering around for an hour or so in the long grasses and ferns and thick broad-leaf woodland on the plateau, I get completely lost – stupidly I'd left my compass back in my tent, thinking I was merely out for an afternoon's sightseeing. On first reading *The Lost World* I'd felt scornful of Conan Doyle's heroes getting stuck on a plateau without being able to get down – after all, they got up there somehow, surely the more difficult bit. Now I start to view their predicament more sympathetically. The sides to this plateau are *sheer*, with a vertiginous drop to the surrounding plain. 150 metres may not sound much on paper, but it's more than enough looking down. There are plenty of marked hiking trails up here – but when you want to be alone with Nature and don't wish to see signs for marked trails you can't get away from them, and when you're lost and actually need one they're nowhere in sight. Eventually I spot a family of tubby South African holidaymakers waddling through the trees with a large map; surreptitiously I follow them back to the surrounding plain below, keeping a dignified distance by pretending to study the Waterberg flora whenever they slow down.

After dark I walk beside the plateau back towards the Okakarara Road, followed for part of the way by a local madman who sings and dances behind me before dashing off abruptly, straight into the thickest bushes where there is no path. But I guess he knows his own business. Perhaps by no coincidence the full moon tonight is huge, an incredible globe of cool molten yellow, almost close enough to touch, shining over the open bushland like a giant floodlight. I stop to gaze at it for a long time, still half expecting the crazy guy to spring out of the nearest thicket to continue his performance where he left off. Namibia has extraordinarily clear skies at night – there is so little pollution here, and for most of the country there's virtually no glare from city lights. Traditionally the Bushmen worship the new moon, which often illuminates their hunting expeditions in the desert. This strange and beautiful moon would make a prize-winning photograph, but my limited ability with a camera would merely turn it into a distant blob of yellow light, like a fake UFO picture.

The following morning is cool and overcast. As I start back towards Otjiwarongo a small family of warthogs trots briskly across the road in front of me, but not before their mother stops her brood to look left and right as though she's following a road safety programme.

Back again in Otjiwarongo I visit the Nature Conservation Office, where I discover my proposed route through Bushmanland is legal but unworkable. Even though winter is approaching in the Kalahari, for vast distances there is no water and no proper road; the few scattered villages marked on the hugely detailed farming maps of the country periodically change their location completely, their inhabitants moving to the next available water supply. Without a support team for emergencies I might well vanish off the face of the earth. Instead I'll have to cross the West Caprivi Game Reserve on foot, although this will bring its own share of problems – chiefly the promise of lions, bandits and unexploded landmines.

7. Squashed Snakes and Cold Ditches (Namibia: Otjiwarongo to Rundu)

I was once present when a fellow missionary attempted to sing among a wild heathen tribe of Bechuanas, who had no music in their composition; the effect on the risible faculties of the audience was such that the tears actually ran down their cheeks.

David Livingstone, *Missionary Travels*

I spend several hours in a German café in Otjiwarongo, huddled over a succession of sweet coffees. I feel tired and ill, with a bad stomach and headache. It's bloody cold outside, and at this time of year night-time temperatures can fall below freezing. I realize I'm trying to put off the moment when I have to start walking again, and order yet another coffee.

When finally I drag myself back on to the road to Otavi the first afternoon is horrible. The cold penetrates four layers of clothing; at one point I'm convinced I'm coming down with malarial chills, which turn out to be no more than normal cold symptoms. After a whole day of hard work I've covered only about twenty kilometres.

The following day I stop at a trading post on one of the big ranches, and buy some thick soured milk and heavy-duty biltong. This industrial-grade biltong is much cheaper than the wimpy variety available in bite-sized, bar-coded packs at coastal supermarkets; while the latter could be chewed successfully by someone with no teeth, my newly-purchased biltong is so tough it leaves my jaw painfully stiff for the next two days.

Because of the roadworks on this stretch of highway, my nights here are characterized by excruciating bumps under my back – huge digging-machine tracks have churned the mud into exotic configurations that have then set like concrete. On a few occasions the only flat place I can find to pitch my tent for the night is in a ditch. Despite their negative associations, sleeping in a ditch is a very economical way to live. Once you fall asleep – if you ever get that far in a freezing cold ditch – you're just as much asleep as if tucked up in the finest suite at the Hilton. And however uncomfortable your chosen ditch, morning finds you surprisingly reluctant to get out of your sleeping bag and leave it. My sleeping mat is lightweight but thin, and I wish I'd invested in one of the latest self-inflating mats; at the end of an exhausting day's trekking the sight of a sleeping mat inflating itself independently must seem as marvellous as one of Ray Harryhausen's special effects monsters rising from the earth.

Towards Grootfontein I begin to notice a better class of ditch. Even so, you can have enough of them, and a comfortable bed has always been important to me. Back at home I could never face the world if I didn't like my bed, and regarded it as my only true place of retreat. Often the state of my bed has had a huge effect on the rest of my life. I remember the closest I felt towards someone special was when she confessed she felt the same. When we split up I thought: 'Now it's just my bed.' Which of course it always was.

On the journey so far I've been getting about ten hours' sleep a night, far more than I did at home – but I'm working so hard each day I literally can't get by on less. Out in the bush I'm not missing much by turning in early; by the time I crawl into my tent most nights I'm wiped out. The only form of exertion I can still manage is raising a cigarette to my lips; usually I just lie there moaning, with a big pile of gear on top of me. Sometimes I'm so tired that eating inside a dark tent becomes a real challenge; occasionally I miss my mouth completely, and spill food everywhere. I don't understand this, as I didn't usually need a mirror to eat with back at home, even when I was pissed.

I'm relieved that I don't miss a stove at all – fuel is heavy to carry, so my stove was one of the earliest victims of my weight-reduction purges on starting inland from the coast. After walking thirty or forty kilometres each day, the last thing I want is to start cooking and washing up – and both activities require water I can't afford to carry. I'm so tired at the end of each day that I'm quite happy eating cold food; a big fry-up and hot coffee would be wonderful, but not if I have to get off my arse and make it myself.

After eating each night in my tent I often try to read, but usually I'm too tired even to keep my eyes in focus; I just lie in my tent as though hypnotized, staring at nothing. Tiredness like this feels like a mild dose of anaesthesia. By now I'm getting used to doing stupid things in the dark at the end of an exhausting day. One night when I finally summon the energy to brush my teeth in my tent I gradually realize that something is not quite right; lighting a candle, I notice I've been using my tube of Fiery Jack Deep Volcanic Heat Rub as toothpaste. I'll have to be more careful as my gear includes several tubes of things I wouldn't care to brush my teeth with, including a toothpaste-sized tube of extra-strong contact adhesive. Such things do happen; just before I left England the broadsheet press reported a true case of a short-sighted elderly gentleman mistaking a tube of superglue for his haemorrhoid ointment and super-gluing his buttocks together.

Despite my best intentions, smoking has already established itself as a recurring leitmotif on this journey. Routine and habit quickly merge, and cigarette breaks do tend to punctuate a long day's trekking. I can understand why soldiers often smoke, or indeed anyone whose day-to-day existence involves some degree of hardship. Local matches make smoking in Africa even more hazardous; each time I strike one, burning sulphur shoots off like a comet, often right in my face. This happens even if I strike the match directly away from me, which seems to contradict the laws of physics. I try lighting them with my eyes closed, but in a tent this only makes it more difficult to find the red-hot match-head burning a hole through my groundsheet.

While smoking in a tent scores highly on any scale of foolishness, especially when tired, burning a candle in my tent every night makes things even more risky. But as with so many things, the line of least resistance is rarely the most sensible – torch batteries are heavy to carry, and after a day's hard trekking there's no way I'll find the self-discipline to get up out of my tent for a bedtime fag. But it does trouble me, especially since over the years I've already had several unfortunate experiences around naked flames. Once I set all my hair alight while brushing my teeth, having failed to notice a candle on the bathroom ledge, placed there as an uncharacteristically romantic touch by my girlfriend at the time. I only realized something was amiss when a big flame shot up from the top of my head like something out of *Struwwel-peter*. The foul smell of burnt hair lingered in the flat for days, and for the rest of the time we spent together any suggestion from her that I needed a haircut became: 'It needs burning down again.'

I dream of doing many things on reaching Grootfontein, which will be my first day off in a town since leaving Kokkie's farm – well over 400 kilometres to the southwest, the equivalent of walking from London to Newcastle. My imagination runs riot: as soon as I've found somewhere reasonable to stay for once instead of camping in ditches, I plan to lie in a hot bath for several hours in a state of semi-aquatic torpor, moving only to avail myself of a large bag of chocolates.

Unfortunately my map underestimates the distance from Otavi to Grootfontein: it's about ninety-two kilometres, not seventy-six. At first I tell myself the distances on the signs beside the road must be wrong. When these hopes evaporate, I think positively by concentrating on the surrounding countryside, which is turning more and more picturesque – this northern edge of Namibia's central plateau is very different from the sparse desert scrubland to the west. Although the landscape here is still semi-arid, in parts it's lovely, the road passing small mountains and farms as German in appearance as those on the Rhine. The weather remains idyllic, cool and bright and perfect for walking. A slight breeze sweeps gently over the maize fields, while the stalks of grain nod gently as though in private conversation.

By early evening I still haven't covered nearly enough distance to reach Grootfontein on schedule. The thought of arriving there at lunchtime on Saturday – just after the shops have closed for the weekend – is soul-destroying. To avoid this I walk for over two hours in the dark, which is almost as bad.

After a bitterly cold start, the following day is hard going and the evening is dreadful. I make further empty promises to myself never to walk at night again on the trip. The moment the sun goes down the temperature plummets, and soon it's below zero. The night sky is exceptionally clear; I can see Grootfontein in the distance, hundreds of lights twinkling invitingly, lending the town all the appearance of a mini Las Vegas at night. Anyone who knows Grootfontein by day might laugh at the idea of the town arousing such raw *desire* in a traveller, but tonight it fills me with real longing. How I want to be there, instead of shivering here in the cold, alone with only the glow of a cigarette for comfort. I'm not enjoying myself at all right now, and there's enough walking still to do tonight, at least another fifteen kilometres if I'm to reach town before the shops close tomorrow.

God, it's cold. Even the moon looks frozen. I pull so hard on my cigarette that sparks fly off its tip into the freezing night air. I wish I'd bought some alcohol.

With another ten kilometres still to go to reach Grootfontein, I've had enough for tonight. I stop under a bridge, my fingers so numb I can hardly get my tent up. When I finally get inside my tent it still takes me ages to warm up. Apart from wearing all my clothes inside my sleeping bag, there's little I can do to raise the temperature. I try huddling around a cigarette for warmth, and consider just striking some matches. A guy I meet later in Grootfontein tells me that further north the temperature fell to minus eleven degrees in the night, and by morning all the vehicles were covered in thick ice. I didn't come to Africa to shiver – I can do that back in England well enough. But at least in such temperatures the mosquitoes stay at home, tucked up in bed, or whatever the little bastards do when it's freezing.

I'm on the road by six, the morning crisp and clear. I wish I'd brought gloves, the one thing I didn't even consider packing for Africa. I walk into the icy wind, my fingers hurting so much I have to keep stopping to warm them, which means shoving them down the front of my trousers; passing motorists can draw their own conclusions for all I care, but it's no coincidence that for once no one stops to offer me a lift.

I reach Grootfontein shivering and completely knackered. I've covered the 210 kilometres from Otjiwarongo in a week – certainly not breaking any land speed records, but I've not been feeling especially well, and I really need to rest for a couple of days. Energized only by the immediate prospect of a comfortable bed, I find the nearest cheap hotel. After all this time on the road, hot running water feels like a gift from heaven. After the cold and sleeping in ditches for weeks, there's something so lovely about standing barefoot on a carpet warmed by the sun through the bedroom window, like some distant childhood memory. True, the carpet in question is threadbare, with a nauseating 1970s floral pattern – but this doesn't stop me standing there for a good ten minutes, savouring these comforts like a Victorian street urchin suddenly finding itself alone in a gentrified townhouse.

I spend most of my time in Grootfontein stuffing my face at a German café. When I've proved myself a good customer by ordering a succession of large fry-ups, the haughty female proprietor condescends to give me a confectionery sort of smile – sweet enough, but containing no more warmth than the meringues sitting obediently in her refrigerated display. I suspect she thinks I lower the tone of the establishment, limping in like some kind of rough type and then eating like a pig. Perhaps because of the boss's disapproval, the black waitresses seem to like me and regard me as something of an ally in adversity. But as far as I'm concerned the manager can think what she likes, provided there's hot food and plenty of it. The civilized clink of a teaspoon against a saucer feels extraordinarily comforting after long weeks on the road, almost part of another world.

Grootfontein itself is a small colonial market town of around 10,000 inhabitants, at the centre of the region's cattle ranches and maize farms. Its name means 'big fountain' (the more exotic Herero name *Otjivandatjongue* translates as 'The Hill of The Leopard'). For me the town's most noticeable feature is the sheer number of locals gathered outside every *drankwinkel* (bottle store). It's the last weekend of the month, so scores of thirsty customers are investing their monthly pay packets without delay. Some of the drunkards here are the genuine article, not just ordinary guys who happen to be pissed on this occasion; it's as though someone has turned off a switch in their brain and nothing there still functions. I notice a real difference between the street-corner drunk here and those back at home. An English wino absolutely must have a drink in his hands at all times – even an empty can is better than nothing; without this badge of office (a can of super-strength lager or cider) the poor guy has no identity, he's just someone standing around on a street corner. But his African counterpart can't afford to have a bottle to hand so constantly, and usually drinks what he has even faster, and is left simply standing around staring into space.

Back in my cheap hotel I read in the bath for about three hours, sipping a bottle of cheap red wine as my toes turn an absurd shade of pink in the hot water. I make the most of that rare occurrence on this journey, a pleasant evening in. Later I spend ages trying to turn off the light without getting out of bed, prodding ineffectually at the switch with a fully extended trekking pole. After several minutes of this foolishness it becomes a real challenge: it's obvious from the word go it would be far quicker and easier just to get up and turn the switch off at the wall, but where's the fun in that? I don't remember giving up, but when I wake up the following morning the light is still on.

Some people insist that watches are superfluous while you're trekking in the wilderness, and that you should time yourself according the rhythms of nature. I can't be bothered with all that, so I buy my third cheap watch so far on this trip. It stops an hour after I leave the shop, but after I've booted the bloody thing around my room a few times it's in good working order again. It starts falling to pieces shortly afterwards, but runs after a fashion all the way to the east coast, then stops permanently the day after I reach the Indian Ocean, like the grandfather clock in the children's song. Spooky.

I'm still unsure which route to take on leaving Caprivi, the far eastern corner of Namibia. Four countries converge at this point, so potentially I could cross into Zambia, Botswana or Zimbabwe; the pros and cons of each feasible route are endless. The guy at the immigration office at Grootfontein tells me I won't be able to walk through Chobe National Park because of the lions; he does, however, suggest yet another little-known border crossing I could use. He adds as an afterthought that to reach it at this time of year might involve wading through flooded swamps full of crocodiles – after good rains over half of eastern Caprivi may be under water, the rivers and swamps full of bilharzia. I'll make a decision when I get there.

Several people have warned me that a lot of thieving takes place in Grootfontein, often by gangs in broad daylight. Sure enough, as I'm leaving town a local guy befriends me while his dopey accomplice tries to pick my pocket. They're so obvious and incompetent I have to laugh – Laurel and Hardy would have made a more professional job of it. But when I think about this later I regret not giving the less dopey one a thick ear.

The first night out of Grootfontein I set up my tent beside the road. A white farmer stops his car, demanding to know what the problem is. He becomes more reasonable when I explain the situation; he just didn't want his farm burnt down. After he's gone I pick up a stone to hammer in my tent pegs and a lizard runs into my tent, resulting in a high-speed chase. I fall asleep to the rustle of snakes and small rodents; at least the long grass makes a comfortable bed.

Although it's winter in this part of Africa the days are warm again. Even so, the early mornings are cool enough for me to feel the chill of sweat on my back whenever I stop for ten minutes or more. At such times I feel far more rested if I more or less lie down flat, though I have to be careful where I do this: apart from the snakes, broken beer bottles often litter the undergrowth, hurled from passing vehicles. On the road itself squashed snakes are becoming more common, some of them quite large. But the most common road casualty here is some kind of flattened rodent, crushed so utterly that it's extremely difficult to guess how it looked before it came to grief. I see dozens of these large gerbil-like creatures, but only in their present condition – before long I'm imagining them alive looking like this, waddling across the road like inverted dinner plates.

The road to Rundu is long, over 250 kilometres, the same distance as walking from London to Cardiff. As I get further north the bushveld gradually turns denser and greener. After several days I reach the Red Line, an animal disease control checkpoint, designed to stop the spread of rinderpest and foot and mouth disease. Strict laws forbid taking cattle across the checkpoint from north to south, or even selling of them abroad. The Red Line has had great political significance as the dividing point between the white-owned commercial ranches to the south and the communal grazing lands of black Africans. In 1923 the land was very unequally divided by the Native Reserves Commission. Despite the fact that they constituted over ninety per cent of the population, black Namibians were assigned only two million hectares of land towards the Angolan border, nowhere near enough for them to live on. To compound the problem, harsh laws were brought in to control where black people could live and work and to restrict their movement in white areas; since they could not support themselves on their own land, this forced many into contracted labour for the whites. This humble barrier, then, can be seen as one of the symbols of deep injustice in Namibia's history.[1]

At the checkpoint I find a small caravan selling horrible food and sweets, where I buy some dreadful Russian sausages. My only sensible purchase here is a small bottle of Rhumba, a cheap local spirit made from the residue of the rum-making process. That night in my tent I sip it carefully, my tongue turning numb. I light a cigarette cautiously, wondering if this is a good idea with Rhumba fumes on my breath – to be on the safe side I keep my tent door wide open in case a great blue flame leaps two metres across space and my tent goes up in a fireball.

Days elapse before I can face the last Russian sausage, and it hasn't improved with the delay. It may have been fine in its youth, while still fresh and sizzling, but its journey in my rucksack has left it cold and perspiring as though unwell, with big lumps of slimy fat to chew on. But despite its shortcomings it's infinitely better than nothing.

After some time on the road, I'm once again looking forward to reaching a town with real shops. The moment I arrive in a town these days I start throwing money around like a sailor on shore leave, though admittedly not on quite the same thing. I spend hours fantasizing about all the food I intend to devour within an hour of reaching Rundu. Jelly and custard tops the list, gradually becoming a fixation until it assumes the proportions of a Holy Grail. I don't understand this at all, as back at home I've always detested jelly and custard. I must have regressed to some vague childhood conviction that jelly and custard is somehow a good thing, a special treat – an idea almost certainly instilled by adults for reasons never properly divulged. As a child I was always given the impression that if I didn't like jelly and custard then I bloody well ought to. But I never saw any grown-ups eating it.

Moving steadily northeast across Namibia I leave behind the open spaces of the huge white-owned cattle farms and game ranches; instead, the road is now lined with subsistence farming villages, divided into small kraals and rondavels, the distinctly African circular thatched huts, surrounded by small vegetable patches and fields of maize and millet. The whole region is far more heavily populated, and virtually the only white people I see now are those speeding past in their vehicles. The change of scenery seems to extend to the people, who seem friendlier than those further south. Just outside the villages the trees and bushes are usually decorated with Coca-Cola cans, the best-looking ones resembling Christmas trees. Outside the villages are ramshackle little stalls selling vegetables and woodcarvings; elsewhere, large melons with prices carved on their sides sit sunbathing beside the road. This trade in melons must be conducted entirely on trust, as I never see anyone collecting money from passing customers.

'Welcome, friend!' reads a little home-made sign outside one village. I find this touching – how many European villages would display such a sign and actually mean it? Those big signs back at home announcing that a town has been twinned with another are hardly the same thing.

The change in landscape makes walking after sunset much more complicated, with human settlements and domestic animals never far away. When darkness falls my progress now is slowed by repeatedly stepping in cow shit. Passing any village at night I invariably set all the dogs barking; it's Walvis Bay all over again, but without the sensible middle-class gates to keep these savage creatures where they belong. On a few occasions the usual terrific barking is accompanied by the sound of several sets of paws charging out into the road towards me. At these times I back off cautiously, in the process treading in even more cow shit. It would help if I knew the correct expression for 'Nice doggy!' in the local language, or some other calming expression. The dogs are certain in their own minds that I don't smell right; after days on the road I'd agree with them on this, but I've no wish to discuss it with a pack of yammering dogs in pitch-blackness. Dogs charging at me in daylight are bad enough, but I really start to worry when I can't even see what kind of creature is attacking me. My bare legs and ankles feel very exposed, and there's a real possibility some of the dogs here carry rabies. I'm grateful for my trekking poles, which prove extremely useful in fending off normal-sized dogs without doing the animals any damage or provoking them or their owners to further unpleasantness. But I escape with my skin intact, thankfully without having to resort to a good kick in the teeth to send some crazed mutt howling through the night.

During daylight hours I often ask local people how far I have to go to reach the next village; sometimes the reply reveals the difference between European and African concepts of distance and time:

'It's too far.'

'Yes, but how far?'

'No ... it's *too* far.'

For the first time on the journey I begin to feel I'm in black Africa, rather than walking though some vast white man's playground.

One afternoon a young white man stops for me, getting out of his car looking concerned. I ask him if he has any spare water.

'I'm sorry, man, I don't,' he says, looking even more concerned. 'But tell me, are you a Christian?'

'Actually, I'm not.'

'Then you should think about becoming one – you especially, because you have the courage to carry on. Jesus loves you, man.'

He talks to the black guy with him as an equal, which makes a nice change – but then he does explain that the latter is some kind of minor chief. They both depart slightly nonplussed that I don't share their religious conviction, yet they seemed decent fellows, and genuine in what they were saying.

These two guys would not be the first to find converting strangers in this part of the country an uphill struggle. The Reverend Samuel Hahn, the dominant German missionary figure in Namibia in the nineteenth century, found his Herero congregation reluctant to embrace Christianity. 'Murder, immorality, lying, the three banners of Satan's empire waved freely ...' ran one of his milder observations. A poor speaker, the uncharismatic Hahn found it difficult to retain his audience's attention; after he'd been preaching for a few minutes the Hereros usually wandered off in search of something to eat. Once an old man seized Hahn by the beard and kissed him several times, declaring: 'If the others do not want to hear you, I do!' Hahn immediately launched into one of his best sermons, only to have the old man interrupt him to ask whether he had anything to sell. On another occasion the congregation listened with uncharacteristic interest when Hahn assured them God gave man life by blowing into his nose. Hahn indignantly had to refuse to blow into another old fellow's nostrils to prove the theory.[2]

Early missionaries in Africa often found it extremely difficult to express concepts from the Bible in the local language. It's easy to gloss over the tremendous obstacles in their paths, but they almost certainly would have made greater progress had they shown more sensitivity towards existing tribal beliefs and social structures. The amused reaction of Africans sheds light on how they really perceived the European colonists and their strange ways and religion. In twenty years among the Hereros, Hahn failed to make a single convert – a track record worse even than Livingstone, who did at least manage to make one temporary convert during his career, the Bechuana chief Sechele, who later lapsed.

To Livingstone's credit, unlike many of the missionaries he genuinely loved the Africans, and he could usually see the funny side. Like Hahn, he also had his share of problems retaining order during sermons. Sometimes the congregation – often smoking wild hemp throughout the service – would lose interest and instead start 'dancing and roaring at the top of their voices'.[3] The Makololo women, on the other hand, 'behaved with decorum … except at the conclusion of the prayer. When all knelt down, many of those who had children, in following the example of the rest, bent over their little ones; the children, in terror of being crushed to death, set up a simultaneous yell, which so tickled the whole assembly there was a subdued titter, to be turned into a hearty laugh as soon as they heard Amen … When preaching on the most solemn subjects, a woman might be observed to look round, and, seeing a neighbour seated on her dress, give her a hunch with the elbow to make her move off; the other would return it with interest, and perhaps the remark, "Take the nasty thing away, will you?" Then three or four would begin to hustle the first offenders, and the men to swear at them all, by way of enforcing silence.'[4]

Livingstone's attempts to liven up his services with music did not go smoothly: a slight speech defect combined with a particularly broad Lanarkshire accent made him difficult to understand at the best of times, even for his fellow Scots. The Makololo tribe found his preaching and singing of the psalms a memorable performance, and called his psalm-singing *bokolella* ('to bellow like a bull').[5]

The day before reaching Rundu I stop at a village to get water. A large group of women are busy filling their containers from a huge communal tank. As I fill my own bottle they draw my attention to a collection of vicious thorns sticking to the seat of my pants; I hadn't even noticed these, though presumably would have done the next time I sat down. One lady kindly pulls them out for me while her neighbours burst into laughter. At such times one feels the genuine kindness of so many Africans towards strangers. Livingstone always maintained a joke carried far more weight in Africa than 'solemn assertions', and so it still does.

102

'His shoes are genuine!' whispers another lady to her companions, who start discussing my appearance good-naturedly.

'You have too much power!' shouts one guy as I walk past his hut. I only wish it were true. Variations on this theme become common; sometimes the locals shout 'Hey, Big Man!' to me, although I'm never entirely sure if this is a put-up or a put-down. But the comments I get in Africa are almost invariably good-humoured. When local guys see how tough the journey is they assume I must be a decent fellow – some of the women, on the other hand, appear to want to mother me, or at least feed me when they see how thin I am these days.

By late afternoon I sit beside the road outside a village some twenty kilometres before Rundu. Within minutes I'm the unwilling centre of attention. The people here are friendly but I'm dead beat; all I want is peace and quiet by myself. Few people here speak English, but everyone's interested in me, especially when my cheap watch decides of its own accord to start playing 'Happy Birthday to You', something it has never done before – I had no idea it could play tunes, and to everyone's great amusement I can't get the bloody thing to stop.

At this stage the attention from local people still feels something of a novelty; I don't yet dream of the level of constant attention waiting for me in Malawi and Tanzania, where at times it reaches the proportions of a nightmare, with villages seemingly stretching out for ever.

8. Lion Country
(Namibia: Rundu to Kongola)

I saw the lion just in the act of springing upon me … Growling
horribly, he shook me as a terrier dog does a rat. The shock
produced a stupor similar to that which seems to be felt by a mouse
after the first shake of the cat. It caused a sort of dreaminess, in
which there was no sense of pain nor feeling of terror, though quite
conscious of all that was happening. It was like what patients
partially under the influence of chloroform described, who see all
the operation, but feel not the knife … The shake annihilated fear,
and allowed no sense of horror in looking round at the beast. This
peculiar state is probably produced in all animals killed by the
carnivora; and, if so, is a merciful provision by our benevolent
Creator for lessening the pain of death.

David Livingstone, *Missionary Travels*

I pitch my tent a dozen kilometres or so before Rundu. Tonight there
are so many rustlings in the grass outside, I have to bring my rucksack
into the inner tent instead of leaving it in the porch as usual – I don't
want any unpleasant surprises in the morning when I shove my hand
inside. In my sleeping bag I dine on a can of curried beef, rice and gravy,
intended as a special treat but which turns out to be almost entirely
gravy; when eventually I find a small shred of vaguely beef-like substance
near the bottom of the can it's like chewing a piece of cotton wool fished
out of a muddy pond.

Being hungry so much of the time effectively solves the problem of
unappetizing food. I've stopped asking questions about the food set before
me; in some cases a truthful reply would only upset me. This happened to
the nineteenth-century traveller-sportsman Arthur Donaldson Smith,
whose chef once served him fish fried in Vaseline.[1]

Most things I'd turn down flat back at home are more than welcome
now – and after all, there's enough dreadful food back in England. Some
people might consider the worst food in Africa far worse than its English

equivalent, but I'm not convinced. Just before leaving England I read in the papers of a hamburger seller in London facing prosecution after a potential customer caught him pissing in his onions.

Almost all the white people I encounter in Namibia have one thing in common at mealtimes: the staggering amount of meat they put away, at least by European standards. Attitudes here to eating meat differ from those back at home. In Europe you're expected to be slightly apologetic if you admit to eating meat regularly, but in Africa vegetarianism is usually viewed with incomprehension. In Namibia this is understandable, as most of the land can support only livestock. The *braai* (barbecue) is a real social institution for whites, and I can't think of anything comparable based around eating in England. Almost every campsite and picnic spot in Namibia has a special pit for people to set up their *braais*. This is partly because it's a huge country with a very low population – bars as such are scarce, so when people get together they take the opportunity to cook up as much *boerewors** and steak as everyone can eat without actually exploding like Monty Python's Mr Creosote.

The taste for meat isn't restricted to white folks, even though they tend to have more money to indulge their appetites. On the great African safaris the prospect of high wages and plentiful meat was hugely attractive to enlisting porters. At home a man counted himself lucky if he ate meat on special occasions; as a safari porter he could offset his back-breaking and dangerous work by stuffing himself with five kilos of meat a day, or more if the hunting was particularly good. On occasion Livingstone had to stop shooting antelopes when his men started becoming 'fat and dainty'.[2]

Rundu is a relaxed, pleasant little town of around 20,000 inhabitants, on the banks of the Kavango River opposite Angola. Its character is very different from that of the other towns I've passed through so far across Namibia, with none of their overtly German feel. Instead, its strong Portuguese influence originates from the other side of the Angolan border, and the area is still home to thousands of Angolan refugees who fled the violence in their own country.

I head straight for the nearest supermarket, where a litre carton of

---

*Afrikaner sausages of beef or game, seasoned with rosemary and thyme.

UHT custard sets me back three US dollars – at that price to hell with the jelly. Since I'm in the mood for pampering myself, while I'm in town I'll have to stock up on any luxuries I can afford to carry; there's little in the way of shops for the next 500 kilometres to Katima Mulilo on the Zambian border.

In Rundu for the first time on this trip I encounter large numbers of beggars, soon to become a regular occurrence in every town and village. Later I find it difficult to reconcile compassion with a responsible attitude. Ultimately shortage of money makes the decision for me, and I strike a compromise of sorts with myself: if anyone asks me for food I'll always give them food, if I have any. If they ask for money I decline politely. It may not be right-on enough for some folks back at home, but I can live with that for now. Even so, it's impossible not to feel guilty turning down some poor beggar grovelling in the street and then stuffing my face at the nearest Portuguese restaurant.

Over a big Portuguese fry-up, the kind popular with English football fans breakfasting abroad, I watch cable television, hoping for some news from England. Instead all I get is a handsome presenter with implausibly white teeth, smarming over the weather forecast and warning me of unstable weather conditions over the South China Sea.

Although many people I meet on this trip assume I'm reasonably brave, in fact I'm scared of most things, including dinosaurs. The truth is I'm worried about crossing the West Caprivi Game Reserve on foot, so I visit Rundu's Nature Conservation Office to get some up-to-date information on lion attacks. The staff here are extremely helpful; we consult a map of the park, which covers an entire wall. 'You will have to be careful over the last forty kilometres – all the reported lion incidents have been in that area,' the officer tells me. I never realized before how sinister the word 'incident' can sound. Lions recently killed a road worker in the reserve, leaving only a soggy scalp for his colleagues to bury

Equally unwelcome is the prospect of unexploded landmines in the game reserve, a legacy of the bush war. I'll have to stay close to the road and be bloody careful about wandering around in the undergrowth. The guy also warns me of former UNITA soldiers out poaching in the park, still armed to the teeth; at night they cross from the Angolan side of the Kavango River, taking any spoils back with them. 'For safety you should camp on the south side of the road through the game reserve,' he tells me. 'And if you get into trouble with the locals you should pretend to be a witch doctor. Man, you think I'm joking? I tell you, even today some of the local people are still that superstitious.' I'm not entirely convinced by this – and even if it's true, I didn't come to Africa to cure people of spiritual ailments or raise the dead.

But the big cats are causing me the most anxiety. In reality the threat from lions in Africa is often exaggerated in many people's minds. Lions usually have far more reason to fear humans than the other way around, which was always the case, even before the African lion was hunted to its current levels. I'm more likely to get killed by a drunken driver, yet I didn't hear any well-meaning individuals back at home warning me not to go walking in Africa in case I got run over. Despite the thousands of Africans they kill each year, drunken drivers are less well-established in popular folklore than lions. Even so, it doesn't pay to act too cavalier in one's attitude towards the big cats – enough people have died over the years through doing exactly that.

I'm still not sure what I'll do if I meet a lion along the road. I could always try the springbok ploy of making balletic leaps in the air to show I'm fit, healthy and hard to catch. Springbok leaps of this nature are known as 'pronking'; but how do you pronk with a heavy rucksack? I can hardly compete on equal terms: lions themselves are excellent jumpers, and when charging can easily leap twelve metres in their final bound. Quite apart from its teeth and claws, a lion can deliver a blow with its paw of sufficient force to break the neck of a fully grown buffalo.[3]

Some people advise me that if I'm attacked I should distract the lion by sticking my arm in its mouth; as soon as the lion gives its full attention to my arm between its teeth I should stab it behind the shoulder. Resistance to the bitter end is recommended, as lions occasionally turn away or release their prey. This sounds wonderfully straightforward in theory, without the lion in question crunching my arm to splinters. Other people insist passive behaviour is the key to surviving a lion attack: apparently the laid-back approach spares the body stress without encouraging the lion to further unpleasantness. Either way, one factor may work in my favour – like most wild predators, lions haven't yet realized that humans can't smell properly. So if I pay attention to the wind I'll have at least some idea from which direction an attack might come – downwind.

In the most famous lion attack in history, Livingstone opted for a mixture of both the aggressive and the passive response, resorting to the latter only after the more traditional approach of shooting the angry beast several times at close range had failed. On this occasion Livingstone was helping a party of Tswanas in the Northern Transvaal hunt a troublesome lion that had killed an ox. Only a short way into the hunt he found himself in the jaws of the very lion he'd been searching for. Livingstone's life was saved by the timely arrival of a native teacher, Mebalwe, who courageously seized a gun and attempted to fire it at the lion. The gun misfired; the creature immediately dropped Livingstone and attacked Mebalwe, ripping his thigh open, and then bit the shoulder of another native who entered the fray. Eventually the bullets originally fired by Livingstone took effect, and to great relief all round the lion dropped dead.

A lengthy and excruciating convalescence gave Livingstone ample time to reflect on his lucky escape. He remained convinced his tartan woollen jacket had prevented poison from the lion's teeth infecting his wounds. Even so, he never regained proper use of his badly set arm; a false joint formed, and for the rest of his life he had to set his rifle against his left shoulder. After his death, when Livingstone's followers carried his body to the coast, the corpse's distinctive damaged shoulder proved beyond doubt the body was indeed that of the great explorer.

At one village Livingstone met a *pondoro*, a person who can change his form at will. The man insisted he could change himself into a lion, a story that Livingstone's Makololo companions found wholly convincing. Livingstone instructed them to ask the *pondoro* to change himself immediately into a lion, and he would give the man a cloth for the performance. 'Oh no,' they replied, 'if we tell him so, he may change himself and come when we are asleep and kill us.'

Sometimes *pondoros* would appear no different from ordinary men; at other times they could easily be recognized by their sharp pointed fangs and the unusual number of flies surrounding them, attracted by the strong smell of carrion; furthermore, their eyes would turn yellow at the sight of cattle, exactly like those of a lion.[4] As this particular *pondoro* displayed none of these characteristics, Livingstone felt disinclined to believe his story. Aside from his other peculiarities, this *pondoro* also imagined he suffered from a strange allergy to gunpowder: smelling a discharged gun in Livingstone's party he started 'trembling in a most artistic manner, but quite overacting his part'. The villagers insisted he regularly changed into his leonine form and then disappeared into the woods for days. 'His considerate wife had built him a hut or den, in which she places food for her transformed lord, whose metamorphosis does not impair his human appetite.' On his return to the village he would say to the villagers: '"Go and get the game that I have killed for you." Advantage is of course taken of what a lion has actually done, and they go and bring home the buffalo or antelope killed when he was a lion, or rather found when he was pursuing his course of deception in the forest.'[5]

In the final years of the nineteenth century another celebrated survivor from a lion attack was the traveller-sportsman Lord Delamere. Like Livingstone, he owed his life to the courage and prompt action of his native companion, in this case the Somali gunbearer Abdullah Ashur. Delamere's first shot merely enraged the lion without killing it; while Delamere prepared himself for a second shot the lion seized him by the leg, breaking the bone. With almost suicidal courage Abdullah distracted the lion by grabbing its mane; at this unexpected move the lion turned its fury on its new assailant, who then went one better by seizing it by the tongue. The lion took a few moments to recover from the shock of this gross personal affront, by which time Delamere had recovered sufficiently to shoot it again, driving the creature away. Both Delamere and Abdullah survived their severe mauling, and Delamere showed his appreciation of his employee's bravery when, on a later occasion, the captain of the ship on which they travelled spoke abusively to Abdullah; Delamere punched the man so hard he fell overboard into the Gulf of Aden.[6]

Sipping a cold beer in a lodge bar on the banks of the Kavango, I reflect that getting killed by a lion would certainly prove a sensational exit from this world – and an extremely uncomfortable one. Frederick Courtney Selous, the most famous white hunter of all time, was sceptical of Livingstone's claims of divine intervention in making the encounter painless. Selous had many conversations with survivors of lion attacks, who all assured him the experience had been agonizing. He wrote: 'I can but conclude that this special mercy is one which providence does not extend beyond ministers of the Gospel.'[7]

Lions usually hunt at night to frighten and confuse their prey, to me a deeply unsettling image. But I should be reasonably safe asleep inside my tent. Many hunters have considered lions far more dangerous during storms, when their usual laziness vanishes: having no fear of thunder and lightning, they hunt aggressively while the storm disturbs their quarry.[8] Thankfully the weather forecast for the next few days is good. There's a significant difference between myself and most visitors to Africa: for purely practical reasons I don't actually wish to see a lion at all. In all honesty I'd love to have seen one in the wild, or even to have been chased by one and escaped unscathed to tell the tale. I just don't want to see a lion in front of me right now, and not know if it's hungry, or not until it sinks its teeth into me.

Statistically the chances of getting eaten by a lion in Africa are pretty low. Yet someone has to get eaten once in a while for such statistics to exist. While preparing to cross the game reserve on foot, I have to remind myself repeatedly that most accidents happen at home – though not, admittedly, accidents involving lions.

Leaving Rundu, I head east towards the Caprivi Strip. Once known as 'The Devil's Finger', this panhandle-shaped stretch of land once formed part of the German colony. It derives its un-African name from the even more un-African name of the nineteenth-century German chancellor, General Count Georg Leo von Caprivi di Caprara di Montecuccoli, thankfully shortened. Germany acquired the territory from the British in 1890 in exchange for Heligoland and Zanzibar, and were delighted with this strategically important link through the British colonies to German East Africa. In the First World War, however, it became the very first German territory to fall to the British. At the outbreak of war, the unsuspecting German governor was dining with an equally unsuspecting British official from Rhodesia, the two men on the best of terms. The meal ended on a sour note when the British official's aide passed him a letter announcing the start of the war – he immediately arrested the German governor and annexed the Caprivi Strip back to the British crown, all within the time it took to serve the brandy and cigars to the remaining diners.

I trek through the bushland along the Kavango, looking vaguely trainspotterish with my compass hanging on a string around my neck. This stretch of river resembles the Thames below Richmond Hill; even the trees look similar from a distance. Although heavily vegetated, with green fields and dense woodlands of teak, much of the Caprivi Strip is covered with Kalahari sand. The whole area was once a desert, but now it's the most fertile region in Namibia. Caprivi is so lush I find it hard to imagine it's part of the same country as the Namib Desert. So much of Namibia is arid: the country has enormous problems with water shortage, countless adverts proclaiming water as 'our most precious resource'. Yet here in the north of the country the Okavango system alone has more water in it than all the rivers in South Africa put together. And when the region floods, it really floods – the vast Caprivi swamps are sometimes known as Namibia's 'water country'. Local people often travel by means of *mekoro*, dugout canoes skilfully propelled by long poles – 'He who digs his pole too deep will be stuck forever,' runs a local proverb.

My progress through the sand slows to a weary plod; as if to taunt me a flock of tiny black birds repeatedly whizz past at breathtaking speed, back and forth over my head like miniature Red Arrows. I head back towards the main road and immediately make much better progress. By necessity I've become something of an expert on walking surfaces, judging which offer the firmest footing, which prove kinder to your feet, and above all which allow the least expenditure of energy. Rough gravel roads tend to tear sandals to ribbons; in some ways they're worse than walking through the bush, especially when the road is a mixture of loose sand and sharp stones. Carrying a heavy pack, I sink up to my ankles in the sand while the sharp stones hurt my feet through my sandals.

A well-to-do black family stops and presents me with a can of ice-cold 7UP, which right now tastes more like the elixir of life. Later some less affluent locals fill my water bottle from the innards of their car, a gift just as welcome – although I suspect this last offering has something to do with my coming down with giardiasis later. The heat meanwhile turns my reading candles into wax bananas.

Before the entrance to the game reserve I stop for a day's rest. I want to get moving through the West Caprivi Game Reserve as quickly as possible, rather than sitting around here worrying about lions up ahead, and I'm half-tempted to carry straight on. But I've just walked 200 kilometres from Rundu without a break to get here, and the road through the game reserve itself is the same distance again. It would be foolish to set out immediately when I'm already worn out; the lions can wait another day for their dinner.

I pitch my tent in the campsite beside Popa Falls. 'Popa' translates rather redundantly as 'it is here' – although you could say that about most places with some degree of confidence. The Kavango River is over one kilometre wide here, although the falls themselves are little more than rapids, and fail to entice the hordes of visitors away from the spectacular Victoria Falls downstream. But it's a peaceful place, surrounded by forests of jackal berry and buffalo thorn; the noise of the river tumbling over the cascades is lovely in this heat, with plenty of shade around the thatched wooden bungalows. If this were Europe I'd be swimming by now – but there are too many crocodiles and hippos to make this a viable option, not to mention the bilharzia.

Instead I sit in a lodge bar a couple of kilometres downriver from Popa Falls, watching two crocodiles who in turn are showing a keen interest in a family of hippos. But the latter can look after themselves; hippos may appear to be peaceable creatures most of the time, but they kill more people than any other animal in Africa. Anyone reckless enough to place themselves between a hippo and its young – or even just the water – is likely to see it transformed into a three-ton engine of destruction, and a charging hippo can flatten most living things. They're denser than water, so they can waddle on the floor of a lake or river with their lungs full of air; since they can manage this, I can't understand how they can also float to swim, but they've obviously worked it out somewhere down the evolutionary line. Despite their size and weight they can also tiptoe through a campsite at night without snagging a single guyline.

Although Namibian law prohibits local people from trapping hippos in this area, it still goes on, the temptation of so much free meat inevitably proving irresistible. Livingstone was often impressed by the courage of hippopotamus hunters, especially the Makombwe on the Luangwa River. Often a wounded hippo would attack the hunter's canoe and crunch it with its great jaws 'as easily as a pig would a bunch of asparagus'. To escape with their lives the natives would swim frantically for the shore, keeping underwater while the angry hippo searched for them on the surface. 'We have no sport, except perhaps Indian tiger shooting, requiring the courage and coolness this enterprise demands,' Livingstone wrote. The moment the hippo's blood is shed into the water 'all the crocodiles below are immediately drawn up stream by the scent, and are ready to act the part of thieves in a London crowd, or worse'. He often saw 'frightful gashes' on the legs of people who had survived hippo attacks.[9]

But it's the lions rather than hippos that are causing me sleepless nights, and my anxiety about them is getting worse. Sitting watching hippos in a comfortable lodge with a cold beer in my hand isn't helping me cross the game reserve in one piece. Rest or no rest, I've run out of plausible delaying tactics, and I simply have to get moving without any further stalling. Crossing the bridge over the Kavango River, I pass a police checkpoint then start the long trek through the game reserve.

Within hours my rucksack has started chafing against my back, rubbing a hole through my skin that hurts like hell. I can't face this for the next 200 kilometres, so I spend ages trying to stick a plaster over the exact spot right in the middle of my back, contorting myself like a yogi. It proves so awkward to reach that I have to give up and grit my teeth instead. I wish that lady who pulled the thorns out of the seat of my trousers were here; she'd know how to deal with the situation.

I pass countless signs warning me about the danger from elephants. I'm hoping any elephants I meet will be friendly, as I haven't brought any buns for emergencies. I'm disappointed that I don't encounter the real thing, apart from the occasional huge pile of elephant crap in the middle of the road. I steer well clear of these – apart from anything else, guerrillas have an unpleasant tendency to put landmines in them along this stretch of road. As in so much of Africa, poachers have hunted the animals mercilessly; the destructive effects of the long bush war have only compounded the problem. Even so, conservation efforts are making some progress, and a number of herds of between 300 and 500 elephants can be seen in Caprivi during the winter months. There are no fences so the elephants can range vast distances, back and forth across Caprivi and often crossing into Zambia and Botswana.

I pass the turn-off to Omega, a village several kilometres off the road, and the only sizeable settlement in the whole game reserve. Until recently it functioned as a military camp; today it's still home to the Bushmen trackers once employed by the white South African army. During the War of Independence the Bushmen trackers found a new use for their skills, hunting SWAPO fighters through the bush. The legends surrounding the Bushmen's incredible tracking skills have a strong basis in fact. Frederick Selous observed the Bushmen teaching their young children to track by giving them tortoises to play with; when the tortoise was released and crept away, the children crawled after it, following the creature's almost invisible claw marks on the rocks.[10]

The hunting skills and courage of the Bushmen inspired terror in their quarry. Livingstone observed that the lions living to the south of the Caprivi Strip seemed to have a 'wholesome dread' of the Bushmen, and with good cause. Whenever the Bushmen found evidence of a lion having eaten well they would track it 'so quietly that his slumbers are not disturbed. One discharges a poisoned arrow from a distance of only a few feet, while his companion simultaneously throws his skin cloak on the beast's head. The sudden surprise makes the lion lose his presence of mind, and he bounds away in the greatest confusion and terror.' The effects of these poison arrows were horrific. The Bushmen prepared a virulent toxin from the entrails of the N'gwa caterpillar, or sometimes from a particularly venomous species of tarantula; after poisoning their arrows they always cleaned their nails scrupulously: 'a small portion introduced into a scratch acts like morbid matter in dissection wounds'. The agony induced by this poison became so intense that a person affected would slash themselves with a knife, call for their mother's breast, or 'fly from human habitation a raging maniac'. The effects on the poor lion were equally terrible: 'He is heard moaning in distress, and becomes furious, biting the trees and ground in rage.'[11]

The road through the game park itself is remarkably flat, crossing a landscape of broad-leafed deciduous woodland, with all kinds of trees I'd never heard of before, from Zambezi teak to wild raisin and bush-willow. Birds flit though the branches in bright metallic hues – Caprivi is a birdwatcher's paradise, with over 400 species seen here regularly. But my thoughts are more focused on the prospect of meeting a lion on the road, to the extent of not paying enough attention to where I put my feet. As a result I nearly step on a puff adder sunbathing in the middle of the road. Puff adders are big and fat and should be easily noticeable on a tarmac surface; but I don't see this fellow until he's almost under my foot. Despite my heavy pack, I jump straight into the air and what feels like several metres backwards in a completely involuntary Fosbury Flop.

Like the danger from lions, the threat to humans from snakes is often exaggerated in Western minds. Even so, travelling on foot I see a lot of snakes, and many Africans die from snakebites every year. Whereas the average snake encountering a human wants only to disappear as quickly as possible, the puff adder's laziness makes it far more dangerous: they rarely bother to get out of your way, and as a result kill more people than any other snake in Africa. Their venom causes extensive internal bleeding, followed by respiratory failure. Despite their sluggish natures they strike with incredible speed – later a guy tells me he once saw a puff adder bite the same tyre of a moving car twice as it passed. To me this sounds like those apocryphal stories of angry black mambas overtaking a galloping horse, which they definitely can't, unless the horse in question is due for a visit to the glue factory. But without question puff adders can put on an impressive turn of speed when they lash out, so I give this one a wide berth.

For me snakes arouse a mildly horrified fascination, but without the loathing they inspire in some people. I find them beautiful creatures, and I can't agree with the many individuals here who kill a snake on sight, presumably thinking they're doing a good deed. Of course, if I found a snake sharing my sleeping bag I'd take a less reasoned stance, at least until the creature made some other arrangements for the night.

For all his machismo Hemingway confessed to a strong fear of snakes. Livingstone shared this phobia, recording how once he accidentally 'trod on a serpent' in his bedroom at Mabotsa Mission Station: 'The moment I felt the cold scaly skin twine round a part of my leg my latent instinct was roused, and I jumped up higher than I ever did before, or hope to do again, shaking the reptile off in the leap. I probably trod on it near the head, and so prevented it biting me, but did not stop to examine.'[12]

Many theories on treating snakebites are rubbish, particularly the better-known ones; experts now claim that sucking out the poison is a waste of time, and tourniquets are likewise frowned upon. The Victorian explorers went in for predictably dramatic ways of preventing the venom spreading: 'explode gunpowder in the wound … cut away with a knife, and afterwards burn out with the end of your iron ramrod, heated as near to white heat as you can readily get it. The next step is to use the utmost energy, and even cruelty, to prevent the patient's giving way to that lethargy and drowsiness which is the usual effect of snake-poison, and too often ends in death.'[13]

Grogan had his own theories on the subject, and when a porter was bitten by a night adder Grogan plunged the man's hand into a cauldron of boiling water laced with permanganate of potash. The unfortunate porter lost all the skin on his hand and his yells were 'fearful'; even so, Grogan noted that the swelling on the man's arm and chest reduced. Reluctant to continue with Grogan's course of treatment, the porter deserted, taking his own load and as much as he could carry with his remaining good arm. Surprised and hurt, Grogan brooded on the man's response, and for the rest of his life remained convinced Africans were incapable of gratitude.[14]

After four days' trekking I've covered around 120 kilometres across the game reserve, but I'm slowing down alarmingly; I feel weak and nauseous, so I stop early for the night. By the following morning I feel genuinely ill, and have to stay put for the day. It's obviously a bad attack of giardiasis – not serious, but mildly debilitating. For a short while I become so racked with aches and pains and diarrhoea that I wonder if I've got malaria as well. On reflection it was stupid of me to set off into the park when I was still tired from walking all the way from Rundu, and I should have rested at Popa Falls for a few days; but I was in a hurry to get across the park without meeting a lion, and now I'm paying the price.

I can't even find the energy to move my tent into the shade, which is just as well – I don't want to go wandering around in the bush here for fear of stepping on a stray landmine.

The midday sun in Africa becomes a real enemy when you're ill. I spend a horrible day wallowing under its scorching rays, with hardly a breath of wind to make it bearable. I can't eat, and smoking makes me want to throw up. To add to my woes a strange and irritating bird sings all day in a nearby tree, sounding like an old man gargling. All this might be bearable if I could spend the day inside my tent out of the sun, but it's too small and stuffy. Joseph Thomson summed up the problem perfectly: 'To be shut up ill in your tent, with your face close to the roof and your hands touching both sides, means an addition to your tortures of no mean account.'[15] Galton offers little practical help for my physical symptoms, suggesting for an emetic I drink a charge of gunpowder in a tumblerful of warm water and tickle the throat.[16] I resolve to carry on walking the next day, however bad I feel – I can't go through another day like this, sprawled full-length like *The Death of Chatterton*, with the appropriately ghastly pallor to my face.

Fortunately by the following morning I feel slightly better, even though my pack feels five times its normal weight. I still can't eat, which is just as well as the biltong I've carried as iron rations is now covered in green mould. I throw it away – there's more likelihood of lions here than anywhere else in the park, and I don't want anything even resembling meat in my tent tonight apart from myself (there isn't a great deal I can do about that now). I've still got to walk another eighty kilometres to reach the other side of the park, so I set a blistering pace.

Towards late afternoon I notice deer tracks in the sand beside the road, closely followed by lion pads. And this is more or less the spot where lions killed the two tourists and ate the road worker. Lions allegedly start getting hungry around tea time; keen to avoid the early starters, tonight I pitch my tent in record time.

Halfway through the night, loud growls issue from the bushes close by, deep and very gruff. I tell myself that maybe it's not a lion at all, just some other large growling creature that inhabits lion country. I'm puzzled at my own calmness: I'd imagined that if I heard a lion nearby I'd start cowering in my sleeping bag, or even worse, especially with the giardiasis. Instead I feel more curious than anything, and also an irrational temptation to stick my head out of my tent to check it really is a lion out there in the moonlight. Thankfully common sense prevails and I stay inside.

People have assured me a lion won't try and get into my tent in the night. I only hope the lions themselves are aware of this veto. In 1898 the Man-Eaters of Tsavo, a famous pair of lions in Kenya who killed at least twenty-eight Indian railway workers, entered a different tent or building every night to drag off their human prey. And there have been other isolated cases of lions invading tents. I lie in darkness, wondering what I'll do if the flimsy walls of the tent are suddenly sliced open by big claws and a lion shoves its head through the aperture, the rest of it silhouetted against the moonlight. Then it strikes me that if this happened there wouldn't be much point wondering what to do – the decision would be rather taken out of my hands.

On a less life-threatening level there's still the urgent problem of giardiasis. Lions or no lions, a couple of hours after all growling activity has long since ceased I have to leap out of my tent stark naked without another second to lose. Of course, if I was reasonably sure a lion was still waiting outside I would make some other desperate arrangement inside my tent, however unpleasant. As it is, I'm willing to take my chances – I don't even have time to get a few steps away from my tent. By this stage I'm utterly fed up with this explosive diarrhoea, and I wouldn't care to share a tent with someone with giardiasis. It's a shame none of the *Boy's Own* stories of gung-ho African explorers brought in realistic details like horrendous attacks of giardiasis every time the hero attempts some feat of derring-do. Or perhaps they did, euphemistically referring to these unhappy episodes as 'the point where our hero's fortunes fall very low'. But at least I'm not an astronaut in a space suit suffering from the same condition.

These last two days in the game reserve are *tough*. If things had been this hard at the beginning of the trip, I might even have given up. Carrying a heavy pack when I'm ill is no joke; even most soldiers don't march forty kilometres a day carrying this weight when they should be in the sickbay.

I reach the eastern side of the game reserve just before nightfall, but it's a close-run thing; I really didn't want to spend another night in the park with lions about. Slowed down by illness, it's taken me a week to walk the 200 kilometres across the park, and now I'm completely done in. But this is offset by relief and a modest sense of triumph. After the Namib Desert, this is the second big obstacle I've crossed – or the third, if I count Tsondab. I certainly haven't forgotten him.

This page:
The Skeleton Coast, Namibia's
'waterless land', where the
journey began. 'Death ... would
be preferable to banishment in
such a country', wrote an early
explorer on this coast.

Henry Morton Stanley (1873), christened by the Africans *Bula Matari* ('The Smasher of Rocks').

Four years later, Stanley white-haired and emaciated after completing his 1874-77 traversa, the greatest single journey in African history. He was still only 36.

Dr David Livingstone, whose dour exterior belied a distinctive wit and humanity.

'Doctor Livingstone, I presume?' Stanley's celebrated meeting with Livingstone at Lake Tanganyika (1871).

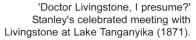

'*Kina bomba*', the boisterous Zambian greeting that so upset Livingstone.

Chuma and Susi, who carried Livingstone's body 2,500 kilometres through hostile territory to the east coast.

Slave traders revenging their losses on the march.

Livingstone mounted on his cantankerous ox, Sindbad.

Livingstone's famous mauling by the lion.

Tsondab at The Spawning Ground, Walvis Bay.

Tsondab at The Alternative Space, Swakopmund.

The *Lady Alice*, the most beautiful donkey cart in Africa.

Marieke, my gigantic mule. (Usakos)

Hagen: 'You need a trolley to carry all your gear.'

The Waterberg Plateau, where Europe's attempt to exterminate the Herero, in one of the earliest attempts at genocide in 20th century history, began in 1904.

Caprivi, Namibia's 'water country'.

African children, Caprivi.

Fellow traveller on the long road through Caprivi.

Ill and exhausted after crossing the West Caprivi Game Reserve.

Typical village water pump.

The Zambezi. Livingstone dreamt the mighty river would become 'God's highway to the African interior', but his hopes were to end in fiasco.

Afternoon tea, Zambia.

Victoria Falls (*Mosi-oa-Tunya*, 'The Smoke That Thunders'). 'Scenes so lovely must have been gazed upon by angels in their flight …' wrote Livingstone.

Eastern Zambia: the cutest
African children, plus the coolest
man in the world.

Luangwa Bridge: village
restaurant, with bars on the
window to keep the diners in.

Near Livingstonia
Plateau, Malawi.

Ingratiating myself with the local police chief,
Chipata.

Chibuku 'Shake-Shake' beer.

Lake Malawi. Captivated by its beauty, Livingstone called it 'The Lake of Stars'

At the Malawi border.

Kombwe Lagoon, Thomson's 'enchanted arcadia', which became the scene of a Victorian My Lai when Mlozi's slavers massacred the Nkonde tribe here.

Reaching the Indian Ocean at Bagamoyo, near Zanzibar.

9. Tales from the Zambezi
(Namibia: Kongola to Zambian Border)

Europe had always heard that the central regions of southern Africa were burning solitudes, bleak, and barren, heated by poisonous winds, infested by snakes and only roamed over by a few scattered tribes of untameable barbarians. But Dr. Livingstone found himself in a high country, full of fruit trees, abounding in shade, watered by a perfect network of rivers.

London Journal, December 1856

The morning after leaving the game reserve I'm feeling slightly better. I chat with a middle-aged local man cycling towards Katima Mulilo; he's surprised and impressed when I tell him I don't accept lifts, as he can see I look dead beat. 'So,' he says thoughtfully, 'you want to *feel the distance!*' I couldn't have put it better myself. He cycles beside me for several kilometres, looking slightly perplexed, obviously on the verge of posing some question. 'Do you wish to claim my vehicle?' he asks finally, gesturing towards his bike, which seems an almost ludicrous act of generosity. Obviously I haven't fully explained the rules of my journey, so I try again. 'You have really walked through the game reserve?' he demands. 'But it's very dangerous, full of lions and tigers!' I missed those tigers.

A few hours later I arrive at a ramshackle shop doubling as a bar. After the long road through the game reserve, I'm astonished to see so many people together in one place again. Although it's only Thursday lunchtime, the weekend has started with a vengeance; the bar is packed with people of all ages, from seven to seventy, already drinking heavily and dancing to deafening reggae. As soon as I walk in, a young woman turns and sneezes right in my face; she then apologizes, and suggests I buy her a beer to make amends. Two men engaged in a loud argument choose this moment to start beating each other up right in front of me. Although no one else in the bar appears particularly interested in the

119

fracas, I'm still feeling very unwell and in no mood for watching a punch-up. Hastily I buy a couple of cans of drink en route to the nearest exit; there's an excellent chance one of the combatants will miss his opponent completely and break a chair over my head by mistake. It's like being in a western movie in a one-horse town, the saloon brawl scene. Outside I lose no time in hoisting my pack on to my back, still expecting one of the fighting guys to fly headfirst out of the bar and land at my feet concussed and drooling.

A common sight in Caprivi is the distinctive sausage tree, *Kigelia africana*, its strange fruit hanging like sausages in a butcher's shop window. The local people use them as charms against whirlwinds, but for me its more obvious associations are the main thing: whenever I pass such a tree it reminds me of how much I'd like some real sausages. A whole trough of sizzling *boerewors* would do just fine. On the road to Katima Mulilo I pass several makeshift open-air slaughterhouses, bovine carcasses dangling from hooks while others are dismembered enthusiastically. The locals slaughter their cattle with an axe or shotgun; occasionally this proves an awkward business when the guy dispatching the unfortunate beast has steadied his nerves with Rhumba. In such cases the job tends to get botched, with someone killed or at least horribly injured, and the cow leaves the scene as walking wounded rather than in separate joints.

By the time I reach the outskirts of Katima Mulilo I'm very, very tired. The last proper break I had was back at Rundu, over 520 kilometres to the west.

I camp in the grounds of a lodge right on the banks of one of the world's greatest rivers. This is my first sight of the Zambezi, gliding past surprisingly quickly, its surface dazzling white in the late morning sun. 300 metres across the water lies Zambia. The name 'Katima Mulilo' in Silozi means 'to quench the fire'. On long canoe journeys the local people carried burning embers to save time lighting the evening fire after a hard day's paddling; the rapids at Katima Mulilo often caused such an unsteady ride that the embers fizzled out like damp squibs.[1]

I've arrived at the Zambezi not far from the spot where Livingstone and his fellow explorer William Cotton Oswell first saw it on 4 August 1851. For me the first sight of the river is exciting, and the occasion for some urgently needed rest; but for Livingstone it was a major triumph. When they first arrived here Livingstone and Oswell could hardly believe their eyes; although they had heard reports of a large river, they were unprepared for the sheer majesty of the Upper Zambezi. They stared as if mesmerized, lost for words, and could only exclaim: 'How glorious! How magnificent! How beautiful!'[2] An old man who lived nearby took Livingstone and Oswell out in his canoe. Almost crying with joy, Livingstone recorded that the only thing stopping his tears was the fear that their pilot might demand: 'What are you blubbering at? Ain't afraid of these alligators, are you?'[3]

Livingstone immediately recognized this as a turning point for him as an explorer.* On a personal level his arrival here far surpassed his later and more celebrated 'discovery' of Victoria Falls. Here lay absolute proof that the African interior was in no way the desert imagined by geographers back in England – instead, they had arrived at a rich and fertile land, well populated and teeming with game. The huge blank spaces on the map of Africa were starting to vanish, and Livingstone saw tremendous possibilities opening before him. He dreamt the Zambezi would become God's Highway to the African interior, stretching all the way from the Indian Ocean; this would open the way to Christianity and commerce, thereby ridding the whole region of the pernicious slave trade.

The Zambezi was to completely dominate Livingstone's thinking for the next decade. Years were to pass before this dream ended in failure and bitter disappointment on his disastrous 1858–64 Zambezi Expedition. This government-sponsored venture dissolved into fiasco and almost destroyed Livingstone's reputation, when he discovered that the Cahora Bassa rapids were totally unnavigable – by an extraordinary stroke of bad luck, this was the one single stretch of the eastern Zambezi Livingstone had neglected to explore on his traversa.

*Ironically, although Livingstone received all the kudos for his 'discovery' of the upper Zambezi, once again he was not in fact the first white man here. Some years later, when he met the Portuguese trader Silva Porto for the first time, Livingstone was mortified to learn that Porto had been there three years before him. Fortunately for Livingstone, the British public showed little interest in the Portuguese discoveries, particularly with their strong links to the slave trade. And Livingstone himself went to great lengths to discredit the Portuguese explorers, dismissing them as 'half-castes', thereby making himself the first 'genuine' European to reach the upper Zambezi.

A nice young Danish couple at the lodge are camping in the next tent. I like them – they seem happy together, as young couples often do when you're single. I can't deny that mild jealousy enters the equation. It must be more fun to travel like this, in comparative comfort – young, attractive, bonking your brains out whenever the mood takes you, instead of having to deal with all the shit I've put up with lately, even if most of it is self-inflicted. The girl looks rather like a former girlfriend of mine, the one whose romantic candle set my hair alight. The Danish girl isn't as pretty, but I'm prepared to attribute that to sour grapes on my part because right now I'm on my own.

Before I left England a friend wanted to know if I'd take any photos of old flames along with me in Africa. 'What the hell for?' I asked, sounding more defiant than I actually felt. As it turned out, the only photos I brought were those in a small leaflet on malignant melanoma; if I started getting skin cancer from the African sun I could then identify the problem without delay and seek medical help. There is, after all, a hole in the ozone somewhere over Namibia. But in all truthfulness I did give serious thought to bringing some old snaps with me. I went as far as bringing a tiny elastic hairgrip that once belonged to someone important I was involved with years ago; it still had strands of her hair trapped in it. For months after we split up I could still faintly smell her hair on it; this wore off with time, as do most things. One evening back in London, some time after we'd split up, in a fit of pique I fired it like an elastic band out of my bedroom window; regretting this the following morning, I spent the best part of an hour hunting for it in the long wet grass outside my house. The hairgrip, still with attached hair, came with me to Namibia; the sentimental side of me liked the idea of taking some part of her across Africa. But I lost the hairgrip before I even got halfway across Namibia, which saddened me for a day or two; at which point I reassured myself with the thought: 'Does it really matter so much, anyway?' I've got more than enough problems in the present without getting maudlin about the past.

I arrange a lift for the Danish couple to Victoria Falls, with a family I met back in the game reserve. Delighted at this, they pool their resources to buy me a large beer, and a pleasant evening follows. The guy has just had a very short haircut in town, a drastic remedy after he came to grief at a village barber's shop. The village barber had developed his skills only on local coiffures, and blond flowing Nordic locks proved well beyond him. Using his clippers in the customary downwards direction for several minutes, nothing much was happening until the Danish guy suggested he adjusted the setting; whereupon great clumps of hair started coming out at the roots.

'Couldn't you use scissors instead?' pleaded the Danish guy.

'Scissors!' exclaimed the barber. Whoever heard of using scissors to cut hair? His brave but ultimately disastrous attempt with scissors made an even worse job of it – it would have been better if he'd just made some pretend snipping noises behind his customer, who left the shop looking like he'd been dragged through a hedge backwards.

I go to bed in a reasonable mood for once. In the morning I feel rather sad to see the Danish couple depart. I spend the rest of the day trying not to smoke, and instead eat most imprudently. The giardiasis has not yet cleared up, but I feel better than I did in the game reserve.

Over lunch I talk to a friendly German who tells me how he once travelled in Morocco with a donkey – I'm always pleased to meet a colleague. After making reasonable progress for three or four days, his party came to a desert village with a beautiful fountain sparkling invitingly like something from one of Aesop's fables. But the donkey refused to touch the water. 'I should have been suspicious, if I hadn't been so goddamn thirsty!' the guy tells me. 'Half an hour later I became so sick my friends had to take me straight home, tied face down across the donkey's back like a dead cowboy.' But if he managed to travel four days in one direction with a donkey, he still got further than I did.

He now works on a local environmental project in Caprivi, which seems a good job as it involves flying around most of the day in a bright red helicopter. Every morning I'm woken by the *whup! whup! whup!* of rotor blades as the helicopter comes to pick him up, landing noisily in the lodge grounds, barely metres from my tent. It all strikes me as rather ostentatious, but no doubt I'm just envious. These uncharitable thoughts evaporate only days later, when the helicopter crashes in the bush, killing everyone on board. The German guy had a lucky escape – by a one in a thousand chance he'd been working on a different project that afternoon, the only time he'd done so in months.

From the Namibian side of the border almost all the signs for Zambia look bad. Many white folks here regard Zambia as a risky place to visit, populated almost exclusively by robbers and bandits who spice up their thieving with gratuitous violence. I talk to a middle-aged English guy called Barry, cycling from Ethiopia to Cape Town, who tells me some most unpleasant characters recently mugged his friend just south of Lusaka, exactly where I'm heading. After taking their victim's money and possessions, they beat him up and then burst his eardrums with a piece of rusty wire, purely out of spite.

I consider exactly what I plan to do should I find myself confronted by robbers. The most sensible option would be to do nothing. Travelling alone like this the feeling of vulnerability at times becomes intensely frustrating. Potential robbers, unless they're pretty thick, surely realize my pack has to contain some things well worth stealing, and that I must be carrying money about my person. And I can hardly chase after robbers while carrying a large rucksack. Perhaps I should look on the bright side – if all the reports on Zambia are true I won't be carrying anything for much longer.

Livingstone's experiences with local thieves occasionally resulted in slapstick chases straight out of the Keystone Cops. On one occasion during his traversa, near the village of Chief Ionga Panza, some local guides ran off with two guns and a sack of beads standing in Livingstone's encampment. Livingstone's men promptly gave chase: ' …when the guides saw that they would be caught, they threw down the guns, directed their flight to the village, and rushed into a hut. The doorway is not much higher than that of a dog's kennel. One of the guides was reached by one of my men as he was in the act of stooping to get in, and a cut was inflicted on a projecting part of the body, which would have made anyone in that posture wince. The guns were restored, but the beads were lost in the flight.'[4]

Most nights at the lodge I hear gunfire from the opposite side of the river – slightly disconcerting, considering I'll be sleeping over there in a day or two. In the meantime Zambian robbers paddle across at night to steal any boots left outside tents, or anything else they can carry off. Because of this, armed security guards patrol the grounds of the lodge while a large spotlight turns the campsite into Colditz. While I've no wish to lose my boots, I'd rather this happened than some Zambian wide-boy getting his head blown off in the act of taking them.

But there's always the chance Zambia may confound these negative expectations. Most of the guests at the lodge are white middle-aged tourists, who presumably wouldn't enjoy a trip to Zambia anyway, so there's no reason for them to try to see the country in a favourable light. And the whole country can't be all bad – after all, it's big enough, spread over three-quarters of a million square kilometres. If the entire population was criminally inclined the country would simply grind to a halt. I'll be there for some time, so I tell myself I should start thinking positively.

Hippos sometimes lumber out of the Zambezi to crop the greenest portions of the golf course adjoining the lodge; but only the most dedicated golfers are likely to start arguing with them about it. Prominent signs at the lodge warn guests about the danger of crocodiles. At this part of the Zambezi Livingstone noted the prodigious number of crocodiles, and he considered them more savage than on other rivers. Many children were carried off annually when they went down to play in the water, and many calves were also eaten.[5]

At night a big owl perches on a branch outside my tent, calm and observant, completely unperturbed by the proximity of humans. Like its counterpart in folklore, it misses nothing and gives every impression of cool detached wisdom. African superstition links the owl with bad luck; south of Caprivi they're thought to be the familiars of night witches.

I waste the best part of an afternoon trying to teach the lodge's large talking parrot some rude words in English, although we both lose interest before the end of the first lesson. Parrots are popular pets with white Africans, but I always feel sorry for them; their cages invariably seem far too small, and I can't see any way they can stretch their wings properly. Some of the bigger parrots here seem to be permanent residents in their cages, like convicts languishing in oubliettes. Most of them shriek like the inmates of Bedlam – and who wouldn't, stuck in a cage all the time? But perhaps they do that anyway, back in the forest.

Around this time I find my first tick, firmly embedded in my thigh. At first I try the recommended method of burning it off with a cigarette, which doesn't even impair the creature's appetite let alone kill it. These creatures are *tough*, and well designed; wild animals must find it almost impossible to dislodge them from their hides. After drilling a hole in their host's skin, they fasten themselves by means of a feeding tube; in return for sucking your blood they can give you a dose of tick bite fever. If you tear them off their feeding tube will break off in your skin and fester; it takes me best part of an hour to dig this one out with a needle.

I spend much of my time here reading outside my tent, while a small incontinent dog chases around the campsite grounds. My tent so far has lasted well; even the helicopter landing close by couldn't blow it down. Even so, I wish I'd brought a slightly roomier version, despite the added weight. One of my neighbours at the lodge sleeps in a tent fitted to the roof of his truck; at least no one can drive off with his vehicle at night without him noticing *something*. Couples on camping trips often fail to realize that in a crowded campsite, bonking by torchlight in a tent creates a magic lantern show for any neighbours who might care to watch. No doubt some people just like showing off, or don't care either way. Even so, I can't believe the guy in the next tent is aware that most nights the whole campsite can see a silhouette of his backside going up and down like a fiddler's elbow. I've no desire to witness any of this, even if I can't help hearing it – I'd rather be back in the bush, where there is peace and quiet. I must get back on the road soon, even if it's straight into the arms of the highway robbers waiting on the other side of the Zambezi.

I've been in Africa for nearly five months by now, and I need to start replacing some of my clothes; my trousers in particular have more or less disintegrated. It strikes me that the clothes I brought from home have been fairly good choices, even though before I left London I spent ages deciding what to take. The Victorian explorers weren't much help on this subject; usually they wore Norfolk jackets and heavy boots, and for some reason believed flannel shirts protected the wearer from sunstroke and fever. Few great explorers considered themselves properly dressed without a cork solar topi, although Livingstone habitually wore a small but distinctive consular cap and Stanley preferred a slightly comical high-peaked hat of his own design, complete with brass-reinforced ventilation holes and a cloth flap to shield his neck from the sun. The great traveller Mary Kingsley, who explored much of West Africa in heavy Victorian skirts, insisted: 'You have no right to go about Africa in things you would be ashamed to be seen in at home.'[6] For most of the journey

I tend to forget this sound advice, and after that long stretch through the West Caprivi Game Reserve I'm starting to look disreputable.

Instead of their thick Western clothing and heavy boots, the African explorers might have travelled in greater comfort had they adopted local attire – although for missionaries like Livingstone this was not really an option. He often observed local women in a state of 'frightful nudity', while naked men walked about 'without the smallest sense of shame. They have even lost the tradition of the "figleaf". I asked a fine large-bodied old man, if he did not think it would be better to adopt a little covering. He looked with a pitying leer, and laughed with surprise at my thinking him at all indecent: he evidently considered himself above such weak superstition. I told them that on my return I should have my family with me, and no one must come near us in that state. "What shall we put on? We have no clothing." It was considered a good joke when I told them that, if they had nothing else, they must put on a bunch of grass.'[7]

Apart from buying a Gore-Tex jacket, there seemed little point in spending much money on clothes before I left England. I knew the climate would change dramatically between different regions, so I could buy things as I went, and this plan has worked out well so far. Unlike a lot of people travelling in Africa, I never bothered with any khaki-coloured clothes; growing evidence suggests khaki is not the best colour to wear if you're one of those people who likes to creep up on wildlife unobserved – although throughout the journey I'm more concerned about the wildlife creeping up on me. Despite khaki's long tradition on safaris, and the fact that it camouflages humans from each other perfectly, apparently animals can spot it a mile off. The same theory maintains that wild animals have problems detecting blue; but dark blue clothing attracts mosquitoes and tsetse flies, so whatever you take you can't win.

I stay at the lodge for a week. I need the rest, and preferably some company, yet the sight of all these beautiful young people serves only to compound a real sense of loneliness. I sit watching them, trying not to mope. I've lived twice their lives, more than that in some cases; but right now they're having a much better time than me. Adolescent pheromones whiz through the campsite, with bare legs everywhere – there seem to be more pairs of attractive bare legs on display than there are people present. Mercifully my ardour is dampened when one group gathers around their campfire and starts strumming the obligatory guitar; I'm treated to a medley of Christian songs in Danish, accompanied by much hand-clapping and banging of plastic utensils.

After the Danes have headed off east towards Victoria Falls, peace returns briefly to the campsite. Then a large party of Norwegian high school kids arrives, their bus adorned with slogans informing me in English that Jesus loves me. These newcomers are much louder than the Danes, and shatter the silence like a troupe of circus tumblers suddenly piling into your living room. Before even pitching their tents, they rig up a small stage and launch into a loud impromptu puppet show, like *Sesame Street* in Norwegian.

I wander off and sit beside the swimming pool to give my ears a break. I've been there less than five minutes when the new arrivals realize there's a pool, celebrating their discovery with whoops of glee. Abandoning the puppet show in mid-performance they descend on the pool like paratroopers falling from the skies. I'm feeling rather old in the face of all this. I'm determined not to move, even though I can barely concentrate on my book for all the screaming and splashing. But live and let live, I tell myself; if I'm not careful I'll end up like one of those grumpy old men always chasing kids from their doorstep. After all, there's nothing wrong with people having a good time. I'm beginning to feel rather generous, adopting such a tolerant viewpoint, when the school fatty leaps into the pool and half empties it, mostly over me. Completely drenched, I watch him explode to the surface like a human depth charge. I give him a filthy look; his only response is a loud guffaw.

It's time to get back on the road, though I simply can't resist another couple of days with slap-up breakfasts at the lodge. Once you've paid your money here you can eat as much as you like, which is definitely not in my best interests after living hard in the bush, with the prospect of more of the same ahead. Each morning, after resolving to do nothing of the sort, I eat like a horse and then feel like throwing up for the rest of the day.

In hindsight it's just as well I spend some time gorging myself while I still can. Since the journey started I've walked around 1,600 kilometres to get here, so I've convinced myself that by now I'm becoming adept at this mode of travel. Instead, the next stage on to Victoria Falls comes as a real shock, worse even than crossing the Namib Desert.

10. Hunger March
(Zambia: Namibian Border to Victoria Falls)

> We were surprised the next day by our black cook from Sierra Leone bearing in a second course. 'What have you got there?' was asked in wonder. 'A tart, sir.' 'A tart! of what is it made?' 'Of cabbage, sir.' As we had no sugar, and could not 'make believe', as in the days of boyhood, we did not enjoy the feast that Tom's genius had prepared.
>
> David Livingstone, *Expedition to the Zambesi*

I cross the Zambezi at the Zambian border post at Wenela. For me there's always something exciting about leaving one country and entering another – particularly now that I've walked right across one and I'm about to do the same with the next. After so long in Namibia it feels strange to be in a new African country; everything seems subtly different, and it can't all be my imagination. Things are definitely more run-down: the huts are dilapidated with the thatch falling off, the stone-and-concrete buildings are crumbling, and yet the local people seem friendlier and more laid-back.

I reach Sesheke ('the place of white sand'), once an important Makololo town but today little bigger than a large village. Unlike your average town, this one has had something of an itinerant history, having changed its site at least once. During his traversa Livingstone visited Sesheke in its original location and was nearly assassinated here after being caught up in a local power struggle. Approaching the town with his friend the young Makololo chief Sekeletu, Livingstone was alarmed to see the chief's ambitious kinsman Mpepe running with all his might towards them with an upraised axe. Sekeletu managed to escape to a nearby village, and Mpepe fled in the opposite direction.

To avoid a factional war, Sekeletu and Mpepe met later for conciliatory talks, with Livingstone acting as mediator. Mpepe, now on his best behaviour, was most contrite about his earlier actions, insisting that the unfortunate business with the axe had been merely a misunderstanding.

The talks dragged on late into the night, and Livingstone was delighted when Sekeletu and Mpepe eventually swore vigilant friendship with each other. Livingstone then asked Sekeletu where he could sleep for the night. At this Mpepe's eyes lit up – he'd ordered his most trusted followers to stab Sekeletu the moment Livingstone left the hut.

Sekeletu, however, had no intention of trusting Mpepe; so he rose with Livingstone under the pretext of showing him where to sleep and thus avoided assassination by a hair's breadth. Had Sekeletu been killed in this way, Livingstone as the chief's friend would certainly have been murdered the same night. Instead, after Mpepe himself had gone to bed gnashing his teeth at finding his plans in ruins, the men he'd instructed to stab Sekeletu went straight to the chief and revealed the entire plot. Sekeletu ordered Mpepe's immediate execution; two of his warriors seized Mpepe in silence and led him a mile outside the village, where they speared him to death. Livingstone, sleeping only yards away, heard nothing of this until the next morning; and only weeks later he had to watch helplessly as Mpepe's father and uncle were hacked down with battle axes and their bodies thrown to the waiting crocodiles.

While my own arrival at Sesheke is far less eventful than Livingstone's, it does bring its own share of problems. I discover that the bank no longer exchanges foreign currency, which seems absurd – Zambia's currency is anything but stable, and the country is desperate for dollars. On a personal level this leaves me right in the shit. I've no local money and the nearest town, Livingstone, lies over 200 kilometres away. I consider hitching a ride to Livingstone, where I could change some money and then hitch back here to continue walking where I left off. But on balance, this seems such a waste of time and effort that I make the rather irrational decision to carry on with no local money and no food – something might turn up, and I'll just have to make bloody good time.

For the rest of the day I make reasonable progress, around thirty-five kilometres. But the lack of food quickly becomes a real problem, and the poor condition of the road slows me down considerably. Given the choice, I'd always prefer to work extra hard today than to have to go without food in a couple of days' time. Unfortunately on this long stretch to Livingstone I have to do both. But hunger is a powerful incentive when you need to cover large distances in a short time, especially with the prospect of food at the end. Hunger for anything has usually got me moving in some direction – like many people, often when I haven't achieved something it's simply because I wasn't hungry enough for it. Right now, of course, physical hunger makes all this less of an academic issue, and it grows steadily more real with each passing hour.

Before long I'm fantasizing that something wonderful and unexpected relating to food will happen, but it doesn't, apart from an unexpected gift of a tiny can of pilchards donated by a kind South African family driving a Landrover back from Victoria Falls. I never imagined a can of pilchards could fill me with such pure delight. Pilchards are remarkably good things to eat when you're starving and don't know where the next meal is coming from; they're so horrible and difficult to digest that they stay in your stomach for ages, providing a welcome if temporary solution to growling hunger pangs.

The local people still seem very friendly, and the surrounding countryside is lovely: despite some spoilsport visitors claiming Zambia is boring to look at, the tall, broad-leafed teak woodlands with cool glades beside the road make a refreshing change from the wide open bushveldt back in Namibia. But it's difficult to give much attention to anything other than the prospect of food. I'm so hungry that the idea of eating soon occupies all my waking thoughts. I've heard of people in similar situations spending all their waking hours dreaming about the various foods they intend to devour on reaching civilization; but right now the idea of deliberately fantasizing about food seems to me the worst kind of folly.

Despite my good intentions, a couple of days without food leave me without any choice in the matter: food is constantly on my mind, with or without conscious effort. Trying to think pleasant thoughts on any other subject proves impossible, and everything comes straight back to eating. Trekking fifty kilometres a day with a heavy pack is burning up so many calories that without food there simply isn't enough energy left to do the job properly. But at least being mobile like this means I can do something to extricate myself from this situation – it's much better than being stuck fast somewhere without food, which must be truly terrifying.

Livingstone, a 'heavy grubber' like so many of the Victorian explorers, found it difficult to balance exploration with the demands of his stomach. His nights under African skies were often filled with dreams of favourite foods; he'd then wake to find his pillow soaking wet, having spent the night drooling over visions of roast beef and juicy marrow bones, while chimerical puddings and pies danced their way temptingly through his dream landscape. On reaching Portuguese West Africa in 1854, Livingstone enjoyed his first full meal in four months; he ate so voraciously that he worried he'd appear a glutton, later confessing that if he'd been alone he would have bought even more food to devour in bed throughout the night. Livingstone came close to dying of starvation on several occasions, as did Stanley on both his traversas. At the time of their famous meeting, when the latter arrived with desperately needed food and supplies, Livingstone was so emaciated he described himself as a mere 'ruckle of bones'. 'You have brought me new life!' he said over and over again to Stanley, who at first suspected the great explorer's privations had left him mildly demented.

The appalling state of the road from Sesheke to Livingstone makes it one of the worst tarred roads in Africa. For long stretches the potholes are so extreme that the road's surface is missing entirely, and walking on the loose Kalahari sand exposed by the huge gaps in the road is very hard work with a heavy pack. But this is not my main concern: without food, this part of the journey gets worse and worse. I have to step up the pace, even though I've already been going more or less flat out.

After several days without eating, even recorded music becomes strangely laden with references to food. I have to start selecting CDs carefully to avoid being taunted – when even Otis Redding's *Shake* starts mentioning a bowl of soup I turn him off in a rage. If Freud really thought everything was sex, he could never have been truly hungry; if he was still alive I'd write to tell him he's been talking bollocks, and in fact everything is food.

Right now even a dog biscuit would be lovely.

The night before I reach Livingstone I'm pretty much on my last legs; I've walked 180 kilometres now with nothing to eat except one small can of pilchards. Then a friendly middle-aged white guy called Alistair stops his vehicle for me. He runs a trading post nearby, and presents me with a miniature banana and a small handful of *kapenta* (tiny dried sardines, so salty they guarantee a raging thirst), which is all he has. I'm almost pathetically grateful, and I'm shovelling them down even before he departs, talking to him with my mouth full of half-masticated fish.

Food tastes utterly different when you're truly hungry – which of course is how it tastes all the time, we just don't bother to notice. I never imagined a humble banana could taste so exotic, so divine, so *inexpressibly fucking wonderful* ... The taste of it just *explodes* on my tongue. When I've finished it I try eating the skin as well.

While these few mouthfuls of food are marvellous, they're still nowhere near enough. I'm almost sorry I ate anything – now the floodgates have opened I'm hungrier than ever. I expect to reach town the following lunchtime, but that seems a lifetime away when all the intervening hours will be filled with this gnawing hunger. I'd imagined that the knowledge I can eat my fill tomorrow would lessen the pangs of hunger now – instead, I find that knowing the end is hours away only heightens the obsession. It's like telling someone absolutely bursting for a piss not to worry, there'll be a toilet they can use in a few hours' time.

It's difficult to explain my own attitude to being so hungry at this stage. If I really was as desperate as all that I could try begging something from strangers, or stop every single passing vehicle in the hope of scrounging something. I could always barter some of my kit at one of the few villages I've passed on this stretch: someone surely would take pity on me, and the locals would almost certainly help me. And at any time I could simply hitch ahead to Livingstone, stuff my face, then hitch back to where I stopped walking. What stops me from doing any of these things is some weird bloody-mindedness, which I'm not even sure I understand myself and which rather surprises me. Perhaps it's just ego, trying to fool myself how tough I am – after all, I wouldn't be walking across Africa without some streak of masochism.

Of course, if this went on much longer I would simply *have to get food*, no matter what. I always knew this would only be for a short period, and for me there was always a choice. But it does bring it home to me that enough people in some parts of Africa literally have to live like this, and real hunger – hunger without choice or any real hope of finding food – must be horrifying.

Even so, by normal standards, I'm still bloody hungry.

Late the following morning I reach the town of Livingstone, with one thing only on my mind. Several people along the road have recommended a hostel called Jolly Boys, which sounds delightfully camp; I couldn't care less what its guests get up to provided there's food, immediately, and lots of it. When I reach the hostel there's no chance of doing anything mundane like filling out signing-in books or any of that nonsense – food has to come first, *I simply can't wait any longer.* After changing some dollars in record time I start walking quickly the few hundred metres to the local supermarket. Walking quickly proves far too slow and quite involuntarily I break into an unseemly run.

Once inside the supermarket I make a disgusting spectacle of myself – any food will do, the only requirement is that it goes straight into my stomach with a minimum of chewing. I settle for yoghurt and cream cakes, stuffing my face like a pig while still standing in the checkout queue, my face covered in cream, shoving cakes into my mouth with a force not normally associated with eating. The first batch of cakes doesn't even last until I get served; thankfully the girl on the till accepts my word on how many I've eaten. I rush back to the cake counter for more, eating with a peculiar grim concentration that even the finest actor would have trouble faking. I want no distractions of any kind, not even anyone speaking to me until I've finished – the sheer urgency of chewing and swallowing as quickly as possible takes up my whole attention. The security guards exchange glances; hefting their clubs nervously, they watch me carefully as though I'm mad. Sensibly they keep their distance, and we obviously understand each other: if they ordered me to step away from the cream cakes I'd start snarling like a wolverine. Nowhere near satisfied, with all this food suddenly available I start looking for variety: cream cakes aren't enough to get my teeth into, so I buy a huge packet of digestive-like local biscuits and go through the lot like a cartoon beaver chomping through a log.

After a further batch of gooey cakes I'm finally satiated. Too satiated, in fact, and dangerously close to regurgitating the lot. The locals once had an expression for this degree of gluttony; Livingstone heard many a native gourmand 'declare the feast to be so recherché that every step they take homewards will cause their stomachs to say "tobu, tobu, tobu"'.[1] God knows what my stomach says on my slow and sober walk back to the hostel, carefully avoiding passers-by – I'm worried I'll throw up over someone like the scene from *The Exorcist.*

Back at Jolly Boys, the average age of the guests seems to be about nineteen. I'm feeling rather old in the face of this, and presumably looking it, like mutton dressed as lamb. In conversations around me everything is 'awesome', 'chilled', 'wicked' or 'totally cool'. I'm too tired for all these superlatives, and can't enter into the spirit of it right now – and I still haven't ruled out the possibility of throwing up all the cream cakes in front of everyone. But at least there's a bath here, and books as well – and it's only two dollars to camp, in pleasant gardens filled with all kinds of fruit trees, everything from papaya and avocado to lemon, mango and guava.

The Australian who runs the place doesn't like me at all, while appearing perfectly well disposed towards everyone else. It's not that he's overtly rude, exactly – and I'm not suggesting that as soon as I've filled in the signing-in book we should jump into the nearest bunk bed with each other or anything. But he is a little *offhand*. No doubt I'm expecting too much, but I've got on well with the people at every similar place I've stayed at so far. His manner reminds me that I've rather grown to like the quasi-celebrity status my walk is giving me in most people's eyes. When someone clearly couldn't care less, it actually comes as a mild surprise. How things have changed since London.

I get along rather better with an attractive Finnish girl who works for the Salvation Army in Lusaka. Despite much good-natured chaffing from the other guests, she remains adamant she doesn't play in the band. I also get on well with the black cook at Jolly Boys, a nice lady called Mercy, which she pronounces 'Messy'. The kitchen facilities are excellent, and the chance to cook for myself again after so long on the road is such a novelty I find myself cooking three or four times a day while I'm staying here. I become so involved with this that Mercy is soon convinced I'm a chef, and starts treating me as a colleague, asking my advice on local dishes when I've never even heard of half the ingredients, let alone the recipe. But for some reason the food I crave the most is oat porridge, and I start eating it at least twice a day. God knows why – back in England when I was desperately saving to get to Africa I ate enough porridge to sink a ship.

The main attraction in this part of Africa is Victoria Falls, at twice the size of Niagara the world's most spectacular waterfall. Livingstone named it in honour of his queen; the Makololo name, *Mosi-oa-Tunya*, means 'the smoke that thunders', referring to the enormous cloud of mist rising from half a million cubic metres of water crashing every minute into the Zambezi Gorge below. Even from fifteen kilometres away the noise of the falls does indeed sound like rolling thunder.

On the Zambian side of the Zambezi I go right up to the lip of the falls, in the process getting soaked with spray. Close to the edge the water moves deceptively gently before vanishing abruptly into space. A tree stretches out over the big drop – if you're mad you can climb out along it and look right down into the waterfall, although I feel exposed enough standing at its base, right next to the brink. Close to, the sense of the raw power of nature is almost overwhelming; the deep rumble of this vast body of water in motion is now accompanied by an ominous hiss of such force that it soon becomes mesmerizing, a physical presence looming through the mist. I feel very uneasy walking above the falls; the narrow footpath is dangerously slippery with spray as well as vertiginous. I'm surprised more people don't slide over the edge – occasionally even elephants lose their footing while dining on the lush vegetation above the falls and plunge to their death below.

Recently a Japanese tourist chose Victoria Falls as the climactic scene for his video diary. Walking along the narrow slippery path at the edge of the falls and filming as he went, he paid more attention to his movie than to where he was putting his feet; stepping out into space, he took his final work with him.

Even today it's easy to see how water has always attracted mystical associations; how waterfalls and rainbows have been regarded as the abode of spirits, a link between this world and the next. The small islands on the edge of the falls were once used as places of worship, and the early Tonga people sacrificed animals here to their rain god, launching the unfortunate creatures into the thundering abyss below.[2]

The sheer size of Victoria Falls can hardly fail to bring out some feeling of humbleness in even the most cynical visitor, a sense of personal insignificance. Some people on the edge of the falls have reported an unmistakable urge to hurl themselves over, but I'm relieved to feel exactly the opposite. I start wondering what it would be like to plunge into the falls – I imagine there would be little sensation of falling as such, and instead one would be plucked into nothingness by the vast curtain of water, and life crushed out within moments. Amazingly, one man actually survived such a plunge. In 1904 a certain Trooper Ramsay lost his paddle while kayaking above the falls, and was swept over the edge. A policeman later fished Ramsay's drowned body from the Zambezi; to the officer's amazement the corpse woke up, spitting water and barrack-room curses in equal measure, and very much alive. Ramsay escaped with mere bruises, and an unbeatable yarn to tell his mates down the pub.[3]

Occasionally people have been given a helping hand in this direction. Livingstone records how a group of Makololo warriors once pursued some fugitive Batoka tribesmen right to the edge of the falls; unable to stop the impetus of their flight, the unfortunate Batoka were literally dashed to pieces at the bottom. Their task completed, the Makololo then 'beheld the stream like a white cord at the bottom, and so far down … that they became giddy, and were fain to go away, holding on to the ground'.[4]

Livingstone's descriptions of the Victoria Falls are among the best known of all his writings: 'Scenes so lovely must have been gazed upon by angels in their flight … The morning sun gilds these columns of watery smoke with all the glowing colours of double and treble rainbows. The evening sun, from a hot yellow sky, imparts a sulphurous hue and gives one the impression that the yawning gulf might resemble the mouth of the bottomless pit. No bird sits and sings in that grove of perpetual showers, or even builds its nest there … The sunshine, elsewhere in this land so overpowering, never penetrates the deep gloom of that shade. In the presence of the strange Mosi-oa-Tunya, we can sympathise with those who, when the world was young, peopled the earth, air and river with beings not of mortal form. Sacred to what deity would be this awful chasm and that dark grove over which hovers an ever-abiding pillar of cloud?'[5]

But despite such lyrical treatment, when Livingstone first arrived here in November 1855 he was far from completely bowled over. He'd first heard reports of a gigantic waterfall five years earlier, when he was only several days' march away at Sesheke, yet he hadn't even bothered to investigate. His first sight of the upper Zambezi, with all its thrilling possibilities, was of much greater personal significance – and in purely practical terms the last thing Livingstone wanted to find on God's highway to the African interior was the world's biggest waterfall. Significantly, although by nature a precise man, Livingstone completely misjudged the size of the falls: at over 100 metres high and 1.7 kilometres wide, they are twice the size of his first estimate (and also twice the size of Niagara).

Although to this day Livingstone's name is inextricably linked with Victoria Falls, as with so many of his 'discoveries' he was probably not in fact the first European to come there. The Portuguese traders knew of the falls, and almost certainly visited them, as did the occasional Boer hunter – those hard-riding gents covered immense distances in southern Africa. Their stories are long forgotten, while Livingstone's lives on.

The site of the Zambezi Bridge was chosen personally by the empire builder Cecil John Rhodes, who planned it to be the star attraction of his great dream, a railway stretching all the way from Cape Town to Cairo. Something of a showman, Rhodes insisted the bridge must be built so near the falls that spray would drench the railway carriages. Surprisingly, he never visited the Zambezi himself. During the construction of the bridge a huge safety net was stretched across the gorge, dangling some ninety metres above the river, designed to keep fatalities among the workforce to a minimum. This sensible precaution backfired on the first day: convinced they were expected to leap into the net as part of the job, the horrified native labourers called an immediate strike.

Those involved in this early example of Zimbabwean industrial action might today be amused to find bungee jumpers paying handsomely for more or less the same experience. Bungee jumping has become one of the main attractions at the falls; at 110 metres it's still one of the highest commercial jumps in the world. I wouldn't mind trying it some time, but eighty dollars is expensive for a ten-second buzz; if I want to reach the east coast I can't afford entertainment I can measure in moments.

After resting for a few days at Livingstone my whole body seizes up. For a day or two any movement becomes difficult, and I wonder how I'm going to continue walking. At such times I find it easy to descend into weedy fantasies about things I'd like to happen on my return to Europe. These usually revolve around some form of romantic encounter, preferably involving eating oat porridge the morning after, or even better during.

For much of Namibia it proved all too easy for me to eat crappy

Western food rather than local African meals. So at Livingstone's curiously named Twatasha Kiosk I have my first proper dollop of *nsima,* the stiff porridge made from maize flour boiled in water. Similar to European polenta, it forms the staple diet of most Africans south of the Sahara; before long I acquire a taste for it, which is just as well, as from here to the east coast it's usually the only thing on the menu.

After another couple of days at Jolly Boys my stiff joints start to loosen up. Instead of lazing around in a weary stupor as usual, I devote a morning to shopping in Livingstone. This sleepy little colonial town, once the country's capital, is now time-worn and rough around the edges; many of the Victorian houses built by English settlers are crumbling, their corrugated iron roofs in need of repair, their wooden verandas almost rotten. The streets and African shopfronts are more recent but equally shabby – even so, the town has character, and its friendly, relaxed atmosphere is just what I need.

In a local pharmacy I buy some suspiciously cheap malaria tablets, so cheap they're a bargain even if I later catch cerebral malaria and die horribly. The pharmacist insists they have no side effects whatsoever, which raises my suspicions even further. It's worth being cautious on this – malaria still kills more than a million Africans every year, and the real danger of catching it is growing steadily the further east I get. Unfortunately malaria tablets don't work particularly well; sometimes they create more problems than they solve, masking the first symptoms and preventing early diagnosis. The only sure way to avoid malaria is to avoid getting bitten by mosquitoes, which of course is the difficult part.

All the African explorers knew that malaria was by far their worst enemy, and the greatest single obstacle to any European presence in Africa. During his own researches as a medical doctor Livingstone made some very astute guesses on malaria. He observed that mosquitoes were particularly common in areas badly affected by the disease, and he was the first explorer to recognize the full significance of quinine in opening the African interior. Without quinine African exploration had been an almost suicidal undertaking, and even when using it every single European explorer in nineteenth-century Africa still suffered horribly from malaria.[6] By trial and error Livingstone developed his own medication for its treatment, quinine-based tablets known as 'Zambezi Rousers' or 'Livingstone Pills'. He wrote: 'If I can only discover a healthy range of country and means to foil that terrible plague, I shall be content to let the unicorn sleep in everlasting oblivion.'*

Even when he was prostrated with malaria himself, Livingstone was always prepared to listen to native doctors, remarking: 'I make it a rule to keep on good terms with my professional brethren.' At times he regretted this, after being 'stewed in their vapour-baths, smoked like a red herring over green twigs, and charmed *secundum artem*'. His friend Chief Shinte offered Livingstone this advice on the subject: '"Drink plenty of the mead, and, as it gets in, it will drive the fever out." It was rather strong, and I suspect he liked the remedy pretty well, even though he had no fever.'[7]

Some things in Africa are moving in a positive direction. A poster in Livingstone's Maramba Market bears the slogan: 'A government without women is like a pot sitting on one stone.' A few metres away a stall sells a framed picture of two grinning black men beating up a local woman, dragging her around by the hair. The caption reads: 'Men shouldn't fight each other when they're double crossed by a woman – instead they should teach the silly girl a lesson!' I find myself wondering who would buy such a picture, let alone where they would put it.

I notice a huge difference between African markets and the shopping culture back in England. For all the hassle of African markets, people here still behave like human beings when they're out shopping. It's so much less fun back at home, with everything moving steadily towards the impersonal, with Internet shopping and soulless shopping malls identical in every town. The supermarkets in this part of Africa are surprisingly Westernized, though they're fairly small affairs. Their freezers are crammed with frozen fish with long pointed faces and huge reproachful eyes still intact; beside them lie frozen ice-pops, here called 'slurps'. Outside, the market stalls are filled with shoddy copies of Western training shoes, emblazoned with names like *Redbok* and *Reebuh*.

Before I left England one or two people asked me in all seriousness if I intended to live off the land during my trip across Africa, hunting wild

*Livingstone had been dead for quarter of a century when in 1897 the British physician Sir Ronald Ross finally proved beyond doubt the connection between mosquitoes and malarial transmission.

game and plucking luscious fruits from jungle trees. Despite the temptation to send them postcards confirming these fantasies, in reality I spend as much time as possible pushing a shopping trolley around supermarkets, searching for special offers and reduced items – it's a kind of hunting. The same people back at home worried that my journey might well end in someone's cooking pot; I'd arrive weary and unsuspecting at some remote village, and after receiving the warmest of welcomes I'd be served up for dinner within the hour, or even sooner if the cannibals preferred me slightly *al dente*.

Cannibalism was a favourite Victorian fascination with the 'Dark Continent', and in popular imagination every explorer ran a serious risk of being eaten. The reality was rather different; in fact it was widely believed by natives in the interior that white men ate black people. Sometimes the Arab slavers used this idea to enlist the help of their captives; often when their dhows were pursued by the Royal Navy, the Arabs would persuade their prisoners to pretend to be members of the crew; pointing to the smoke billowing from the pursuing British cruiser, they claimed the white men were lighting a fire to cook negroes.[8]

Yet cannibalism did occur, and frequently in some areas. Livingstone often encountered ambivalence towards the practice; one man told him his tribe ate only those killed in war or revenge, as 'the meat is not nice; it makes one dream of the dead man'.[9] By contrast, Stanley frequently saw the clearest evidence of a taste for human flesh; his expeditions were characterized by countless battles with cannibals along the River Congo, their attacks usually heralded by loud cries of '*Nyama! Nyama!*' ('Meat! Meat!'). One particularly determined cannibal tribe even tried to catch Stanley's flotilla in a giant net strung across the river.

Grogan encountered horrifying scenes of carnage in the Mfumbiro Range on the borders of Rwanda and Zaire; cannibals had massacred entire villages, leaving skeletons everywhere, their extraordinary postures graphic evidence of extreme violence. Entering hastily abandoned cannibal villages, Grogan's party found gnawed human bones with half-cooked flesh still attached, hands toasting on sticks, a human head with a spoon left sticking in the brain, and warm cooking vessels containing soup with bright yellow fat. Many years later Grogan was still having nightmares about these sights.

141

I have to cross over to the Zimbabwean side of the river to pick up some mail from the post office at Victoria Falls. The town itself is crowded and touristy, expensive and not particularly interesting; on the plus side, the post office seems organized and leaves me with the impression they will actually send my letters. In some parts of Africa it's unwise to post a letter without first getting the cashier to stamp it in front of you – if you don't, the stamps will later be steamed off and resold, and your letter binned or used as bog roll.

While it seems strange that the great explorers could occasionally receive mail while exploring, this was less of a contradiction in terms than it may sound. Often the journeys of exploration were made to establish new routes between two known points, such as Bagamoyo on the Tanzanian coast and Ujiji on Lake Tanganyika, and the mail by contrast would follow the existing caravan routes. The postal service was anything but reliable; and sometimes the existence of a mail service was a mixed blessing, with hopes dashed after long months on safari when no mail appeared. On reaching Ujiji on his 1874–77 traversa Stanley was bitterly disappointed to receive no mail at all, not even from his American fiancée, Alice Pike. In fact she had not even bothered to write, having just married someone else back in New York.

Livingstone was more impressed with native messengers, who carried messages of considerable length great distances, rehearsing the message around the campfire each night to keep to the exact words. These verbal messengers were one of the native objections to learning to write; Africans advised him that if a person wanted to communicate with someone else, the best plan was to go to or send for them: 'And as for corresponding with friends very far off, that is all very well for white people, but the blacks have no friends to whom to write.'[10] Galton recorded that messengers in Damaraland were 'greased before they set out on a journey, and greased again when they come back'.[11]

Reading my mail from home while sinking a 'Mosi' beer in the campsite bar, I get stung by a large hornet. The injection of the sting is actually audible, like a miniature staple gun being fired: *kaa-chunkkk!!* For a few minutes the sting becomes more and more painful, until I start getting really worried. The last time I was stung by a wasp in England it caused an extreme allergic reaction; the pain was excruciating for hours, and for the next two days my chest was covered by a huge red patch the

142

size of a dinner plate – and that was only a feeble European insect. Fortunately this Zimbabwean species doesn't seem quite so bad, and the pain wears off quickly. Maybe I'm getting tougher. Livingstone's observations on African hornet stings are uncomfortably accurate: 'The sting, which it tries to inflict near the eye, is more like a discharge of electricity from a powerful machine, or a violent blow than aught else. It produces momentary insensibility, and is followed by the most pungent pain.'[12]

I need to find some way of padding my sandals, but at short notice I can't find any suitable materials. Back at Jolly Boys, Mercy the cook presents me with a large piece of foam rubber. 'I've been keeping it for a special occasion,' she tells me. I can't think of any special occasions requiring foam rubber, but I'm still grateful. After adding two big slices of foam, my sandals now resemble a pair of giant cheese sandwiches strapped to my feet. They're extremely stinky too.

Sheer embarrassment on this has so far prevented me from getting my sandals repaired, but they're wearing down at an alarming rate. A shoe repairer in Livingstone market replaces the soles of my sandals with two pieces of old conveyor belt; he's stoical about the stinkiness, assuring me he's 'smelt worse', but I suspect he says this to all his customers. While this work is being done I have to sit next to a rival shoe repairer, an old man who earlier tried to overcharge me. I know it's pathetic, but the latter looks so crestfallen I feel guilty, and hope the job is finished quickly.

A young crazy fellow approaches me, weaving slightly as he gets nearer, obviously stoned, and stands swaying over me. 'How's your Clinton?' he asks several times, before wandering off giggling. 'That guy smokes too much dagga!' says the shoe repairer, presumably referring to the crazy guy.

Smoking cannabis is hardly a new phenomenon here; Livingstone found the habit widespread across the continent, although as a non-smoking missionary he declined to join in. Using a huge water-pipe made from a calabash or kudu's horn and a metre-and-a-half length of split bamboo, the smokers would sit in a circle and take turns on the pipe before 'uttering a string of half-incoherent sentences, usually in self-praise'. Sometimes a particularly good blast on their giant bong would bring on 'a species of frenzy, which passes away in a rapid stream of unmeaning words, or short sentences, as, "the green grass grows", "the fat cattle thrive", "the fish swim". No one in the group pays the slightest attention to the oracle, who stops abruptly, and, the instant common sense returns, looks rather foolish.'[13]

Late one evening at Jolly Boys I'm about to turn in when female screams pierce the night, coming from somewhere outside the gate. The shrieks are accompanied by loud barking; naturally I assume someone is being attacked by a dog. While I'm keen to avoid getting bitten, I decide to do the gentlemanly thing and go to the assistance of this anonymous damsel in distress; hopefully this will require no more than offering advice to run, shouted from a safe distance.

It turns out some demented local has whacked a young Danish guy around the back of the head with a brick. The injured party is now lying in the road, surrounded by his backpacker friends. At first it's difficult to work out what's going on in the darkness; it looks as though one of the bystanders might be the person who hit him. But it soon becomes clear that the locals are trying to help; the fellow with the brick took to his heels when one of the girls launched a surprise counter-offensive by throwing a small empty plastic bottle at him.

The Danish guy is helped to his feet and taken inside the hostel. I'm hoping my pocket first aid handbook will come in handy at last, having carried it all the way from the Namibian coast. I'm disappointed to find it contains nothing on head injuries other than advising the removal of dentures. But he's not seriously injured, and looks likely to recover quickly. I look at it philosophically; it could have been worse, the fellow with the brick could have hit me instead. But I resist the temptation to share these thoughts with the patient, at least until he's feeling better.

Early the next morning I'm already stuffing my face with the usual oat porridge in the lounge at Jolly Boys when a friendly and very attractive American girl called Julia arrives. I fancy her like crazy so make sure we get chatting, and she seems to rather like me. At one point I mention the guy with the brick. 'Imagine the resentment he must feel!' she says, which strikes me as a very analytical way of looking at it. She's travelling around Africa on her own, and goes on to talk about her reasons for travelling: 'After this trip I'll never again travel without some *purpose*, some fixed goal, you know?' I tell her I've got the opposite problem, that of having too much purpose. A set goal, a difficult one, always introduces the possibility of failure, and is it worth the added pressure? For a few ridiculous moments I fantasize about her travelling with me. Then reality reasserts itself; I don't have much to offer on this trip. I'm damn sure I'd have much more fun if she were with me; but she'd have to be mad, or stupid, or desperate to do so, and unfortunately she seems none of these things. Realistically, I couldn't walk across Africa accompanied by someone I was having a relationship with. Too much temptation would get in the way; there are far more pleasant ways to spend a day than walking with a heavy pack in the African heat. We'd never see the east coast, unless we took the bus.

So it's not to be. I walk her to the bus stop and know I'll never see her again.

11. The Joys of Chibuku
(Zambia: Livingstone to Lusaka)

The boyaloa, or beer of the country, has more of a stupefying than exciting nature; hence the beer-bibbers are great sleepers; they may frequently be seen lying on their faces sound asleep.

David Livingstone, *Missionary Travels*

I leave Livingstone after nearly two weeks' rest, salving my conscience by telling myself I bloody well earned it. As if to punish me for recent slacking, the midday heat is now oppressive, the flies maddening.

Despite all the bad press the country often receives, the vast majority of Zambians are amazingly friendly and welcoming. While a few individuals here do show a certain weakness for plunder, and would jump at the chance of stealing everything short of your underpants, only a small percentage of the population actually wants to beat your bloody head in. Most folks back in England – even wealthy people or those living at odds with society – rarely experience anything like the temptation staring many Africans in the face. And this happens every time Africans see a foreign visitor loaded with expensive gear they could well live without. Inevitably, far more fuss is made about travellers getting robbed than of their excellent chances of keeping most of their belongings until they get home. Little attention is paid to the fact that so many desperately poor people in Africa wouldn't dream of stealing from a stranger, however stupidly or insensitively some foreigners behave, however obvious their comparative wealth. To many Africans, even some of the poorest, stealing is as unthinkable as giving your grandmother a good punch. And in some African countries the penalties for theft are harsh; shouting 'Thief!' in the street may well result in a medieval-style hue and cry, and if bystanders catch the robber there's a good chance he'll get beaten to death.

So far I've avoided serious trouble of any kind, but walking alone I know I'm taking risks. Camping alone here is always potentially danger-

146

ous, particularly doing it night after night, often by necessity in places I shouldn't be. It would be less of a problem if I could always pitch my tent far from human settlement, but this is becoming increasingly difficult without making huge detours. Even so, two factors work to my advantage. I always arrive at places unannounced, so potential thieves don't know when I'll turn up (as they do with people getting off the tourist buses) and consequently have less time to think up ways of fleecing me; and many of the locals I meet are so surprised to see a white man walking alone like this that they assume I must be some kind of tough guy. My trekking poles help bolster this image: no one here has seen anything like them before, and some people assume they're a weapon, like Matabele fighting sticks. Later I'm mistaken for a ninja.

Overall, the vast majority of people here want to help me rather than cause me problems. I'm constantly surprised in Zambia how rarely people overcharge me, which would never have been the case had I just stepped off an overland truck. It's only in the touristy places I get ripped off. Everywhere else, I find myself treated not so differently from the locals, or even like one of them – one bunch of young men cooking beside the road invite me to share their dinner, even though clearly they're already living on short rations. Shopkeepers in villages and small towns often give me small gifts of food and milk when they learn of the nature of my trip.

Part of the appeal for me of travelling in this way is the very hardship and the problems it creates. Travelling in a comfortable vehicle sets you apart from the local people; the hardship of walking means at least one barrier is lowered. It's easy to be self-righteous, but I don't want to follow the example of rich tourists shielding themselves from every reality. Obviously when the rich tourists in question are being kind to me – as indeed they often are – I take a more charitable view of them. It's easy to make judgements when you're too short of money to have much choice in the matter. But even that's only comparative. Back in England I may be a poor man; but a poor man in England and a poor man in Africa are not the same thing. At times like this it all gets very politically correct ...

'I will try!' claims a sign outside a hut, advertising the services of a traditional African doctor. Local schools in this part of Zambia usually have signs outside proclaiming their excellence: 'We lead, others follow';

'Knowledge persued [sic] is knowledge attained.' For me, the most endearing of these mission statements is the humblest: 'Trying to do the best for everybody.' Zambian buses display more strident messages painted on their sides: 'No retreat! No surrender!' or 'We have the eyes of an eagle!' One reads: 'How am I driving?' – presumably a rhetorical question, as no one has spray-painted some witty reply beneath it. On the back of the same bus is the message: 'I believe in God!', which is just as well in this case. The strangest of all reads simply: 'Your nigger!' – either intended as self-deprecation or possibly an inflammatory remark aimed at people travelling with rival bus companies.

Around 190 kilometres after leaving Livingstone I reach the small market town of Choma. I chat with the Indian owner of a garage shop, who tells me the road from Lusaka to the Malawi border is swarming with bandits. While I suspect he's exaggerating, I'll still have to be careful. He also says there's a lot of game on the road I've just come along, including lions, who obviously keep a low profile during daylight hours.

A more immediate problem on the road to Lusaka is that of blisters: my feet have somehow turned utterly wimpy during the rest in Livingstone. My right foot is particularly painful, and towards the end of each day's walking feels like it's squishing around on a bunch of overripe grapes. Whenever my blisters burst spontaneously on the road my socks are suddenly soaking wet. Blisters on my heels tend to be more incapacitating than those on my toes, especially since I'm usually wearing sandals. The worst blisters are those under hard skin, as it's almost impossible to do anything about them. Each night in my tent I burst my prize blisters, an operation usually leaving a wet patch the size of a saucer on my groundsheet.

Experts on the subject recommend immediate action the moment you even suspect a blister might be forming; in theory this is good advice, but so far I've found it better not to spend too much time inspecting the damage; in any case, the sight would only upset me. Galton's advice on the subject ranges from soaping the inside of the stocking before setting out, to changing socks to the other foot, or even to breaking a raw egg into a boot before putting it on.[1] But apart from using sticking plasters, I let my feet sort out their own problems even if this approach brings its share of grief all the way to the Malawi border.

The nights I spend in African woods are filled with pops and cracks as dead branches fall to earth, tortured creaks and groans punctuated by the occasional pistol shot when a bigger branch parts company with the tree. Each night I have to check that no large branches are directly above my tent, even apparently healthy-looking ones. Yet African woods and forests are enchanting places to sleep. Many Africans consider them the home of spirits, often evil, from demons and ogres to malevolent ghosts.[2] Familiarity allows me to ignore the cracking of dead branches and the noise of insects; the woods at night are often as quiet as a churchyard. But on a few evenings the wind howls through the woods like a living thing, which of course it is. I find the roaring hiss of wind through trees strangely soothing.

Less soothing is the local farmers' habit of burning the long grass in their fields, especially alarming after dark. Some nights I'm on the point of going to sleep when I hear the distinctive crackle of flames only a couple of hundred metres away, a truly horrible sound. When I'm dead tired at the end of the day and already in my sleeping bag, the thought of having to get up again to pack my tent and gear in the dark before moving to safer ground is soul-destroying: the prospect of getting burnt to death where I lie seems only marginally worse. Fortunately I never have to move.

A casual observer might think this periodic burning a haphazard process – and accidents do happen from time to time, with perfectly sound villages reduced to ashes. But there's wisdom behind the process. Many trees and shrubs here are long accustomed to frequent fires from natural causes such as lightning, and they've ingeniously adapted. After the old dead grass perishes in the flames, new flowers and seeds quickly appear, taking advantage of the greater space and available rainfall, and the field then flourishes. But while this may suit Mother Nature's plans for the Zambian countryside, it's really pissing me off – whenever I camp in a recently burnt field I'm black with soot by the time I climb into my sleeping bag. If this goes on for much longer I'll reach Lusaka looking like an itinerant chimney sweep.

'You look like Neil Armstrong!'

This observation comes from a friendly middle-aged man in a village restaurant just outside Pemba. Not entirely understanding the remark, I take it as a compliment.

'You have come here to see how poor we are?' the guy continues without a trace of self-pity, his eyes twinkling as he dunks a handful of maize porridge into his watery-looking bean stew. Then he notices my trekking poles: 'You are in training for some competition? Perhaps you are a skier?'

Around this time I lose my bush hat, a disaster to rival running out of sticking plasters. I console myself with the thought that it did make me look ridiculously gung-ho. Unfortunately several days without a hat leave my face the colour of new English bricks. A nice Indian guy in a general store at the village of Monze gives me a piece of material for a bandanna. This material is too thick for the job, and covered in pictures of BMX bikers; when I wrap it around my head it looks and feels like a tea cosy. But it's better than nothing, and will have to suffice until I reach Lusaka.

I start acquiring a taste for the local beer, Chibuku. Brewed from maize and millet, it's also known as 'Shake Shake' – before quaffing it you're supposed to agitate its pale-brown murky contents into something palatable. It's sold in one-litre cardboard cartons, appropriately known in Zimbabwe as 'scuds'. In taste it's slightly acidic, and in texture more like kefir than normal beer. Westerners often find it disgusting, but I become rather fond of it. It's popular in all the African countries I cross, and most towns and villages have special bars that serve nothing else. Its strength varies; sometimes it gets you pissed remarkably quickly, at other times you could sink ten litres with impunity, although you'd be sick anyway if you did that. The small brown chewy bits floating in its murk are the sort of thing English food manufacturers add to their wholefood ranges to suggest rustic charm; on one occasion I get halfway through a carton before finding a drowned false eyelash.

The first time I buy a Chibuku the cartons are swelling in the heat to the point of explosion, although the man selling it has carefully packed bottles of Coca-Cola and Fanta in cooler boxes under his stall. Naïvely, I ask if he has a cold Chibuku for sale. He gives me a funny look, followed by an anxious whispered conversation with his friend. Later I realize that asking for a cold Chibuku is like an English wino buying a bottle of meths at a hardware store asking the shopkeeper if there are any cold ones out the back.

I may be drinking too much, but at least I'm managing to keep off the cigarettes temporarily, which is just as well as the local brands are as rough as sawdust. The non-smoking Livingstone noticed the same thing: 'The Batoka tobacco is famed in the country for its strength, and it certainly is both very strong and very cheap: a few strings of beads will purchase enough to last any reasonable man for six months. It caused headache in the only smoker of our party, from its strength, but this quality makes the natives come great distances to buy it.'[3] Significantly, the region today still displays a high incidence of lung cancer.

I reach the outskirts of Mazabuka, a small farming town surrounded by sugar plantations. I'm so tired that a field of sugar cane seems as good a place as any to sleep. But although the sugar plants stand several metres tall, I still find it difficult to find somewhere out of sight. To draw less attention to myself I try for once to get to sleep without bothering with a tent; within minutes the seething cloud of mosquitoes is so unbearable that I have to get up and pitch my tent anyway.

The following morning I spend ages trying to get served at Mazabuka post office. When the postmaster finally appears behind the counter he's a little *strange*. 'We're not serving the public today,' he tells me in a confidential whisper. 'We're waiting for a bus.' I can think of no logical interpretation of what he just said – unless he's working out his notice, having been sacked for being mad. I hope his bus arrives for him before the van does.

On a more practical level I simply must rest for a day; since leaving Livingstone I've walked around 350 kilometres without a break. Unfortunately the only guesthouse I can find is a horrible run-down slob of a building. While council rest houses in Zambia are reasonably cheap, they're gloomy places and so noisy that rest is the last thing you get for your money. A roof and a bed are all I need, but there's something about these places oppressive to the human spirit. The room here is dismal and stinky – an en-suite toilet sounds fine in theory, but in a cheap African guesthouse the reality is awful. The overall impression of crumbling decay is encouraged by the rats and mice scurrying above the ceiling, playing some game with a chase theme. And the walls are painted in horrible colours, murky blues and sludgy browns; whoever chose this colour scheme must have been on some form of medication at the time.

I'm also feeling very unwell; more accurately, I feel *dreadful*, as though

151

I've been put through a giant mangle. I can't even breathe properly. I wish I was still smoking, so I could give up and feel better. I spend the day lying in bed moaning like a sick cow, and the next morning I still feel ill and exhausted. But this guesthouse is so depressing I decide to carry on anyway, so I continue east.

Whenever I camp near any settlement I'm woken in the middle of the night by cocks crowing; obviously no one has explained to them that they're not supposed to start until just before dawn. Similarly, late-night drumming is popular at almost every village I pass. With these two factors combined I've no idea how anyone ever gets any sleep. Livingstone remarked of the natives on the Tamba river: 'some thrum a musical instrument the livelong day, and, when they wake at night, proceed at once to their musical performance'.[4]

The night after Mazabuka I camp next to the railway track. In the dark the trains seem about to thunder right over me, and they're *loud*, like Thor driving home after a good night out, and the earth trembles. As one train passes it gives a terrific hoot, like an inexpert blast on an alpine horn. I can hear drums from a couple of tiny villages a few hundred metres away; before long I'm convinced their drum rhythms are deliberately mimicking the sound of a train, which makes a weird kind of sense; or maybe I'm just tired. Every African village has at least one drum, and they're often surrounded by ritual. The spirit of the tree from which the drum is made lives on in the finished instrument, and the sound the drum makes is the voice of the spirit. When dancers become completely involved in the rhythm of the dance, the drum's spirit has entered them and the spirit itself dances.[5]

In the morning I wake to find I've been sleeping on top of some big hairy caterpillars who somehow sneaked into my tent while I was putting it up. My back and arms have come out in an itchy stinging rash, like *War and Peace* written in braille, which I can only put down to the caterpillar hairs. After walking for an hour or two I discover yet another giant caterpillar squashed against my back, and we part company immediately.

By midday I reach the town of Kafue ('Hippo River'). The overhead sun is intense; even the street market traders lie snoozing in the shade beside their stalls, reclining in wheelbarrows. It strikes me that if a stallholder wanted to eliminate the competition he could remove sleeping rivals by simply trundling them away in their own wheelbarrows. Arriving everywhere unannounced like this is for me one of the joys of travelling alone; my sudden appearance at Kafue causes barely a raised eyebrow from the shady depths of the vendors' wheelbarrows. Had I arrived in a tourist bus the scene would have changed to pandemonium, every market trader pouncing on me to sell me their woodcarvings, everything from tiny masks to giraffes only slightly smaller than life-size.

I'm now halfway across Africa.

To continue east I have to pass through Lusaka, but I've no great desire to stop here – much as I like reaching towns and cities, I can't justify another rest break so soon after the last. Lusaka is one of Africa's fastest-growing capitals, sprawling over seventy square kilometres. It's home to around 2.5 million people, the recent population explosion caused mainly by the hundreds of Zambians arriving daily from the countryside in search of a better life. Whether they find it or not is open to doubt; over sixty per cent of Lusaka's inhabitants are unemployed, and many journeys here end in a life of poverty in the city's growing shanty towns – a general drift from the countryside to the capital has turned in recent years into an unstoppable flood. The city has a reputation as an excellent place to get mugged or else to take part in a riot – the overcrowding and poverty here mean that crime is higher than in other parts of the country.

Just outside the centre a wealthy-looking black woman stops her four-wheel drive. 'You mustn't go into Lusaka,' she insists breathlessly. 'There's rioting all the way down the Chachacha Road … they're a lot of savages!'

I can't face making a huge detour around the city, at least not until someone confirms her report or I hear screams and shouts dead ahead. If the worst comes to the worst and I become involved in a riot, I can always abandon my rucksack and run off myself in the opposite direction. But I suspect that once again Zambia has had an unfairly bad press, and that most of the people in Lusaka are as friendly and law-abiding as anywhere else.

As it turns out, instead of violence and disorder I find Lusaka extraordinarily *busy*, crowded and vibrant even by African standards –

compared to any other African town I've passed through on the journey it's full of frenetic energy, a world apart from quiet, reserved places like Windhoek or Swakopmund. The impression is heightened by the peace and quiet of months on the road – but despite the warnings there are no flying missiles today, or people breaking one another's heads. I walk right through the city, from the desperately poor outskirts, past the rich modern shopping malls of the centre and back through the shanty towns on the other side. In all this time I don't see anything that could be described as rioting, apart from a couple of kids fighting over a game of marbles in the dusty street.

As I leave the eastern outskirts of Lusaka, I wash my face in a garage toilet and see my reflection properly for the first time since leaving Victoria Falls. It strikes me that apart from excruciating blisters the main problems I'm encountering at this stage of the journey are cosmetic rather than life-threatening. Walking east day after day in the southern hemisphere like this can leave a white-skinned person looking slightly *odd*. Most of the time the sun lies on my left side, which has resulted in a very curious suntan, since I'm always facing east: the left side of my face has turned dark but the right side has remained comparatively pale and pasty. If this process continues I'll reach the Indian Ocean looking decidedly *With The Beatles*.

12. Crossing the Luangwa
(Zambia: Lusaka to Malawi Border)

Night is a dead monotonous period under a roof; but in the open world it passes lightly, with its stars and dews and perfumes, and the hours are marked by changes in the face of Nature. What seems a kind of temporal death to people choked between walls and curtains, is only a light and living slumber to the man who sleeps afield. All night long he can hear Nature breathing deeply and freely ... The outer world, from which we cower in our houses, seemed after all a gentle habitable place.

Robert Louis Stevenson

The first night out of Lusaka I'm approaching a village in twilight when a hundred metres ahead I notice a strange group of dwarfish Easter Island statues standing staring into the road, their stillness and concentration eerie. On closer inspection I realize they're no more than oversized sacks of charcoal, set out for sale beside the road. I must be tired.

Passing a small village the following morning I talk to a local called Joseph. Although only in his early twenties, he already has five children. He's convinced that white people have everything all worked out, and takes the fact that my family is small as proof of this (six children or more is common in Zambia). He knows better than ever I could that while a poor family in Europe may face problems with the expense of extra children, an African family may face disaster.

'I have to make a decision soon,' he tells me, 'and I want your advice on this matter. I am thinking of taking an engineering course, which might help me get a better job one day. So should I carry on working as a farmer, when I am not interested in farming? Or should I take this course?'

Knowing nothing about farming or engineering, I'm reluctant to offer him advice. With five kids he's taking a serious step whatever he does. It's all very well to urge others to follow their dreams, but Africa doesn't provide much of a safety net if you make the wrong decision. With virtually nothing in the way of a welfare state here, people have to rely instead on their families helping them out in times of particular hardship. Many of the farmers in Zambia earn no more than twenty US dollars a month, sometimes even less. But this young man is determined to get my opinion, and won't let me off so lightly. He obviously wants to take the course, so I tell him he should do that; he seems pleased by this reply. I hope it was the right answer and that he gets what he wants.

Although the Great East Road is the main highway between Zambia and Malawi, it could hardly be considered a main road in the European sense, apart from its sheer length – over 600 kilometres from Lusaka to the Malawi border, the same distance as from London to Edinburgh. Traffic passes at the rate of only about one vehicle every two or three minutes or so. Every time this happens red dust billows into choking clouds around me, especially when the big trucks thunder past carrying enormous loads of cotton poised ready to topple off at any moment. Recently one clot of a driver threw his cigarette out of the cab window straight back into his cargo; thankfully no one was burnt to death in the resulting conflagration, although a local tells me the driver is currently looking for another job, with the emphasis on immediate relocation.

The surrounding hills bring to mind Hemingway's *Green Hills of Africa*. Some stretches of the Great East Road are filled with a strange and delicate fragrance, rather like English honeysuckle, a pleasant change from inhaling Zambian dust. Stalls are scattered at intervals along the roadside near villages, selling mainly sweet potatoes and tomatoes; some offer four-metre lengths of sugar cane or doughnuts, while apples tend to be restricted to larger settlements. The small kiosks beside the road sell mainly biscuits and soap; they look like Punch and Judy stalls made of twigs and dried grass.

During daylight hours I start encountering a large kind of bumblebee with black and white stripes, like a flying Everton mint. It makes a nice change from the usual black and yellow variety you get back in England. Black and white seem to be very much the 'in' colours this season for Zambian insects. On one occasion a black and white dragonfly pursues me for almost a kilometre down the road, like a miniature fighter plane buzzing an unidentified aircraft invading its airspace, which in effect I am. At night outside my tent the larger insects combine to sound like an orchestra of high-pitched didgeridoos.

The highway east of Lusaka crosses a gently undulating plateau, although when travelling on foot these undulations feel anything but gentle, becoming more pronounced by the hour – which is all very well for admiring the scenery, but less welcome if you're trying to conserve energy. At times I feel like a tiny ant walking laterally across a gigantic sheet of corrugated iron – and always with the sun beating down, until my head starts thumping like a blacksmith's anvil.

And the blisters are back with a vengeance. Walking downhill with blistered feet is far more painful than walking uphill with them, even if it requires less effort. For the entire length of the Great East Road, from Lusaka to the Malawi border, my feet by the end of each day feel like I've been walking barefoot on a cinder path. I'm still having as many foot problems as I did during the first week on the Namibian coast; after all this time on the road my feet haven't toughened up at all, which seems most unfair.

At the end of each exhausting day all I want is to find somewhere discreet to camp and to get to sleep with a minimum of fuss. Often at this point, even when I'm in the middle of nowhere, a local will appear from behind a bush requesting a 'discussion' with me – not to hassle me in any way for crashing out here, but merely to have a friendly chat.

Two days after leaving Lusaka I pitch my tent earlier than usual, having for once found an ideal secluded spot away from the road, surrounded by tall trees. Then a big truck breaks down at the exact spot where I left the road, and for the next couple of hours the woods around me are swarming with young men apparently playing Cowboys and Indians. I've absolutely no idea what they're up to, and I daren't draw attention to my presence by asking. I'm amazed they don't see me, as at times they're only metres away in the twilight – although my dark brown tent is practically invisible in the dark, as I've found to my cost when trying to find it in campsites while pissed. When they finally depart the peace is marvellous.

Five days east of Lusaka I reach the village of Rufunsa, which looked much bigger on the map. I buy armfuls of doughnuts and buns and soggy cassava until my rucksack groans with the weight, then stop for a cheap meal of chicken and *nsima*, served by a friendly woman with a wall eye. I tell her I'm walking across Africa; her response is a great squawk of laughter, completely without malice.

'What, with all this luggage?'

I start to explain that it's not 'luggage', it's essential equipment needed at all times; then I realize she's quite right. Since the first family of cave dwellers went on holiday as part of the evolutionary process, sensible travellers have always placed travelling light at the top of their list of priorities. On this journey I've somehow always failed at this. And yet by definition I must be strong enough to carry all this weight, because I've been doing it for months now – I've walked a bloody long way to get here, around 2,400 kilometres, big pack or no. Even so, the walking is almost nothing – it's carrying a heavy rucksack constantly that's wearing me out. These days I'm carrying less than I did in the desert, but I still have to think repeatedly about saving weight. Sometimes all this worrying about weight seems pointless – I feel like someone on a diet counting every single calorie, and once or twice I'm tempted to go mad and buy some inert and useless object like a sack of cement, just to break the monotony. Maybe I'm doing it all wrong, and I should take a tip from the locals: in Zambia, bags are usually carried on the head, even if the handles are still intact and perfectly serviceable.

Livingstone once met a man who single-handedly carried an ivory tusk weighing five frasilahs (eighty kilos) from his home in Zambia to the coast. While Livingstone himself often decried taking excess baggage, and by the standards of his day he did indeed travel light, this was largely a case of making a virtue out of necessity. Had he been richer he would certainly have taken a lot more trade goods with him on his traversa – although he quite rightly observed that 'a large array of baggage excited the cupidity of the tribes'.[1] Stanley's better-financed expeditions were a different story; on his 1874–77 traversa he set out from Zanzibar with no less than eight tons of provisions, trade goods and arms – although he and his surviving companions were still to reach the Atlantic starving and clothed in rags.

The soggy cassava I buy at Rufunsa market soon smells most unappetizing, and becomes progressively more disgusting; but at least it's filling. The preparation is important; this batch seems to have been boiled then burnt for a while, until the end result tastes and smells simultaneously sodden and smoky. It's heavy to carry, too, having absorbed a lot of water in the cooking process, as well as all the smoke. Cassava is widely grown throughout Zambia, as it flourishes on poor soils; as a result, it can be harvested throughout the year, which can literally fend off starvation while the villages wait for the main cereal crop. But it has little real food value, lacking essential vitamins and minerals. Many people here are malnourished, living as they do on a diet of *nsima* and cassava and little else.

I'm not exactly glowing with health myself, even though I'm just passing through. My own diet through Zambia consists almost entirely of *nsima*, biscuits, stale buns and green bananas, washed down with foaming scuds of Chibuku. I've got more or less permanent acid indigestion from eating all this crap; my whole system is turning into a seething mass of free radicals, and eating rubbish for months on end is giving me a complexion like a sun-bronzed junkie. Apart from the bananas, the one comparatively healthy thing I do eat occasionally is baby cereal, which requires no cooking and is reasonably light to carry. I stock up whenever I reach a town, the shop assistants often giving me knowing smiles, no doubt suspecting I've been sowing my wild oats along the way.

By now I've grown to enjoy maize porridge – despite its blandness, *nsima* has become as familiar to me as potatoes or bread back at home. It's eaten here with most other foods, but especially with meat or vegetable stew, sometimes beans, fish or pumpkin leaves. Following tradition, most Zambians eat with their hands – away from the tourist trail foreigners are rarely offered a knife and fork, or even a spoon. A small handful of *nsima* is formed into a ball, in which you make a depression with your thumb before filling it with stew. It also has other uses: according to Zambian tradition night witches navigate the skies in ghostly flying machines made entirely from porridge; these strange animal-shaped craft are powered by special medicines. Sceptics should note that *nsima* is at least easy to mould.[2]

During his travels Livingstone by necessity became a connoisseur of *nsima*; his usual diet out in the bush involved staring into a seething cauldron of maize porridge every evening, if he was lucky. He particularly disliked the Balonda variety made from manioc, which hunger alone forced his party to eat: 'It is very unsavoury ... exactly like a basin of starch in the hands of a laundress.' Livingstone thought his Makololo companions always undercooked the *nsima*, which gave him heartburn: 'Their porridge is a failure, at least for a Scotch digestion that has been impaired by fever ... It was rather difficult to persuade the men to boil the porridge for us more patiently; and they became witty, and joked us for being like women.' But like sensible people everywhere, the Makololo cooked their *nsima* the way they liked it, wherever possible preparing it with milk. Ultimately this preference led to a degree of porridge snobbery, with the Makololo looking down on neighbouring tribes as 'mere water-porridge fellows'.[3]

Just east of Rufunsa a young white man wearing Ray Bans stops his Landrover beside me, gunning his motor.

'Do you want a lift?' At this point he still seems reasonably normal.

'That's very kind of you, sir, but I'm on a long walk.'

'Well ... *FUCK YOU THEN!*'

'I beg your pardon?'

'*YOU'VE GOT A LONG WAY TO GO, FRIEND!*' he snarls, before roaring off in a cloud of red dust. What a strange young man. I wonder what made him so overwrought – and such shocking language, too.

My exchanges with the locals are generally more polite, with people usually shouting: 'How are you?' This is often when I'm limping along in the midday heat, hobbling like I'm a hundred and ten, dripping with sweat, my face crimson with exertion; when one of the big trucks has just passed I'm powdered with the distinctive local red dust as though I've been dipped headfirst in a giant tub of paprika. Thankfully on these occasions I avoid giving an honest reply; I am travelling in this way by choice, after all.

In Zambia a minor accident such as dropping something usually results in the people around you saying: 'Sorry, sorry, sorry!' This indicates empathy rather than apology, of an endearing kind scarce in England these days. Africans are as fond as anyone of seeing people slip on banana skins, but in my experience they prefer laughing with someone rather than at them. They also like to clap in greeting or approval; elderly women in particular often shower me with applause as I pass – at first I thought they were just enjoying the show. Livingstone often observed mothers teaching their young children the proper etiquette of

160

hand-clapping, as good manners were drilled into him in his own childhood, with different sequences used depending on the situation and level of politeness required.[4]

'You are too strong!' shouts a woman from the doorway of a hut, clapping enthusiastically. 'You are a man!' shout two guys in unison as they pass me on their bikes. I'd love to believe even half of this.

One night I'm kept awake by a most irritating crow squawking in the tree above me. I try shouting at it, which only makes it screech back in derision. I can't sleep through this, so I try throwing stones at it, without success – and as the creature is sitting directly overhead, there's every chance one of my missiles will land on my own head. Eventually the bird gets bored and moves away on business of its own; the resulting peace is startling. Then for the rest of the night I'm woken repeatedly by a sinister frond, waving and tapping gently at my tent door; the plant obviously wants to come in, like an African triffid.

It's always possible some other creature will try to join me inside my tent. Livingstone recorded one such incident while travelling in Barotseland with the female chief Manenko and her entourage. In the middle of the night he heard a terrific shriek from one of Manenko's ladies: 'She piped out so loud and long that we all imagined she had been seized by a lion, and my men snatched up their arms, which they always place so as to be ready at a moment's notice, and ran to the rescue; but we found the alarm had been caused by one of the oxen thrusting his head into her hut, and smelling her: she had put her hand on his cold wet nose, and thought it was all over with her.'[5]

Sleeping in a tent can be a spooky experience when you're camping somewhere you shouldn't be. In the woods at night it seems almost inconceivable that a stranger will be as scared of you as you are of them. Shadows seem to move, while large bushes begin to resemble huge hunched figures; and you can't escape from the sound of things crawling through the bush, small rodents or the occasional snake. But I much prefer them to a night-time visit by armed robbers.

The dangers are not completely imaginary, and were even less so in Galton's day. He extolled the superiority in dangerous country of bivouacking over sleeping in a tent: in the latter 'a man's sleep is heavy; he cannot hear nearly so well; he can see nothing; his cattle may all decamp;

while marauders know exactly where he is lying, and may make their plans accordingly. They may creep up unobserved and spear him through the canvas … Tent life is semi-civilization, and perpetuates its habits … a man who has lived much in bivouacs, if there be a night alarm, runs naturally into the dark for safety, just as a wild animal would; but a man who travels with tents becomes frightened when away from its lights, or from the fancied security of its walls.'[6]

I'm stuck with a tent for now, the mosquitoes having left me with no choice. Unfortunately, I'm finding it progressively more difficult to camp away from people without straying miles off my route, as the spread-out village huts often stretch out endlessly. My ears have become highly sensitive to the murmur of human voices approaching, even from some distance. I once read that when you're straining your ears to catch the faintest sound you should keep your mouth open – the ear has an inward entrance as well as an outer, like the fish's gills from which it originated. So I spend at least part of most evenings gaping like a half-wit. Before I bed down each night I take great pains to try to ensure I'm as far as possible from human habitation; unfortunately in the short African twilight a tiny group of low thatch huts is often well concealed and practically invisible until true darkness falls and the cooking fires light up. Some nights I realize too late that I'm only a few hundred metres from the nearest group of huts, by which time I've already pitched my tent for the night and can't face moving; singing and laughter start as regular as clockwork, then someone whips out their bongos to drum up a storm.

Around this time disaster strikes: I run out of sticking plasters. For all my bravado about blisters I'm lost without plasters, as nothing else I've done to treat blisters has made the slightest difference. You can get sticking plasters of sorts in the local shops here, but they're undeserving of the name, and would barely stick to human flesh under laboratory conditions. They're not cheap, either. Fortunately, I don't realize at this stage I'll have to walk all the way to the Malawi border before I can find any decent ones.

I can't think of any reasonable substitute for plasters. Experienced walkers may disagree, but I find the special blister kits for hikers virtually useless. These 'second skin' dressings look ingenious in the packet, but

I can never get the bloody things to stay in place for more than a few minutes. But for all their virtues, sticking plasters can be a mixed blessing. After several days of heavy trekking, whenever I peel off an old plaster from my foot it often tears off a big strip of skin with it; during this process I discover that I can swear continuously for several minutes without apparent repetition.

I never understand why sticking plasters in Africa are the same colour as those found in Europe, the supposed colour of Caucasian skin. Presumably plasters the colour of dark skin would look ridiculous – it would be almost impossible to get them in exactly the right shade for each individual here. That said, I've yet to see anyone with skin the colour of European sticking plasters, except a few daytime TV presenters.

Apart from sticking plasters, so far on the trip I've used hardly anything from my first aid kit except needles to burst blisters and dig out thorns and splinters, and various creams and ointments to soothe the cracks and cuts on my feet and places where my rucksack has rubbed my skin off. This has worked out well – in a first aid kit it's easy to take a score of things you'll never use in a million years, so I've settled for the absolute minimum, on the possibly spurious reasoning that so long as I can bandage major lacerations until I reach the nearest town or village I'll be all right. Having once been a Boy Scout – admittedly not a very good one – I reckon I should be prepared. After all, most of the emergencies born of pessimistic imaginations simply don't happen: it's the bad things you haven't anticipated that catch you out. On one of his safaris in the 1920s the white hunter Denys Finch Hatton (played as an American by Robert Redford in the movie *Out of Africa*) saw fit to take a medical outfit with which his party could do a major operation if necessary. Later on the same safari Finch Hatton was thankful for his foresight, when during his morning wash in a river a crocodile took a big bite out of his arse. Unfortunately the safari's surgeon proved unable or unwilling to deal with this crisis, so poor Finch Hatton had to rush to Nairobi to get his backside patched up. I don't remember seeing that bit in the film.

While so far I've avoided medical emergencies, by far the biggest problem for me is still that of blisters. The soles and sides of my feet now resemble the clear plastic bubble-wrap used for packing fragile articles. One huge recurring blister between my toes tends to burst repeatedly as

I walk, squirting a fountain of clear fluid into the air at each step for the next few dozen metres. Even when I wear socks my blisters sometimes burst spontaneously: after a momentary sharp sensation like an insect sting my sock starts squelching with fluid. Curiously, when this happens the blisters make a far more thorough job of emptying themselves than when I do the honours with a needle each night in my tent.

In bygone days English tramps would avoid blisters by putting fresh dock leaves in their socks every morning, but I never find the African equivalent. And this situation isn't the same as having sore feet back at home; although I failed to appreciate it at the time, in England you don't have to do much with your feet if you don't feel like it – even tramps can spend much of their day sitting. To make matters worse, the trainers I bought a couple of weeks back are useless for anything more athletic than loafing around on street corners; for long-distance walking they're a joke.

The road through Zambia from Lusaka to the Malawi border is one long stretch of agony for my feet; at times it's *awful*. And white tourists I meet on the road still ask me if I'm having a good time. It doesn't matter that it's not for ever, it's *now*. By the end of each day my face has set in a permanent grimace. I may have some streak of masochism, but this is too much. And to think that some sexually adventurous folks back at home pay good money for this kind of agony.

I try telling myself I should stop moaning – the local guys are stoical enough, and generally always have been. Livingstone commented on their fortitude during surgery: 'Both men and women submit to an operation without wincing, or any of that shouting which caused young students to faint in the operating theatre before the introduction of chloroform. The women pride themselves on their ability to bear pain. A mother will address her little girl, from whose foot a thorn is to be extracted, with "Now, Ma, you are a woman; a woman does not cry." A man scorns to shed tears.' In all his African travels – and he often encountered dreadful suffering in the wake of the slave trade – Livingstone saw only a single native man cry. For me it's one of those tiny snippets of history involving long-forgotten individuals that strikes a deep chord, while tales of thousands perishing can leave one relatively unmoved: 'When we were passing one of the deep wells in the Kalahari, a boy, the son of an aged father, had been drowned in it while playing on its brink. When all hope was gone, the father uttered an exceedingly great and bitter cry. It was sorrow without hope. This was the only instance I ever met with of a man weeping in this country.'[7]

The Luangwa is one of the largest rivers in Zambia, rising hundreds of kilometres away to the northeast, near the Malawi border. The Great East Road crosses it on a big suspension bridge. Here I'm delighted to find a row of local restaurants and shops, obviously having sprung up to provide for the lorries and long-distance buses. I stop at a restaurant run by a very friendly family. I'm so hungry that the usual meal of *nsima* and fish isn't enough, so I order a second, which puts me in something of a quandary: should I feel guilty about such overt gluttony? It's tantamount to showing off – many people here can barely afford one dinner, let alone two. On the other hand I'm bringing business to this establishment, which must be welcome. And walking like this means I'm burning more calories than most folks, so I have a legitimate excuse. Then I realize I'm over-intellectualizing the whole issue – if there's food I'll eat it, as simple as that. There are no difficult decisions involved here.

Lacking a bottle-opener, the female proprietor opens several bottles of Coca-Cola for me with her teeth, each time spitting the metal top straight into the bin on the far side of the room with remarkable accuracy – thank you, madam. Her uncle gives me a lecture on the difference between English and African food: '*Nsima* gives you proper energy for walking, but English food, ha! It's just like water.' He refuses to explain how he became such an expert on English food. He also warns me of the pitfalls of Chibuku on long journeys: 'It will give you false energy, my friend! And you know that professional footballers are disqualified when drug tests show they've been drinking alcohol.' All this time he's knocking back sachets of raw cane spirit like there's no tomorrow, so perhaps he should know. On a more practical note, his son warns me of bandits and lions on the road east.

I cross the Luangwa on its suspension bridge, my blisters by now reducing me to an undignified hobble, so painful I can hardly concentrate on anything else. Yet the problems I'm experiencing here are mild compared to those faced by Livingstone when he crossed the same river on his traversa, slightly further south near Zumbo. Surrounded by a large band of hostile tribesmen, and with only one canoe to ferry his men across, a serious attack seemed inevitable. To avoid splitting his party in such a dangerous situation, Livingstone postponed the crossing until darkness fell. Of all the difficult situations he faced on his African journeys, this was one of the most dangerous. It looked certain that the moment his party divided itself to cross, the local tribesmen would fall on those remaining and slaughter them.

For all his courage, as night approached Livingstone felt the end was near. Resigning himself to his fate, he drew out his Bible. At the first page he opened, he read the words of Jesus: 'I am with you always, even unto the end of the world.'[8] Livingstone's courage came flooding back, and his spirits soared; the idea of crossing by stealth at night now seemed unthinkable: 'It would appear as flight, and should such a man as I flee?'[9] The party would cross the following morning.

Livingstone's account of this incident reveals his unshakeable belief that he had been personally chosen by God to open the African interior. His writings on such occasions contain almost fanatical self-belief and ego, curiously tempered by quiet courage and humility. That night he wrote in his diary: 'See O Lord how the heathen rise up against me as they did to Thy Son'[10] – this from the same man who could also write less grandiosely but with equal conviction: 'If I am cut off ... my efforts are no longer needed by Him who knows what is best.'[11]

When dawn arrived, Livingstone amused the hostile warriors with his mirror and burning glass while his party crossed the river. Himself the last to cross, Livingstone thanked the chief courteously and the following day sent back gifts. Once again his courage and calm dignity had averted bloodshed. He reflected that the local tribes had reason to be distrustful of white people.

A later crossing of the Luangwa at Zumbo in June 1860 also brought Livingstone its share of danger; but this time with an element of slapstick comedy involved. Instead of a band of hostile warriors to oppose Livingstone's party, now the only people to help or hinder them were 'three half-intoxicated slaves'. Unimpressed by Livingstone's claims to be an explorer, they 'began to clamour for drink; not receiving any, as we had none to give, they grew more insolent, and declared that not another man should cross that day. Sininyane was remonstrating with them, when a loaded musket was presented at him by one of the trio. In an instant the gun was out of the rascal's hands, a rattling shower of blows fell on his back, and he took an involuntary header into the river. He crawled up the bank a sad and sober man, and all three at once tumbled from the height of saucy swagger to a low depth of slavish abjectness. The musket was found to have an enormous charge, and might have blown our man to pieces, but for the promptitude with which his companions administered justice in a lawless land.'[12]

East of the Luangwa hordes of flies begin to assume the proportions of an Egyptian plague. I start wondering what the hell do they want from me, exactly? I don't know much about flies, even though I'm spending so much time in their company I should be an expert by now. But at least they vanish at night, apparently viewing the approach of darkness in much the same way as Dracula regards the approach of dawn. I assume they just fly home – but then where is home, to a fly? Do they live in nests, possibly in the fly equivalent of a nuclear family? I can't believe that when night arrives they simply fall asleep wherever they happen to be, as though they've been nerve gassed. And do flies ever go hungry, or ever starve to death? It must happen, even though they're hardly the choosiest diners in the world, and must always be able to find *something* to eat. In African folklore the fly often plays the spy, entering any human dwelling without detection and showing a great fondness for eavesdropping.[13] I resolve to do some research on flies when I get back to Europe. But by then I won't care any more – they certainly won't have the same relevance when they're not tormenting me on an hourly basis.

The big ants swarming by the roadside show an unwelcome interest in my rucksack every time I put it down; they're so loud you can hear them distinctly from several metres away. They show amazing discipline, working with the team spirit favoured by totalitarian regimes as they carry home pieces of bracken or crumbs of food, apparently without the slightest temptation to stop to eat en route. On one or two occasions they start dragging off my matches one by one; I leave them a few so they can carry on practising tossing the caber.

Livingstone had his share of ant problems, and the species fascinated him – he made notes on no fewer than fifteen different varieties. 'It is really astonishing how such small bodies can contain so large an amount of ill-nature,' he wrote, observing that one of the few reliable ways of repelling their furious attacks was to put hot ashes on them. Once an entire army of red ants attacked Livingstone when he accidentally stepped on their nest, his attention occupied in viewing the distant landscape: 'Not an instant seemed to elapse, before a simultaneous attack was made on various unprotected parts, up the trousers from below, and on my neck and breast above. The bites of these furies were like sparks of fire, and there was no retreat. I jumped about for a second or two, then in desperation tore off all my clothing, and rubbed and picked them off *seriatim* as quickly as possible. Ugh! They would make the most lethargic mortal look alive. Fortunately no one observed this *rencontre*, or word might have been taken back to the village that I had become mad …'[14]

Livingstone was fortunate – the nineteenth-century traveller Duff Macdonald once saw a half-mile column of millions of red ants actually kill a fully grown elephant. Entering its nostrils, the ants drove the unfortunate creature berserk; after several minutes of this torment the elephant committed suicide by charging a particularly solid tree, leaving the ant army to strip its carcass to the bone.[15]

One afternoon I stop for water at a remote village, so small it doesn't have a name – at least according to a friendly local, who smiles and merely shrugs when I ask him where we are. He tells me there isn't even a water pump; instead, the people who live here fetch their water from a stream behind the village. I follow him to the stream in question, and I'm relieved I have a purifier: the water is green and cloudy and completely still, more of a pond than a stream. The only thing moving about it is its large population of frogs: fascinated by my water purifier, they splash joyfully around its gurgling intake pipe, jostling each other to get as close to it as possible. I had no idea a simple water pump could give so much pleasure. It must be the most exciting thing that has happened in their pond for ages.

Despite its capacity for entertaining frogs, my filter isn't working properly. I can pump only half a litre at a time before having to dismantle it and wipe all the crap from its ceramic filter: this water is filthy. Pumping water under a hot sun is hard work, and before long sweat is pouring out of me almost as fast as the water is going into my bottle.

My companion proves sympathetic: 'I know what it is to carry a heavy pack,' he tells me, drinking a cup of my freshly pumped water. 'I served in the Zambian army in the 1970s. I was one of the last soldiers to be trained in the British tactics. This was before President Kaunda ordered that the army must be trained in Chinese tactics.'

'Why Chinese?'

'Kaunda thought that since there are so many Chinese they must be right ... But I tell you, it was a bad idea. Those Chinese instructors taught our soldiers a lot of stupid old-fashioned tactics, from before the Second World War, so we were worse off than before. But I was fortunate – unlike these young boys now, I had learnt the British tactics.'

In all the villages along the Great East Road the water pumps are hard work. If you pumped water for an hour every day you'd soon have shoulders like the Incredible Hulk, and it's usually the women who perform this task. The pumps are usually crowded; despite the hard work involved, there's a definite social aspect to fetching the water, without any of the village men present to spoil the conversation. If I was alone I'd be tempted to stick my head under a pump to cool down in the heat, although wasting precious water like that would be regarded as the height of bad manners. The water from these pumps often tastes slightly metallic, as though it's been sitting in an old tin can for weeks. But after a day in a water bottle – should it ever last that long – the taste improves slightly. I can't be bothered to purify water from the village pumps, reasoning that if it doesn't kill the local people it won't kill me either. Even so, I can't rule out the possibility of spending Christmas in the London Hospital for Tropical Diseases. To be on the safe side I could drink nothing but Chibuku – but then I'd reach the east coast a drunken shambles, and have to spend Christmas in the Betty Ford Clinic.

Around halfway between Lusaka and the Malawi border I reach the large village of Kacholola. It's late afternoon, and I'm still trying to save money by not paying for any accommodation unless I can take it for the whole day and night, so I walk on past the village, looking for some secluded spot to camp. This takes me well over an hour. Most of this time is spent playing an unwelcome game of hide and seek in the bushes, trying to avoid the persistent attention of a couple of local wide-boys who seem worryingly interested in my immediate plans. The only place I can find with absolutely no risk of unwanted company lies halfway up a steep hill strewn with thorn bushes, a couple of kilometres from the village with barely enough level ground to lie flat. So once again the feng shui of my tent is all wrong.

The following day I stay at the pleasant and peaceful Kacholola Hotel, which is far less depressing than the average Zambian Rest House. My room on this occasion has a large population of tiny ants, and we all get off to a bad start when I give them a generous blast of 'Doom' insect spray; within a couple of minutes they lie in slaughtered heaps, like several pounds of dried tea sprinkled across the floor. I'm amazed at how quickly I declimatize. After only an hour in a cool room I step outside the hotel at midday and find the heat outside really oppressive – and it's not even the hot season yet. But I'll deal with heatstroke as and when it occurs.

The elderly gardener here wears a curious wig, obviously designed for a woman. In broad daylight this makes him look like James Brown, though I suspect on a dark night he'd look more like Norman Bates wearing his late mother's gear. Late that night I'm woken by loud footsteps outside my door, back and forth, *clump, clump, clump*, turn, *clump, clump, clump* – followed by a long pause each time right outside my door. It's actually quite spooky – I'm convinced it's Wiggy the Gardner coming to murder me in my bed for laughing earlier. This image becomes so powerful that I haul myself out of bed in case the door comes crashing open and an angry old man in a wig springs inside. Finally I dare to peer out of the window; the loud footsteps turn out to be from a hefty security guard wielding a truncheon the size of a medieval club.

East of Kacholola the heat becomes a real problem. More accurately, it's not so much the heat itself as the lack of breeze, combined with the fact that I'm working so bloody hard. If I could laze around in the shade with a cold beer I wouldn't mind if the thermometer rose by five or ten degrees. But when I'm carrying a bloody great rucksack all day I often find myself panting like a dog in the heat. By now my baseball cap is caked white in salt from dried sweat, my piss the colour of English marmalade.

Towards the Malawi border the breeze arrives like a blessing.

Walking experts claim hikers should maintain a constant pace, which apparently is less tiring. I've always found constant paces deadly dull; in the past I felt the same about marathon running and cycling, always going at whatever speed suited me, even if it was no more than a snail's pace. And I usually managed to get where I was going.

In long-distance walking, as with most things, an early start means you make far better progress. So I'm up at dawn and on the road as soon as I've packed my gear. On a typical morning I start walking still worn out from the previous day, with my feet killing me, my back aching, the day already baking hot and it's only six-thirty in the morning. Usually I walk for nine or ten kilometres at a stretch, averaging around six kilometres an hour, then rest for anything up to three-quarters of an hour. This means I usually cover about forty kilometres a day, sometimes fifty at a push. After walking for nine or ten days I take a couple of days off; when I reach some major stopping-off point I stay put longer, doing absolutely nothing that involves walking. In this way a pattern sets in, veering between backbreaking work and sprawling indolence.

I'm not breaking any records for speed, but over time this pace is eating up the kilometres. I've no desire to force myself to follow any ridiculous schedules, I'm pushing myself hard enough as it is. Even the tough Roman legionaries – no slouches when it came to covering huge distances on foot – would generally march only for three consecutive days before calling a rest day. I think if I had to time myself as I went I would despair of ever reaching the other side of Africa. The only way to complete this long trek without going crazy is to take it in manageable stages, focusing on how I feel at any particular time, rather than on the overall picture, the fact that I'm crossing a continent on foot.

The explorers held different views on covering distance. Thomson, one of the milder of the bunch, always favoured leisurely marches, and his journeys were notable for their absence of bloodshed. In contrast the belligerent Stanley usually set a blistering pace; as a result, his expeditions were marked by extremely high fatality rates, even by the standards of African exploration. Very much in character, Livingstone favoured the slow but sure approach, travelling no more than five hours a day, which usually meant covering around fifteen to twenty kilometres: 'This in a hot climate is as much as a man can accomplish without being oppressed; and we always tried to make our progress more a pleasure than a toil.' He contrasted his own approach to that of other travellers: 'To hurry over the ground, abuse, and look ferocious at one's companions, merely for the foolish vanity of boasting how quickly a distance was accomplished, is a combination of silliness with absurdity; the pleasure of observing scenery and everything new as one moves on at an ordinary pace, and the participation in the most delicious rest with our fellows, render travelling delightful.'[16] But considering the realities of African travel, especially in Livingstone's day, this was far too good to be true; through his writings Livingstone desperately wanted to encourage Europeans to follow him to central Africa, not to put them off with an accurate portrayal of the real dangers and hardships of travel in the interior.

In a dimly lit but friendly restaurant in the small town of Nyimba, I talk to a couple of young locals. They're impressed when I tell them I'm walking across Africa, although like most people here they assume I've walked only from Lusaka.

'I couldn't walk from Lusaka,' declares one of the pair, eating a large doughnut. 'It's too hard!'

'Yes, you are a hard worker!' agrees his friend, also with his mouth full of doughnut. 'Lusaka is too far!'

I can't imagine why they think I would choose to walk from Lusaka to Nyimba – though it probably makes as much sense as walking here from the Namibian coast. Perhaps to many Zambians all memorable journeys begin or end at their burgeoning capital.

I buy dozens of buns in the market, enough to feed an elephant; to get my rucksack closed I have to crush them into a solid mass of squashed dough. Leaving town I pass a barber's kiosk advertising various styles of coiffure: 'English', 'Wave', 'Table' and 'Bildso'. All these options sound promising; I ask the hairdresser for further details on his house speciality, 'the Potato'. 'It's a haircut,' he says grumpily, refusing to elaborate. I'm disappointed, as I liked the sound of it. Even if it proved disastrous I wouldn't look any more of a mess than I do already, and I could always keep my hat on for a few weeks. But I'm behind schedule, and I don't feel I can trust this surly fellow with his Potato or any other style: he loses a customer, while I lose out on a whole new image for crossing into Malawi.

I get three-quarters of the way across Zambia before getting my first tsetse fly bite – considering the number of the bloody things buzzing around here, I've been amazingly lucky so far. The tsetse's bite feels like a hot needle being sunk into your skin. It often develops into an unlovely chancre and can cause lethal sleeping sickness in humans, or permanent damage to the central nervous system, although the danger is far greater for cattle. Until the twentieth century most of Zambia had to rely on human porterage for transport, the tsetse fly having wiped out the cattle and draught animals. Paradoxically, from a conservationist's point of view the tsetse has done much to protect many wild areas of the African bush – by seriously disrupting agriculture it has prevented extensive human settlement in these areas. Inevitably tropical medicine has come a long way, but Zambia is still home to some of the most deadly tropical diseases, with sleeping sickness one of the worst and most common.

Whatever the effects the tsetse over the centuries, today I'm surprised at the sheer variety of cattle breeds in this part of Africa. Many have enormous humps at their shoulders like a blunt dorsal fin, while others have slightly comical droopy horns that seem neither use nor ornament. Most cattle here are underweight, as the grazing in Zambia is often poor. Most villages keep dozens of goats, while small black pigs forage energetically most of the day. The young pigs are so cute they'd make nice pets, and even the older specimens look much healthier and happier than the huge fat creatures seen on European farms, wallowing around in filth all day and never getting any proper exercise or having anything sensible to occupy their minds.

One afternoon I find a large silver snake writhing in agony on the road, mangled and bloody, its spine smashed by a passing vehicle. I feel sorry for the poor thing and I'm tempted to put it out of its misery. I've no idea if it's poisonous or not, but it would be pretty stupid to get bitten by a snake that will soon be dead anyway. I leave hoping another car comes past quickly to finish the mess made by the first one, but later I regret not doing the honourable thing and instead leaving it to die in this awful way, flapping around helplessly in the middle of the road.

At one tiny village in eastern Zambia the usual crowd of kids comes running down to take a closer look at me. When they're less than twenty metres away an elderly woman in the doorway of a nearby hut shouts something to them, obviously about me. The effect is instantaneous: the kids flee in total panic, covering ground many times faster in the opposite direction, literally tumbling over themselves in their eagerness to escape. At a respectable distance the bolder ones conceal themselves behind bushes, peering back anxiously to see if I'm pursuing them; the others just continue running into the distance, screaming and waving their arms in the air. I'm tempted to ask the woman what she said – the effect could scarcely have been more dramatic if she told them I ate black children for lunch, which was almost certainly the gist of her remark.

Smiling and waving and saying hello to every Tom, Dick and Harry is exhausting me; I'm not cut out to play the Queen Mother. It's a shame this is all so draining – after all, what's wrong with people being friendly and showing an interest? It's such a different world from London, where no one pays the slightest attention to a stranger unless they're either gorgeous or so ugly they'd frighten a buffalo.

The usual way of attracting someone's attention in many parts of Africa is to hiss. Visitors often find this custom strange at first; to most English people, hissing sounds about as polite as a complete stranger swearing at you to attract your attention. Until now I'd associated hissing with the point in the play where the moustache-twirling villain makes his entrance, or when the tomatoes start flying.

Livingstone had difficulties with the local greetings on the Batoka Plateau: 'They throw themselves on their backs on the ground, and rolling from side to side, slap the outside of their thighs as expression of thankfulness and welcome, uttering the words, "Kina bomba". This method of salutation was to me very disagreeable, and I could never get reconciled to it. I called out "Stop, stop! I don't want that"; but they, imagining I was dissatisfied, only tumbled around more furiously, and slapped their thighs with greater vigour. The men being totally un-clothed, this performance imparted to my mind a painful sense of their extreme degradation.'[17]

I make a small detour to visit the town of Petauke, around 400 kilometres from Lusaka and the last settlement of any size this side of the Malawi border. Such side trips are draining, physically and mentally, and usually accompanied by solemn vows that this will be the last. People assume a three-kilometre detour would mean nothing to someone walking thousands of kilometres; but the very fact I'm walking so far gives extraordinary significance to even the tiniest extra distance, and merely a couple of unnecessary kilometres become the straw that breaks the camel's back.

Detour or no, I have to get to Petauke to post a letter home and buy some razor blades – shaving in a cup of rationed drinking water with a blunt razor has become a real chore. As I approach the town a dark figure cycles towards me, silhouetted against the morning sun with shoulders so hunched that he seems to have no head; under his arm he carries a sinister bundle swathed in rags, the exact size and shape of a human skull. At first I'm convinced he's the Zambian version of the Headless Horseman, the tsetse fly having forced him to swap his horse for a pushbike. And this is in broad daylight – if I saw this character at night I'd jump six feet in the air, heavy pack or not. Then the guy stops right in front of me and looks up. To my disappointment his head reappears in the normal position – he just has very bad posture. He then unfastens his bundle, a heavily wrapped radio, which he then tries to sell to me. Obviously I'm tired.

From Petauke eastwards mosques become a more frequent sight, usually painted in green, the sacred colour to Islam. Their presence is the first tangible historical influence from the east coast – an encouraging sign, and proof of sorts that I'm making progress. Historically, Zambia's central location far from both the east and west coasts meant that until the nineteenth century it had virtually no contact with Europeans or Arabs. The Muslims venturing into the interior had no particular desire to impose their religion on those with whom they traded, so until the arrival of the Christian missionaries like Livingstone the local African religions were almost unaffected.

At a makeshift bar in Kawere, a small village towards the Malawi border, the elderly barman Stan presents me with a big bag of peanuts and refuses to take any money. I find this touching, as the locals here are very poor. He ladles his home-brewed Chibuku out from a big vat behind the bar – I share my cup with a couple of young guys lounging in the shade outside. Unfortunately it doesn't keep well in the heat; after a day and a half in my water-bottle it has all the charm of the liquid found slopping around the bilges of tugboats, with a vomit-flavoured aftertaste. Still, the peanuts were nice.

Livingstone experienced countless examples of real generosity from Africans, and whenever he could tried to reciprocate. Some tribes would present him with an ox, with the words 'Here is a little bit of bread for you' – although the Bechuanas would present a miserable goat with the pompous exclamation, 'Behold an ox!' Livingstone found it inexplicable that some white travellers with plenty of goods would make a present of three buttons or some equally contemptible gift: 'The people receive the offering with a degree of shame, and ladies may be seen to hand it quickly to the attendants, and, when they retire, laugh until the tears stand in their eyes, saying to those about them, "Is that a white man? Then there are niggards among them too. Some of them are born without hearts!"'[18]

The further east I get, the more persistent the insects become. The high-pitched whine of mosquitoes in my tent at night becomes incredibly irritating; the only time they're not whining is when they're guzzling my blood. When they're right by my ear, as they so often are, they're amazingly loud. They may get a good meal out of me, but it will be their last – they're not getting out of my tent alive, particularly as they weren't invited in the first place.

One night I'm woken by the disconcerting sound of loud insect munching next to my head. In the morning I'm relieved to discover that only my homemade insoles have been partially devoured – but what sort of creature would choose to eat those and nothing else? As if to answer my question, the following night giant ants eat a bloody great hole in the floor of my tent. The ants are getting bigger, too, as are the termite mounds beside the road, the two facts presumably related.

As well as ant-damage to my gear, my clothes have started falling to pieces. This is partly my own fault: it's all too easy to put off mending things, even when I know with certainty I'm only creating more work for myself later. I feel absurdly pleased with myself on the rare occasions I repair something in good time. When sewing becomes too much like hard work, I find one of the most useful items on the whole journey is a tube of strong contact adhesive.

On the plus side, my rucksack is bearing up well; I've only had to put a few minor stitches in it so far. Before leaving England I read a guide to solo backpacking by some ex-SAS type, in which he claimed no rucksack he'd ever owned in civilian life lasted him longer than two months of constant heavy use. I'm pretty good at wrecking perfectly serviceable equipment in record time, but two months still seems poor. I can't help wondering what the man did to hasten the collapse of his rucksack; I suspect that at the end of each lonely day's solo backpacking in the wilderness he had some sort of physical relationship with it.

You don't need to be an orthopaedic surgeon to appreciate that carrying a heavy rucksack, even a well-designed one, is to a large extent an unnatural activity. Although my rucksack is serving me extremely well, sometimes I feel real hatred for this ungainly sack of rubbish, riding across Africa on my back like a large ungrateful succubus. Towards the end of every rest break it just sits there in the dust waiting for me to pick it up again, its unfastened hip belt looking for all the world like the outstretched arms of an importunate infant waiting to be comforted. Sometimes I'm tempted to carry it no further than the next big river, fill it full of heavy rocks and then deep-six the bastard.

Throughout the journey, walking big distances is not so difficult – it's carrying a heavy pack that is the exhausting part. While it's impossible to put an exact figure on it, I'd estimate that walking with a thirty-kilo pack requires twice as much effort as walking with nothing to carry; that is, for every thirty kilometres I walk with my pack I could cover sixty kilometres unencumbered for the same expenditure of energy. I've long since stopped wondering why I eat like a pig for most of the journey but remain as thin as a rake.

Near the Malawi border I stop about three kilometres from the small town of Sinda. As usual I find it difficult to conceal myself for the night; just as I'm about to bed down in a suitable thicket, half a dozen locals appear and start digging a hole in the road less than ten metres away from where I'm sleeping. Thankfully they're so absorbed in their excavation work that they don't see me. And in the early hours I'm woken by an ox cart, rumbling past only metres away. For once I'm pleased to be woken, having been dreaming about an imaginary library book still out on my ticket back at home, its fine mounting daily.

The following morning I go for breakfast at a tea shop in Sinda, where the limited menu offers only a straight choice between a 'ban' or a 'ban with bata'. I push the boat out and go for the ban with bata – I haven't eaten anything with butter for months, and suddenly realize I miss it. In Livingstone's day Africans used butter primarily to anoint the skin; when used as food they always melted their butter as a dip, and looked down on Europeans eating it unmelted, rather as Westerners today might look askance at someone eating lard with a spoon.

In the teashop I chat with a friendly local smuggler called Jacob, a handsome guy in his late twenties, noticeably better dressed than most of the other locals. His job involves smuggling unofficial consignments of timber across the Malawi border; the relevant officials turn a blind eye, for the appropriate consideration. While talking to Jacob I mention that I've crossed Zambia without bribing anyone, and he's astonished at this. Many people insist bribery is essential to all dealings in Zambia; it's certainly a widespread problem here, but it's an exaggeration to suggest you can't get anything done in this part of the world without it. Travelling everywhere on foot, I can think of very little that I've actually *needed* to bribe anyone for.

I explain the nature of my journey to Jacob. 'The English are very determined people!' he laughs. 'When they decide to do something, they do it, no matter what.' This seems to be a common opinion here of my fellow countrymen.

Reaching Chipata on the Zambian border (the name translates simply as 'gateway'), I find a campsite more or less in the middle of town. Chipata has a large Indian population, which explains the number of ornate mosques in town. Later I have a drink with a friendly Indian pharmacist and the local police chief, while my feet discreetly soak in a bucket of salty water under the table. The pharmacist takes one look at them and whistles softly: 'You will have to stay put until your feet are healed!' He does have a point – by this stage, strips of flesh are hanging off my feet, and they look and feel as though I've been mildly bastinadoed. But I must reach the Malawian capital Lilongwe before resting for a few days – that's the deal I've made with myself. Despite my best intentions, during the night I decide to take the next day off anyway.

The wind at night in the campsite is terrific; it's like waking to the sound of a roaring sea beating against a craggy Cornish coast. All night the wind huffs and puffs and tries to blow my tent down. But while my tent is cramped and somewhat chewed by ants, its sturdy A-frame will resist anything short of a hurricane. And I love going to sleep to the sound of wild weather outside – even if on this occasion I'm cheating by camping in the middle of a town rather than halfway up Kanchenjunga.

I laze around all the next day, trying without success to soothe my feet with an assortment of local ointments recommended by the pharmacist the previous night. Someone steals my toilet bag, so I hobble into town to replace a few items. But I manage to find some sticking plasters that actually stick, which I count as a real result. Regarding the stealing, I reckon a toilet bag and T-shirt are acceptable losses so far on the trip.

I stock up on more razor blades and also some heavy-duty soap. A popular brand here is Geza Beauty Soap, although the connection between beautiful skin and a geezer is lost on me. Its sister brand is Geisha Beauty Soap, which according to local adverts 'lasts and lasts like a mother's love'. Unlike a mother's love, the local soaps here also tend to leave a thick scum floating on the water.

While I'm at Chipata my remaining T-shirt finally disintegrates, having completely rotted with sweat. Even this is no great loss, as by now it was no more than a collection of holes joined by a few remaining threads. At least T-shirts are easy to come by here, although a surprising number of those for sale display the pugnacious features of Mike Tyson, sporting the Shawnee hairstyle he favoured when he first became famous.

These days I often find myself fantasizing about wearing clean clothes two days running. I'm sick of clothes slimy with sweat. Galton is no help, recording cryptically: 'The sailor's recipe for washing clothes is well known, but it is too dirty to describe.' If I knew what this was I'd be using it by now. Livingstone observed of the villagers on the Upper Shire valley: 'For long life they are not indebted to frequent ablutions. An old man told us that he remembered to have washed once in his life, but it was so long since that he had forgotten how it felt. "Why do you wash?" asked Chinsunse's women of the Makololo; "our men never do."'[19]

Despite not having been washed with shampoo for months, my hair is still in reasonable condition. I suspect I've been doing the right thing – I doubt if Nature intended people to wash their hair, and I've never seen any wild animals soaping themselves down. Livingstone encountered problems using shampoo, when horrified natives assumed he was washing his brains.[20] Even without the shampoo, Livingstone's hair became a curiosity in the interior. He assured the locals that his hair 'was the real original hair, such as theirs would have been, had it not been scorched and frizzled by the sun'. The natives remained convinced that

Livingstone wore a wig made from a lion's mane: "'Is that hair? We thought it was a wig; we never saw the like before; this white man must be of the sort that lives in the sea." Henceforth my men took this hint, and always sounded my praises as a true specimen of the variety of white men who live in the sea. "Only look at his hair – it is made quite straight by the sea-water!"' Livingstone explained to them repeatedly that when it was said that white men came out of the sea, it did not mean that they came from beneath the water. But 'the myth was too good not to be taken advantage of by my companions; so … when I was out of hearing, my men always represented themselves as led by a genuine merman: "Just see his hair!"'[21]

Each day my personal appearance grows steadily more disreputable. Since I started the walk I've grown accustomed to going around covered in grime like a Victorian street urchin, but by now I have to assume I smell worse than an old goat. It's difficult to tell for sure; I'm hoping the very doubt in my mind suggests things aren't as bad as they might be. But it's becoming difficult to reconcile this way of life with any dignity, and I'm growing tired of respectable folks taking me for a rough type when they first set eyes on my toe-rag appearance. If things carry on as they are I'll reach Zanzibar fit to frighten crows.

On the other hand, ending a long journey in rags does add to one's credibility. During the westerly stage of his traversa Livingstone arrived at the Angolan coast looking a complete derelict: 'I made my entrance, in a somewhat forlorn state as to clothing … I was in the same state of mind in which individuals are who commit a petty depredation, in order to obtain the shelter and food of a prison …'[22]

I will add this to my list of things to look forward to. But first I have to cross two more countries on foot.

13. The Lake of Stars
(Malawi: Zambian Border to Nkhata Bay)

Why, if one started when a mere boy to walk to the other end of the lake, he would be an old grey-headed man before he got there. I never heard of such a thing being attempted.

Local chief speaking to David Livingstone,
Expedition to the Zambesi

At the Malawi border a customs officer writes down my details. Despite reports to the contrary, petty officials in African countries are not all out to get you – some are courteous and helpful, and a few are even interested in your problems. As in many parts of the world, this often depends on whether or not the guy in question got a shag the previous night – though of course there's no way of knowing this without risking a night in the cells.

'Occupation?'

'Bookseller'. This may no longer be true, but I'm too tired to discuss my life history. The man writes 'boxer' in the appropriate space, and starts regarding me with more interest.

Often on the journey a conversation or shared laugh with some stranger on the road leaves me feeling energized and optimistic. But when a stranger acts like a complete pain in the arse it drains my energy noticeably. Just across the Malawi border a most irritating young man pursues me with missionary zeal, trying to scrounge anything and everything and to get me to pay for his education abroad. I start walking at top speed – and I've been walking for so long by now that despite my heavy pack I can produce an impressive turn of speed when required. Even so, the guy's determined, and he sticks to me like a human shadow. For several kilometres he manages to keep up, pouring with sweat in the midday heat and pumping his arms like an Olympic speed walker, which makes him look slightly demented. Eventually I have to tell him politely to sling his hook; at this he abandons the chase, panting like an asthmatic dog in the middle of the road.

'We will meet again, if God wills!' he calls after me. Heaven forbid.

I stop at a tea shop in Mchinji and order a mug of tea. The middle-aged proprietor places before me a cup of local powdered milk dissolved in hot water, which tastes like watered-down chalk dust. The man next to me is busy slurping a mug of normal-looking tea, so I ask the boss if I can have some of that instead.

'But that's just the leaves!' he declares.

While sipping my powdered milk concoction I talk to a friendly young woman called Lee. 'Money is easy to find in Zambia,' she tells me, 'but not in Malawi.' As a Westerner, it's easy for me to forget just how little money the majority of people have here. Malawi is still among the world's poorest countries – many people earn less than two US dollars a week and live in utter poverty, to an extent almost unimaginable in England.

The following evening, near the village of Namitete, a white guy called Peter stops his car to ask why I'm walking. I explain my situation, and he drives off, but returns ten minutes later and invites me to stay on his employer's tobacco farm nearby. I accept of course; his boss, Guy Pickering, and his family are extremely nice people, and seem far more fair-minded than some of the white expats living out in Africa.

Later, in a comfortable bed – the first since Kacholola on the Great East Road – I take a look at *Resident Abroad*, a special interest magazine for expats. This edition lists the things most missed by the English living abroad. In the food department, Marmite and sweet pickle top the list; I detest both, and would have had trouble eating them even on that dreadful stretch from Sesheke to Livingstone. According to *Resident Abroad* readers, by far the biggest improvement in Britain in the last quarter of a century has been the introduction of Thatcherism. This disturbing notion must speak volumes for expats, or at least those who respond to *Resident Abroad*'s surveys.

I'm invited to stay another day at the Pickerings' farm. The servants wash my sleeping bag, the first time it's been clean in ages, and the results are so amazing it feels a shame to get in it again. I'd almost forgotten it was red. Guy proves surprisingly enthusiastic about *nsima*, which I find encouraging – some white people wouldn't touch it, considering it 'food for blacks'. Malawian *nsima* differs slightly from that found in Zambia, and several varieties are new to me. One is smooth, oily and vaguely nauseating, while a rougher variety is good with milk and sugar, like breakfast cereal. Eaten neat, it tastes like instant mashed potato made with insufficient water.

I'm embarrassed to admit how much I enjoy watching television again, for the first time in months. Guy's ten-year-old daughter Jessica cuddles up in a blanket in front of the TV, at least until she realizes that a rat has been there first and crapped on the blanket.

I spend my second night at the Pickerings' farm in their tree house, although the idea was more pleasant than the reality. Guy insists that malaria-carrying mosquitoes fly no higher than knee height, but I'm not convinced; while it's true they hunt at ankle height, I've had enough bites over my entire body to make anyone suspicious. Even if he's right, the mosquitoes up in the treehouse are maddening before I even lie down. And hauling my gear up the tree proves harder than it looked, involving several trips.

To complicate matters, one of the guard dogs takes a ferocious dislike to me, snarling viciously whenever I go anywhere near it. When finally I get myself bedded down, it prowls the garden below like an avenging angel, staring up at me and drooling at the thought of sinking its teeth into me. I'm fairly safe for the moment unless I'm reckless enough to climb down from the tree or fall out of it. But the logistics of taking a midnight piss now become a major headache. The window of the tree house is one option, but it's difficult to see if anyone's still up and about in the garden; there's usually the occasional servant or guard at these places. I suspect relieving oneself out of the host's treehouse is frowned upon here as much as anywhere else. And it's so dark I could easily piss on that bloody dog's head. Dogs may not be noted for their climbing skills, but I think if I accidentally pissed on this one sheer rage would propel it right up the tree like a surface-to-air stinger missile. Eventually I have to use my flask: there are definite drawbacks to staying in civilization again after so long on the road.

Despite the savage dog, I'm sorry to leave the Pickerings' farm. The following day, I reach Lilongwe, the capital of Malawi. The city is much smaller than Lusaka, and divided into a new and an old town. The new town is a soulless area of government buildings and small shopping malls; a few kilometres away the old town is much livelier and noisier. The huge crowded market here sells everything under the sun; its large Indian population in particular does a roaring trade in spices and cloth. The cheaper places to stay and eat are all in the old town, and I have no trouble finding a popular backpackers' hostel called Annie's.

As soon as I arrive, the difficulty of not smoking here becomes almost overwhelming. I thought I'd outgrown peer pressure regarding cigarettes; but when everyone else around me is at it I'm a lost cause. While pitching my tent in the garden I find a half-smoked cigarette stub by my feet. After wrestling with my conscience and dignity for at least half a minute, the struggle ends predictably. And it's *so* enjoyable; not having smoked for a while, I feel the instant effects of nicotine in my blood and brain, a pleasurable dizziness. I read somewhere that nicotine is supposed to hit your brain in less than ten seconds after the first drag – I reckon in my case now it's much quicker than that, merely because I want one so much.

I plan to stay in Lilongwe for several days' rest and recuperation. I spend a lot of this time drinking with a young South African guy staying here called Pieter, who looks rather like Scorpio, the crazed assassin in the movie *Dirty Harry*. He makes his money trading gems, buying cheaply from locals then selling for a tidy profit in South Africa and Europe. Work aside, his main purpose in life here is chatting up backpacker women, and tremendous effort over time does seem to bring him results with Annie's high turnover of guests.

Early one evening I find a Jewish guy sitting outside my tent in the back yard, gazing intently at the darkening sky. 'What time do the stars come out?' he says. I've never thought about it until now, and ask him why he wants to know. 'In the Jewish faith you must be able to see three stars before you can pray. To be judged for Heaven you need three witnesses, but for Hell only two. Two intelligent men can disagree – but a third can find a solution without getting involved.'

When the Jewish guy finally gets his prayers underway, I go and sit in one of the cheap plastic chairs near by in the back yard, taking great care; their legs are so flimsy they tend to collapse under you without warning. But it's entertaining enough when the beer is flowing and someone – occasionally me – suddenly sprawls full length on the floor.

The staff at Annie's have the maddening tendency to play the same music over and over. Personal favourites at the start of the evening have become truly hateful by bedtime. I'd prefer it if they played some African music now and again – but then no one travelling in Africa can avoid hearing a great deal of local music. Africans really love their music. And whether you like it or not, most African music is joyful in some way, full of life and energy; they don't go in for mournful stuff, and grunge-like dirges have never caught on here. In the markets the sheer volume of music is almost frightening; distortion is nothing, volume is everything, and the market traders get through a phenomenal number of cheap batteries.

I go out for the night with Pieter and Joe, a rugby player from Manchester who's also staying at Annie's. After visiting all the viable bars in town we arrive at an awful locals' pick-up disco. But at least the beer is reasonable; Malawi is the only country outside Denmark allowed to brew Carlsberg. As soon as we're in the club I can't help thinking that the clichés are true, so many black Africans dance with a greater sense of joy than white people; it seems a more expressive and natural activity here, and probably a lot more fun. Even Livingstone, hardly the life and soul of the party, was aware of this, observing of Sekeletu's village: 'The people usually show their joy and work off their excitement in dances and songs. The dance consists of the men standing nearly naked in a circle, with clubs or small battleaxes in their hands, and each roaring at the loudest pitch of his voice, while they simultaneously lift one leg, stamp heavily twice with it, then lift the other and give one stamp with that; this is the only movement in common. The arms and head are thrown about also in every direction; and all this time the roaring is kept up with the utmost possible vigour; the continued stamping makes a cloud of dust ascend, and they leave a deep ring in the ground where they have stood. If the scene were witnessed in a lunatic asylum it would be nothing out of the way, and quite appropriate even, as a means of letting off the excessive excitement of the brain; but here grey-headed men joined in the performance with as much zest as others whose youth might be an excuse for making the perspiration stream off their bodies with the exertion. As I never tried it, and am unable to enter into the spirit of the thing, I cannot recommend the Makololo polka to the dancing world ...'[1]

After some heavy drinking at the disco, Joe vanishes with a local girl and I decide to leave before getting completely paralytic. If you reach such a state in a place like this – and it's not difficult – you never know who you're going home with, if you're still capable of caring.

The following afternoon, still nursing a dreadful hangover, I sit in the yard at Annie's with Joe and a couple of Irish backpackers. Joe attempts at some length to explain his conduct of the previous evening; he comes up with an extraordinary theory that somehow his travel mosquito net protects him from the advances of local sex workers, and starts referring to it as his 'prozzie net'. Although his logic is lost on us, as if on cue a local prostitute called Lizzie then appears. A regular visitor to Annie's, she announces to everyone within earshot that she wants to have sex with me, or perhaps with me and one of the Irish guys at the same time if I prefer it that way. Both options seem to me a very bad idea; quite apart from any other consideration, Lizzie can't be a day over sixteen. I feel sorry for her; she's always cheerful and friendly, and professional interest aside seems to have taken rather a shine to me. Some of the locals make cruel remarks about her because of her job, but she genuinely doesn't appear to bear anyone ill will. James, the restaurant waiter at Annie's, usually chases her away from the hostel, prompting comments from guests along the lines of: 'James, why are you chasing your wife away?' But he'd be wise not to to antagonize her unnecessarily – although petite she can look after herself, and when she feels strongly about some issue has been known to fight on the floor like a sailor.

I can't help thinking that any man who avails himself of the local hired help here must like to live dangerously. But enough Western visitors do, even though the rate of HIV infection here is so high that there's a reasonable chance of buying a death sentence. You can't help feel sorry for the women and girls who work like this. Incredibly, some wealthy middle-aged European tourists actually pay extra to have sex with Malawian prostitutes without using a condom, presumably in search of some extra *frisson* of excitement. Now that really is mad.

The next day I visit the big market on Malangalanga Road in Lilongwe's Indian Town to get my sandals re-soled. I sit waiting for about an hour in a shoemaker's shop, wishing I'd brought something to read. Then Lizzie walks past, spots me and stops to wave and shout enthusiastic greetings; this results in knowing smirks from the other locals waiting for their shoes, and any attempt on my part to claim I've never even held hands with this young lady would serve only to dig myself in deeper. I start praying that the shoemaker gets a move on with my soles; later it turns out he's made a useless job of it into the bargain.

A change of footwear has now become a priority. One Indian shop-keeper irritates me intensely when I ask to try on a certain pair of training shoes in my size. 'So you're taking them, then?' she demands, before they're even out of the box. Hold your horses, lady. I try them on and they're too small.

'Sorry, they're too tight.'

'They're *not* tight. They are the *right size*.'

I leave her to it.

The shops in Malawi usually have a bigger selection of goods than those in Zambia, although a surprising proportion of the fruit here is actually imported from Zimbabwe. There's still no shortage of products with strange names, such as a hair-straightening paste called 'Placenta'. In the market endless rows of people fry chips and pieces of unidentifiable meat, or hard-boiled eggs in batter. This food is often surprisingly good; sometimes the meat is a little raw, or obviously pieces of some animal's intestine, but usually well worth twenty pence. Fried cassava is nice occasionally, and while you wouldn't want it every day if you have the choice, many people here don't.

A popular non-alcoholic drink is Mahewu, a form of banana milk-shake made without milk (or bananas, for that matter). It's no more than maize and wheatflour in sugary water, with a dash of banana-flavoured chemicals thrown in; but it's palatable enough, especially on the rare occasions it's cold. Like its alcoholic big brother Chibuku, it's sold in one-litre cardboard cartons. The guys selling Mahewu in the market invariably slap the carton as they hand it over, like a midwife administering a newborn infant its traditional welcome into the world. Despite much questioning on my part, no one offers a convincing explanation for this part of the service.

To break the monotony of Mahewu and Chibuku I also acquire a taste for Powers Cane Spirit, a cheap and fiery local path to oblivion. Most evenings at Annie's I'm pissed by seven, or at whatever time Pieter returns from his gem deals, to keep, as he puts it, 'an appointment with Mr Powers'. The affordability of Powers links it with many crimes in Malawi. In Livingstone's day, the same problems in the Portuguese settlements were caused instead by palm-toddy, the fermented juice of the palm-oil tree: 'This toddy, called *malova*, is the bane of the country. Culprits are continually brought before the commandants for assaults committed through its influence. Men come up with deep gashes on their heads, and one, who had burned his father's house, I saw making a profound bow … and volunteering to explain why he did the deed.'[2]

Towards the end of my stay in Lilongwe the sky starts giving subtle hints of the coming rainy season, still some weeks away, and a few token raindrops fall to the parched earth. This reminds me how lucky I've been – this is only the second time I've experienced rain on this trip, and I'm two-thirds of the way across Africa. The last time I was rained on was way back at the Waterberg Plateau in Namibia. But it doesn't stay like this for much longer. Often I prefer gloomy overcast days in Africa to the more usual dazzling ones; I like it when the sun has lost a little of its fierceness, when everything is cool and pleasant, when the air itself seems to hold some trace of magic and mystery.

By now it's becoming obvious I'm staying in Lilongwe longer than circumstances justify. I tell myself I've earned a rest, and that I should stay put until my feet have healed; but I know I should get back on the road as quickly as possible, before I get too used to having people around me again for longer than the time it takes for me to walk past them. Spending all this time in Lilongwe, getting pissed every night and smoking like a chimney, isn't getting me any closer to the east coast.

I decide, however, that before I leave I want to go to a decent party. In Livingstone's day some of the wildest parties were thrown by the Portuguese at Tête, which sounds exactly what I need right now, although Livingstone was appalled at their revelry and immorality: 'The shocking prevalence of intemperance and other vices among the Portuguese at Tette made us wonder, not that they had fever, but that they were not all swept off together. Their habits would be fatal in any climate; the natives marvelled even more than we did; our Makololo looked on aghast at these convivial parties.' Sininyane, one of Livingstone's companions, described one thus: 'A Portuguese stands up … and cries "Viva!" that means, I am pleased; another says, "Viva!" We are all pleased together; they are so glad just to get a little beer.' One night he saw three inebriated officers in the midst of their enjoyment, quarrelling about a false report; one jumped on his superior and tried to bite him; and, while these two were rolling on the floor, the third caught up a chair and therewith pounded them both. Sininyane, horrified at such conduct, exclaimed, "What kind of people can these whites be, who treat even their chiefs in this manner?"[3]

The nearest I get to such an evening in Lilongwe is on my penultimate day here. I go drinking in town with Pieter and his white friends Adam and Hendrik. Adam, a thirty-something coffin manufacturer of short stature, has just acquired the nickname 'Chappie the Chipmunk' owing to a recent bad crew cut that does him no favours whatsoever. Hendrik, in complete contrast, is a largish fellow with a big black beard and arms like a stevedore's. Very hale and hearty, he looks capable of violence should the occasion arise; when he's drunk he's the kind of person who without any bad intention would prefer to kick a door down than open it in the normal manner.

We visit an ex-pat bar known as The Shack. Here I learn that I'm not the only person walking huge distances in this part of the world: three South Africans are attempting to walk from Cape Town to Cairo, raising money for polio research. I think one of them has polio himself, and his bad leg has slowed him down while his companions forged ahead. Apparently they're somewhere near Lilongwe, having eventually caught up with each other, and are now busy reviving their spirits with alcohol.

I look around the bar at the rest of the clientele. Friday night has started with a vengeance, and several lard-arsed Lotharios are already out on the pull. At this point a very pretty blonde girl appears briefly, long enough for me to fall in love with her. Then she vanishes like Cinderella, just as I'm about to speak to her. She was lovely, and even looked like a nice person; I wonder if I merely imagined her. Either way, it's back to the proverbial drawing board. I'm getting very out of practice at this sort of thing, having exiled myself to the bush for all these months. I'm withering on the vine here – I could be having a good time back in London, or indeed anywhere, for that matter, instead of plodding across Africa as chaste as Galahad.

Then a big rugby-playing type comes out of the toilet, ashen-faced. 'Don't go in there!' he warns me. 'There's a *huge* cockroach ...' I go in to investigate; the creature in question looks about half the size of the average Namibian corn cricket, and friendly enough, minding its own business, whatever that might be, sitting on the water cistern and greeting newcomers by waving its feelers in the air. It's actually cute for a cockroach, if such a thing is possible, and I emerge from the toilet visibly unimpressed. 'Don't tell me,' says the rugby player, 'You've spent the last six months in the bush!' A remarkably accurate guess, time-wise. I rather like this guy: at least he's not full of shit.

After several hours in the bar I decide to leave before chucking-out time; if I carry on drinking with Pieter and Hendrik, I'll probably have to witness, at any moment, a big fight erupting between them and some completely innocent stranger. As soon as this thought enters my head I notice the most likely candidate, a wimpy-looking fellow sitting on the next table surrounded by an entourage of pretty women, all discussing whether he should take the bus home later.

'YEAH, GET THE FUCKING BUS HOME RIGHT NOW!' bellows Hendrik right in the guy's face.

I leave at this point. It hasn't been the greatest of nights out.

Late the following morning I wake up frazzled, my hangover like a giant corkscrew being twisted gently through my head. I look the part, too. After the last week I was expecting my features to be somewhat coarsened by drink, but instead I'm greeted by a racoon peering back at me from the bathroom mirror – the dark rings under my eyes are by now so pronounced from recent alcohol intake that they completely encircle my eyes, joining somewhere near my eyebrows. And smoking forty Life cigarettes last night has left me convinced someone has been jumping up and down on my chest.

I'd intended to leave today, but I'm too hungover to move. This may be my last day at Annie's, but Pieter and I both have to give up alcohol – if we carry on drinking like this we'll die, or at least end up in a special home. Unfortunately the absence of alcohol makes my last day at Annie's tedious; we had much more fun while drunk as cossacks. To alleviate the tedium we spend the afternoon behaving like hooligans, hitting each other and smashing plastic washing-up bowls over each other's heads, which fails to make either of us feel better, but does manage to upset a few people.

For some peace and quiet I go for a walk in the small park in the middle of Lilongwe's old town. After dark here everything smells of piss; I walk out on to some rocks in a stream, where things are slightly less stinky. But it's pitch black; however fed up I might be, falling into a river won't help. And this is an excellent place to get mugged – it's hardly wise for a lone white guy to loiter around the poorer areas of town after dark like this. Back on the road I can manage a reasonably convincing impersonation of a hard-case if necessary, but here in my present mood I look about as threatening as a lost puppy. The sooner I get walking again, the better.

Back at Annie's a group of middle-aged Sikhs arrives. They're staying in the dormitory, but spend all evening cooking on kerosene stoves in the yard right outside my tent. I want an early night; I'm not keen on trying to sleep with a big group of people talking loudly only metres away, but it can't be helped. I start climbing into my tent.

'Excuse me! Excuse me!' One of the Sikhs has better English than his companions.

'Yes?'

'My friend here likes you. He likes you *very* much. He wants you to come into bed with him …'

I'm flattered by the attention, really I am, but not tonight. I settle for my own company, keeping a lighter and a can of Doom aerosol handy, just in case I wake to find a turbaned head peering amorously through the entrance of my tent. A makeshift flame-thrower might cool his ardour.

By the standards of this journey it's a late start, but I'm delighted to be back on the road by eight the following morning.

'Ninja! Ninja!'

Several days out of Lilongwe, crossing the mountains near Ntchisi, I'm mobbed at a remote village by a hundred screaming children. The cry of *'Ninja!'* is quickly taken up by all. I've no idea if a ninja is regarded locally as a good thing or a bad thing – whether I'm in trouble or not. Few of these children have ever seen a film or television, so the mistake is understandable; even so, their sheer numbers and persistence are scary.

However much I'd like to escape, I'm forcibly reminded of just how much children enjoy themselves. Adults truly have a lot to learn, or at least I do. Although the kids here can be such a hassle, there are times when I'm feeling even at my absolute worst when they're so funny and

191

likeable they really do wipe the snarl off your face. Children can be so inventive with so little; in dozens of villages I see kids playing enthusiastic games of football with balls made from a scrunched-up polythene sheet tied with string, while other children trundle little cars and aeroplanes made from tin cans and bits of rubbish, or race down the road with a hoop and stick straight out of Dickens. While these children have almost nothing in terms of possessions, I can't help thinking they're still healthier and happier than so many kids back in England, hunched for hours over bloodthirsty computer games and Internet chatrooms, their only form of physical exercise a spot of happy slapping outside the local shopping mall.

But the kids here smile, even the teenagers.

Africans really love their children. Literally nothing is more important or precious in their society, and the lack of children is felt as a kind of death, or even as punishment from the gods. Women with many children are greatly respected in society, while in some areas those unfortunate enough to have had several miscarriages may even today be accused of witchcraft.

Livingstone's skill as a doctor inadvertently brought him into conflict with this overwhelming desire for children. He won great fame for having 'child medicine', after curing a native woman of some complaint which had baffled native doctors. Twelve months after she returned to her husband she bore a son. Livingstone recorded how the delighted woman 'proclaimed all over the country that I possessed a medicine for the cure of sterility. The consequence was, that I was teased with applications from husbands and wives from all parts of the country. Some came upwards of two hundred miles to purchase the great boon, and it was in vain for me to explain that I had only cured the disease of the other case. The more I denied, the higher their offers rose; they would give any money for the "child medicine"; and it was really heart-rending to hear the earnest entreaty, and see the tearful eye, which spoke the intense desire for offspring: "I am getting old, you see grey hairs here and there on my head, and I have no child; you know how Bechuana husbands cast their old wives away; what can I do? I have no child to bring water to me when I am sick."'[4]

Immediately after escaping from the mob of shrieking children, I become lost in Ntchisi Forest Reserve, one of the largest areas of montane forests left in Malawi. With my compass I still have a good idea of general direction, although I wish I had a machete. Perhaps it's as well I haven't, as I'd only start hacking my way even further from any existing path. Stinging plants and brambles hurt my bare legs, while the vegetation claws at my rucksack, more or less bringing me to a halt. As soon as I stop, a family of monkeys starts screaming close by, furious at my uninvited appearance.

People who have lived all their lives in dense woodlands find it hard to grasp how difficult it is for those unused to forests to keep walking in a straight line through woods without a compass. But what seems instinctive to them can be learnt easily: you pick out some conspicuous mark in the distance; as you walk towards it, pick another mark and try to keep it strictly in line with the first, and so on. It still requires practice, however, and the trees here are too dense to distinguish any noticeable landmark.

After an hour or so in the forest I see a fossilized condom hanging dejectedly from a lower branch. I regard this as a good omen – a definite sign of life, or at least of what might have been. Soon after this I stumble across signs of recent charcoal burning, which comes as a huge relief, although I've only been lost for a couple of hours. I have to laugh – this is hardly a Stanley expedition, hacking a path through the deadly Ituri rainforest.

The following morning, for the first and only time on the entire journey, I hire a guide, an eleven-year-old schoolboy called Johann. We travel together for about five kilometres up and down some very steep hillsides, during which time he doesn't say a single word or smile once. Livingstone observed on his Zambezi Expedition that the best guides were often lunatics; his party was 'often under great obligations to the madmen of the different villages: one of these honoured them, as they slept in the open air, by dancing and singing at their feet the whole night'. These poor fellows 'sympathized with the explorers, probably in the belief that they belonged to their own class; and, uninfluenced by the general opinion of their countrymen, they really pitied, and took kindly to the strangers, and often guided them faithfully from place to place, where no sane man could be hired for love nor money'.[5]

'*Muli Bwanji?*' ('How are you?') a few people shout to me. Most people I've met in Malawi so far have spoken to me only in English, and here in the uplands it comes almost as a surprise when people speak only Chichewa, the national language. But sometimes in the mountains my appearance causes real alarm. As I enter one village a kid of about twelve drops his bike in the dust with a great crash and runs off literally screaming with terror. Eventually he sees his father laughing at him, and sidles back shamefacedly. And this was in broad daylight – in uncertain light I must resemble some outlandish figure from local folk tales told to scare fractious children into obedience. Personally I think I look more like a tramp, but then I've had more time to form an opinion on this than the local people I meet for the first time at sudden bends in the path. Whenever I approach a village, most of the women and children run off in panic as if a werewolf has suddenly appeared at their gate. But if the men are similarly agitated at my arrival they usually manage to affect nonchalance, thus retaining some gravitas in the eyes of their fleeing wives.

In some ways little has changed since Livingstone's day. His appearance at African villages often caused 'an agony of terror, such as we might feel if we met a live Egyptian mummy at the door of the British Museum'. Mothers, dogs and chickens would flee in pandemonium until the villagers were 'calmed by the laughing assurance of our men, that white people do not eat black folks … Some of our young swells, on entering an African village, might experience a collapse of self-inflation, at the sight of all the pretty girls fleeing from them, as from hideous cannibals; or by witnessing the mammas holding naughty children away from them, and saying "Be good, or I shall call the white man to bite you."'[6]

I'm looking forward to my first sight of Lake Malawi, a vast inland sea the size of Wales; it's the third largest lake in Africa, and many consider it the most beautiful.

This part of the country is rich in history. For 3,000 years this western shore of the lake was home to the Akafula, Malawi's early pygmy inhabitants, and this long period was a time of peace and plenty. The Akafula were skilled hunters and fishermen; unlike the Bantu who conquered them, they even developed a form of writing. They were famous for their extreme sensitivity about their short stature; the Bantu called them the *Amwandionera Kuti*, meaning 'where did you see me?' – as this was every Akafula man's first question to a stranger. 'I saw you a long way away' was the correct response; on hearing this the Akafula man was delighted, accepting it as proof he was a big fellow after all. If the stranger was foolish or brave enough to give the wrong answer, he ran the risk of getting shot full of poisoned arrows.

The fourteenth century saw the appearance of Bantu invaders along the lakeshore, fierce and merciless warriors with cannibal tendencies. They began a war against their tiny neighbours that ended with the complete annihilation of the pygmies. According to local legend, the beating of pygmy drums can still be heard beside the lake as a warning of doom, like the banshee of Irish folklore.

After the brutal extermination of the pygmies, the shores of Lake Malawi continued through the centuries to witness dreadful violence. Even in times of comparative peace, thousands of innocent men, women and children died each year after being accused of witchcraft – burnt alive or poisoned in 'smelling-out' ceremonies. Witch doctors forced their suspects to drink a lethal cocktail made from the bark of the highly poisonous *mwavi* tree, mixed with owl and hyena excrement. The families of those failing this trial by ordeal, as inevitably most did, were killed immediately.

Eventually the Bantu Amaravi settlers along the lakeshore became almost incapacitated by bilharzia; by the time of Livingstone's arrival in the 1860s their whole society had collapsed under the insidious effects of the disease. Enemies came flocking to the lakeshore, happy to take advantage of their weakened state; after being decimated by Yao slaving gangs, the Amaravi then had to face an even more formidable enemy in the Angoni tribe, whose rapidly growing army swept north from Zululand like an unstoppable force, conquering vast swathes of central Africa. The Angoni *impis* (regiments) slaughtered everyone in their path except marriageable girls and young men who could be recruited into the army. Many Angoni settled here on the shores of Lake Malawi. Using Zulu tactics and weapons, the Angoni's highly disciplined onslaught left the Amaravi paralysed with terror; the latter made little resistance as the raids grew in scale and frequency. During this period of bloodshed only one factor worked in the Amaravi's favour: despite the Angoni's undoubted courage in battle and the fact that they now chose to live beside an enormous lake, they regarded open water with superstitious dread. Local people now saved or prolonged their lives by living in houses on stilts, or on tiny offshore islands, swimming back and forth with their cattle each day. Some escaped the Angoni merely by wading out up to their waists in the lake, leaving their pursuers on the shore.

Livingstone first came to Lake Malawi on his 1858–64 Zambezi Expedition, after his plans for the Zambezi as a navigable highway into the interior ended in fiasco on the Kebrabasa Rapids. At this time he was desperately seeking some great geographical discovery that would salvage his damaged reputation; but he was also here to report on the hated slave trade. Livingstone's arrival at the lake coincided with a period of upheaval and appalling violence in Malawi's history. While the Yao slavers brought destruction to the settlements along the southern shores of the lake, Livingstone found even worse conditions further north, where Angoni raids had left the beaches 'literally strewed with human skeletons and putrid bodies'.[7] This cycle of mindless violence was completed by the arrival of the Arab slavers at the northern end of the lake.*

Although Livingstone is often associated with the discovery of Lake Malawi, again he was not in fact the first European to come here. Like the Spanish conquistadors in South America, the Portuguese in the sixteenth century made brutal inroads into Malawi and Zimbabwe. They convinced themselves that somewhere in the interior lay hidden the fabled Ophir of Solomon, and their frenzy for gold led to years of fruitless searching, all the while decimated by the region's virulent malaria. To revenge their complete lack of success they inflicted dreadful cruelties on the natives, practising widespread murder and mutilation.

As usual, the Portuguese discoveries were little-known in England, allowing explorers like Livingstone to claim they were the first white men to visit remote areas. Livingstone's denial that the Portuguese had beaten him to Lake Malawi is absurd when his friend Candido Cardoso, the Portuguese commander at Tete, had not only visited the lake himself but actually drew a map of it for Livingstone before the latter set out. Livingstone solved this problem by convincing himself and others that Cardoso had drawn a different lake entirely – although it's clear today that on such matters Livingstone could be both disingenuous and mean-spirited towards his fellow Europeans.[8]

I spend my first night beside Lake Malawi with the inside of my tent

*See p. 217.

196

like a sauna. After descending from the cool of the mountain forests around Ntchisi this sweltering humidity is even more stifling. I lie completely still, half-expecting the tent to rise bodily into the air with me in it and float off over the lake like the Montgolfier brothers. While my insect net keeps the hordes of mosquitoes at bay, it also prevents the slightest breeze or breath of air reaching me – my body glows with heat, rivulets of sweat trickling onto my sleeping bag. But it strikes me just how efficient sweating is as a cooling mechanism, even if it does cause problems when you're trying to conserve water. Compared to the desert, this tropical heat makes it much harder to acclimatize; here it's hot twenty-four hours a day, so you can't cool down at night and let your system recuperate.

On the road north to Nkhotakota I learn that the South Africans on the polio walk are approximately one day ahead of me. Some of the local people I meet naturally assume we're part of the same team, and that I've been lagging behind. During the journey I hear of several other foreigners currently making long journeys on foot in Africa, and I guess I shouldn't think of them as 'The Opposition'. Unless of course any of them were walking exactly the same route as me – in which case I'd have to do away with them quietly in some remote corner of the bush.

A Swedish guy is walking through Africa, pushing his belongings in something resembling an ice cream cart. I think he's been walking for two years, heading south with his strange contraption, although I'm not sure exactly where he started or how far he's got. Another contender is a slightly crazy seventy-year-old American, immediately recognizable by the enormous pack he carries and that no one else can lift. His extensive gear includes four throwing knives, a bullwhip and a big staff studded with nails. Reports suggest he has a keen eye for young girls; he often stays at backpacking hostels, which tend not to cater for many seventy-year-olds, and most people who've met him seem to find him hard work.

Just before Nkhotakota, a bus roars past me with an enormous fish hanging out of the driver's window, its head pointing straight ahead and its tail quivering with the motion. I'm sorry it can't enjoy its last ride. Lake Malawi has more than 500 species of fish, more than any other lake in the world, and new species are discovered each year as more of the lake is explored. Even so, at cheap eating places along the lakeshore chambo fish are virtually the only thing on the menu; though they're reputed to make fine eating, every specimen that reaches my plate is bony and tasteless. The only other fish I encounter here are the small sardines known as *usipa*, sold in their sun-dried form in huge mounds at every market; they're too bitter and salty for my taste, and the last thing I need on the road is a raging thirst.

Often I'm perversely curious about places where terrible things have happened in history; but at Nkhotakota I find the small town itself is hot, dusty and depressing, and I feel very little desire to spend any time here at all. Even the prospect of resting for a day or two is strangely unappealing, and I want to get moving again as soon as possible. It's one of the oldest market towns in Africa. Livingstone stopped here in 1863, during his boat journey up Lake Malawi. He called it 'an abode of bloodshed and lawlessness'[9] – the town at that time functioned as a huge slaving emporium with an annual turnover of some ten thousand slaves. The numbers alone give little sense of the human tragedy taking place here over the years, with slaves herded like cattle through the town to the old dhow harbour on the lakeshore, en route to the east coast.

To most Europeans the slave trade from the east coast of Africa is far less known than that from the west coast, because of the enormous legacy of the black populations in America and the West Indies. Slaves taken east were unable to establish similar cultures, for the simple reason that most of the males had been castrated.

Livingstone made the destruction of the African slave trade his life's work; no one did more to bring home its horrors to the Victorian public. 'The subject does not admit of exaggeration,' he wrote. 'To overdraw its evils is a simple impossibility. The sights I have seen, though common incidents of the traffic, are so nauseous that I always strive to drive them from memory ... but the slaving scenes come back unbidden, and make me start up at dead of night horrified by their vividness.'[10] Livingstone estimated that for every slave captured or bought in the interior by the slaving gangs, ten were murdered; only one in five slaves survived the subsequent gruelling march to the coast, and slaving caravans drew in their wake a permanent attendance of hyenas and vultures. 'It is like sending up for a large block of ice to London in the hot weather,' wrote Livingstone's last editor, the missionary Rev. Horace Waller. 'You know that a certain amount will melt away before it reaches you. But that which remains will be quite sufficient for your needs.'[11]

The slaves who survived long enough to reach the east coast were comparatively lucky. Yet their trials were far from over: on reaching the coast at Bagamoyo only one male slave in twenty survived inexpert gelding. And even before the journey to their final destinations there was still the nightmare passage to the slave market at Zanzibar. Hundreds of slaves were packed in bamboo tiers on each tiny vessel, crammed together like rows of spoons in a kitchen drawer, with enormous loss of life.

When Livingstone arrived in Nkhotakota the town was run by the self-styled sultan Jumbe; after preaching here, Livingstone tried unsuccessfully to persuade him to abandon the slave trade. But Nkhotakota's days as a Wild West town were numbered; after Livingstone's death the British managed to stop Jumbe's slaving enterprises by drawing him into an alliance. Negotiations were settled when the pro-consul Harry Johnson offered Jumbe a subsidy of £300 a year, together with a bottle of Chartreuse and a toilet seat inscribed with Queen Victoria's initials.

Late in the afternoon after leaving Nkhotakota I suddenly find myself being interviewed by two young locals who claim to be a journalist and a press photographer. The latter starts taking my picture without so much as a by-your-leave and they both start walking along beside me. At first I'm suspicious, this having all the hallmarks of a scam to distract my attention while my gear vanishes. But a few minutes of their company convince me they're genuine, or at least well intentioned. The journalist starts writing enthusiastic notes on a slightly grubby notepad as he walks. I have to tell him my name several times; he records it as 'Foam'.

'So, Mr Foam, does the government of Malawi know about this journey?'

'I don't believe they do.'

'No! Why? I mean, why not?'

I tell him I'm sure the government has more pressing matters to deal with, which starts a hurried whispered conversation between them; after a minute or so they concur with me on this and depart, wishing me a safe journey. It makes a change to be chased by the paparazzi. But after so long on the road I'm glad there was no camera crew involved to capture on film my dishevelled appearance. Any film footage of me being interviewed would look like one of those videos of kidnap victims instructing their relatives to send the money quickly.

After four days of following the lakeshore north from Nkhotakota, I reach the campsite at Kande Beach. Popular with backpackers and people travelling on the overland trucks, it's still a relaxing spot and very beautiful. The water here is extraordinarily clear, and of a surprisingly intense blue; even better, bilharzia is not a serious problem on this part of the lake, largely because of the action of the waves (bilharzia snails prefer still waters). After the heat of the last few weeks it's marvellous to swim, the first time I've been able to do so on the entire journey so far. I'm enjoying it so much that I consider the possibility of swimming out to tiny Kande Island, which lies temptingly close offshore, but decide against it – I don't want to get washed ashore at Cape Maclear, 300 kilometres to the south.

I prop up the bar at Kande and talk to Dave, a likeable English guy who runs the campsite. He tells me about a rare but memorable natural phenomenon found on Lake Malawi, the aquatic equivalent of a dust devil, a moving column of water spray moving rapidly over the lake surface. This apocryphal freak of nature was last seen at Kande the previous year, when the site was far from complete, and the toilets were mere holes in the ground surrounded by grass shelters. The column of spray raced on to dry land and made straight for the toilets, flattening the grass shelters before moving on swiftly, inevitably leaving in its wake at least one open-mouthed individual with his trousers round his ankles at the time.

Dave has recently built a fence around the campsite, largely to keep out snakes; prior to this, a number of dangerous specimens have been caught here, including green and black mambas and even a big python. While the snakes have taken the hint and no longer venture into the site, other unwelcome creatures still appear occasionally in the neighbour-hood – after all, this is Africa. Earlier this year a big crocodile swam down the Kande River to the lake and attacked a local fisherman at the campsite. At the time of the attack, the fisherman had been sobering up after a massive Chibuku binge; remembering he'd left his nets out while still drunk, he started gathering them in. His impressive hangover must have reduced his awareness of his immediate surroundings, for he completely failed to notice the stealthy approach of a large saurian swimming gently towards him. He certainly noticed it when the crocodile seized him by the leg, nearly tearing it off.

Crocodiles bite in a completely different manner to sharks. A shark's teeth are razor sharp and slice through its prey cleanly, biting off great mouthfuls of flesh, while a crocodile's teeth are designed to hold on tightly while the crocodile drowns its dinner. They can't chew, either; to bite off parts of its victim, the crocodile gets a good grip with its teeth and then spins its whole body in the water by thrashing its tail, tearing off limbs or pieces of living flesh rather than biting through it cleanly. Sometimes crocodiles work as a pair, one holding the unfortunate animal while the other does the dismembering. They generally like to leave their drowned prey for several weeks in their nests before eating it, preferring their dinner slightly high.

When crocodiles attack they move at amazing speed, exploding from the water like a rocket. Sometimes I find merely looking at an African river or lake uncomfortable, imagining some reptilian nemesis dragging me off to its lair. There's something so *primeval* about crocodiles: the species has been around since the dinosaur age, retaining all the ferocity of mythological water dragons. Despite this, crocodiles are remarkably tender parents; in some parts of Africa turtles deliberately lay their eggs near crocodile nests, and the mother crocodiles are so programmed to nurture any small creature emerging from an egg that they gently carry the newly hatched turtles down to the water. This process saves the adult turtles a great deal of time and trouble, not to mention personal risk in areas with a large crocodile population.

While crocodiles kill hundreds of people in Africa each year, the local people have learnt to live with the danger and often bathe in crocodile areas. This strikes me as reckless – yet if the people here were to visit London or New York they might wonder how people could possibly live with so much dangerous traffic careering around and all the cancerous pollution choking the air. After all, more people die from road accidents and the effects of pollution than ever get eaten by crocodiles.

This reassuring thought would have done little to encourage the Kande fisherman while he crawled up the beach with his leg more or less hanging off and a big crocodile in hot pursuit. Hearing his frantic yells the people from the campsite rushed to the man's assistance; the dogs living on the beach also came at a run to investigate the commotion. Domestic dogs in Malawi often vanish in crocodile areas, and crocodiles can develop quite a taste for them but without a second thought the Kande beach dogs attacked the crocodile, which beat a hasty retreat back to the lake. I find it extraordinary that a few dogs could chase off a large hungry crocodile, one that only moments before had already sunk its teeth into its lunch. However, the beach dogs here are unusually fierce when crossed, especially when they're in a pack, and I don't blame the crocodile for suddenly remembering urgent business elsewhere.

The fisherman made a complete recovery; his leg was stitched up, and worked perfectly well again after several weeks' rest and a good few nights drinking out on the story.

The most popular handicraft in Malawi is a distinctive carved chair, made from two interlocking pieces of timber. Shortly before I arrive at Kande, when a girl from an overland truck tried to buy such a chair, her attempts to negotiate a reasonable price triggered off a local tragedy. A slightly sinister local wood-carver with a crippled leg had just started trading in the area. Dave felt sorry for the man on account of his physical problem, and allowed him to set up his stall outside the campsite. Spotting a particularly attractive Malawi chair among his selection, the girl from the truck thought the woodcarver's asking price steep, and attempted to bargain with him. To everyone's surprise the woodcarver merely called the deal off; giving the girl a fierce and meaningful glare he announced he had to go without delay into the forest with his wife to chop more wood for his future carvings.

It transpired later that the woodcarver's personal life was a tragedy waiting to happen. Quite apart from his bad leg, all was far from well in his household; a particular bone of contention was his wife's habit of sleeping with every available man in the village. While hunting for suitable wood in the forest, the woodcarver finally decided that his personal problems could never be resolved. Abandoning all further thoughts of chopping wood, instead he chopped his unfortunate wife to pieces.

Starting back towards Kande with a blood-spattered panga in his hand, he shouted to anyone he passed on the way home that he intended to deal with his infant daughter in a similar fashion. Thankfully someone managed to reach the village minutes ahead of him, and the neighbours were able to hide the baby girl just in time. Thwarted in his plans for murdering his daughter as well, the luckless woodcarver took a coil of rope and limped straight back to the woods, where he promptly hanged himself.

Overland trucks filled with young travellers arrive daily at Kande. Travelling alone, I like to observe the dynamics on these group expeditions, to see what I'm missing on my own journey. They're definitely not for me, with everything arranged for you and countless decisions made on your behalf, often well in advance. On the really long truck expeditions it must be difficult to travel for weeks or months in such close proximity with others – sometimes the passengers split into cliques, which in extreme cases turn into virtual Cold Wars of mutual mistrust and refusal to share cooking utensils. But in defence of these overland trips, they clearly have real potential for character-building; inevitably, good as well as bad qualities come out when people are thrown together with individuals they can't simply ignore for months on end. And if they're lucky with their fellow passengers, many people thrive on the sociability. I still don't fancy it myself, though – I suspect I'd get bundled off the truck before the end of the first week. Even so, I admire people who are laid-back enough to risk travelling for weeks or months with people they've never met before. The problem of course is not knowing how you'll get on with your companions until it's too late.

While today the choice of fellow travellers usually means nothing worse than a crap holiday if you get it wrong, in the time of the explorers the issue was more serious, sometimes turning into a matter of life or death. Livingstone usually avoided the problem by choosing not to travel with fellow Europeans – the occasions on which he did were usually disastrous. Stanley received huge numbers of applicants eager to join any expedition he led; for his first traversa over 1,200 men from several countries applied, including three generals and five colonels. While outlining their suitability for the expedition, many boasted how streetwise they were and 'up to every dodge'; others offered to take Stanley up in balloons or by flying carriages; a train driver suggested he and Stanley cross darkest Africa in comfort by means of a tram and locomotive, both of which he was qualified to drive. A Frenchman offered to interpret at all the hotels the safari stayed in each night, while several applicants proposed to make Stanley's expedition invisible by magic arts and use the 'science of magnetism' to make all the savages fall asleep so they could pass unhindered. One man claimed expert knowledge in poisons, and suggested that instead of paying tribute as they crossed tribal lands they should instead 'poison all the nigger chiefs'. Another candidate thought he and Stanley would do best to cross Africa in disguise, alone and unarmed, with their faces blackened up like music-hall negroes. Eventually the exasperated Stanley picked three individuals he knew already.[12]

When I leave Kande, one of the overland trucks gives me a lift the three kilometres back to the main road, to the point where I stopped walking. The people on this particular truck are very friendly, and their truck is extremely comfortable; this is the first time I've been inside one. Right now I can see the appeal of travelling in this way, and it's remarkably difficult to get out of the vehicle once more into the late morning heat to carry on walking with my heavy rucksack. But soon I'm back into my stride.

The following day, after a pleasant stretch through lush woodland I reach Nkhata Bay. One of a series of small connected bays, Nkhata gets its name from a Chichewa word for a grass head-ring: the shape of the bay was thought to resemble the curve of such a ring. Today it's more like a large village than what you might expect from a busy African fishing port. Westerners often wax lyrical about Nkhata Bay, calling it 'the Caribbean of Malawi', but scenically I think this is an exaggeration – if anything I'd prefer a deserted stretch of lakeshore with a couple of local dugout canoes gliding past in silence. But it's a laid-back place, especially as it's now the hot season, and hugely popular with backpackers diving and kayaking on the lake or just spending weeks here getting stoned while the world goes by. For once on this journey there's a huge choice of Western food and cheap accommodation; I pitch my tent at The Backpacker's Connection, a busy hostel right on the lakeshore.

In the evening I start talking to a small group sitting in the back yard, two Australians and an Israeli backpacker with an unpronounceable name. One of the Australians is a rather irritating fellow in his early thirties, who having travelled continuously for the last eight years regards himself as an authority on every aspect of independent travel, constantly spouting travel tips like a walking guidebook. He even looks like a bespectacled school swot. Because he's travelled for such a long time, some of the newer arrivals here defer to him slightly. Obviously I'm not up for this, so he visibly bristles on learning the nature of my trip, presumably thinking I might steal some of his thunder. He then pointedly avoids any reference to my journey, skirting around the subject with impressive verbal dexterity – particularly as I deliberately keep setting him up to say at least *something* on the subject. I admire his tenacity; eventually we call it an honourable draw and change the subject, which he promptly changes back again to his own travel tips, and why such-and-such a hostel's banana pancakes are infinitely superior to those of another, or which backpacker café sells under-the-counter 'space cake' just like Mother used to make. At one point he spouts on about how much nicer South America is compared to Africa. Everything in South America is better and more interesting, the scenery more spectacular, the food nicer, the girls prettier – there's even 'more history'. I ask him to explain this last point.

'Well, in South America you have the Conquistadors and the Incas, of course.'

So what? Personally, I find the history of the Conquistadors and the Incas fascinating, but what have they got to do with Africa? If South America is so much better in every way than Africa, why doesn't he just clear off on the next flight?

'But Africa has history too.' I offer some examples.

'Oh well, I suppose so …'

Thankfully, the two Aussies go off for a meal, and I cajole the Israeli guy into joining me in propping up the bar. He's chronically shy, and would prefer us to remain sitting in solitude in the near-darkness out the back, but I can't be doing with all that – near a bar there's always the chance some gorgeous woman will appear, you never know. I head straight back to the bar and he follows me. We talk about Israeli history, and he seems astonished that I know anything about his country's past. He's a nice guy, but it's not a great night. A wine bottle standing on the bar buzzes in sympathy to the deafening music, and connected thought becomes difficult. Sleep is totally out of the question; I lie in my tent while the ground beneath me throbs in time to Radiohead.

The following morning I move to a quieter African-owned hostel, which proves so utterly soporific that I spend the evening in a lodge bar a kilometre down the lakeshore. Getting home again proves unexpectedly complicated; it's almost impossible to find my way through this inky blackness, and I'm so pissed I can't tell if a high-pitched shrieking is a cat some distance away or a mosquito right next to my eardrum. I can't remember from passing this way in daylight if there are any sheer drops next to the coastal path; when I reach a bridge of tree trunks over a big dip in the road I've no idea if it's a long way down or not – there's literally no way of seeing what's below me. In my present state, it's frightening.

Somehow I reach the village in one piece, but I still can't find the hostel. Then a figure suddenly lurches out of a doorway right in front of me. I'm convinced I'm being mugged – security along this stretch of the lake is very poor, and several people have been shot dead recently during robberies. Yet he turns out to be a friendly local drunk, and gives me directions most courteously, which saves me from sleeping in the street.

Once inside my room I notice a dozen or so big ants running around. Immediately going on the offensive, I start spraying them with Doom Insect Spray. The more I spray, the more ants appear, until hundreds are swarming over my floor, and now they're cross. Being drunk, I use the entire can of spray in one tiny room. I remember nothing past this point, presumably having fainted from the heady cocktail of Doom and drink.

I wake up around midday, vaguely surprised I'm still alive. When I open the side pocket of my rucksack, a cloud of mosquitoes swarms out, like the inmates of Pandora's box – they must have sheltered in there while I ran amok with Doom. I can't see a single dead ant on the floor; I suspect they only ran off to regroup, and they'll be back in force tonight to get me.

One particularly noticeable character staying at Nkhata Bay at this time is a crazy English cyclist called Dan, another individual who has been on the road in the sun so long that his brain no longer functions properly. He once spent some time in the British army, which clearly did little to help his mental state. Now in his late thirties he tends to talk utter nonsense, usually on the subject of African incompetence compared to what he calls 'English know-how'. Again, if everything here is so awful, why doesn't he clear off back to England and leave everyone here in peace? Obviously he's not so mad as all that, having discovered he can live on the road in Africa very cheaply indeed. And anyone who's met Dan could think of reasons why he might be less than welcome back in his home country, where the authorities would at least compel him to wear a tracking device.

The usual morning protocol at backpackers' hostels is for people to sit around the breakfast table, smoking and talking shit, or sometimes the other way around. Most people nurse hangovers to a greater or lesser degree, so tend to avoid intense or profound discussion of any kind. Such a typical conversation is proceeding lethargically one morning at the hostel when Crazy Dan charges in yelling: 'MY MOTHER GIVES ME LOTS OF MONEY!'

This conversational gambit falling flat, three American backpackers staying here regard this as the last straw. Their aversion to Dan now manifests itself in plans to sabotage his bike. Their planned modifications start with some radical work to the wheels, before sawing the handlebars down to about ten centimetres each side and then replacing the brake levers; cunning adjustments to the saddle will ensure it falls off as soon as Dan climbs on board so the seat pillar sticks right up his arse. If after all this mayhem the poor guy actually manages to get his bike moving at all, the chainset and wheel hubs are set to explode in a hail of ball bearings before he's covered fifty metres down the road. The Americans give a great deal of thought to this, drawing up several blueprints on the backs of fag packets. Fortunately they abandon this rather juvenile scheme when they realize that, if carried out successfully, it would only mean Dan staying here longer. I hope for his sake Dan decides to move on soon – if he remains here much longer it's only a matter of time before he really does get bludgeoned in his bed.

On the beach at Nkhata Bay you're constantly pestered by kids selling postcards or offering to wash your clothes. These children are easy to handle if from the word go you refuse categorically, but if at any point you show the slightest interest in their wares or services you'll get no peace for the remainder of your stay. This is a shame, as some of the postcards are very good; they're also cheap, and the kids selling them are poor. Most of the postcards are so well thumbed they're falling to pieces. Often the kids claim they painted them themselves, which is hard to believe when the picture in question shows a high degree of artistic ability and the child trying to sell it to you is five or six at the most. It's even harder to believe when you know the man who does draw them, a sort of local Fagin who sends the children out doing the rounds with his artwork.

'I can't believe you're walking across Africa,' says Irene, an attractive Dutch girl, as I sit reading on the beach one afternoon. 'You sit there so quietly every day.'

What am I supposed to do to establish my credibility – run around screaming all day or dance on the beach like a whirling dervish? Most of the time I just want to sit in the shade and read. Sometimes I find myself slightly compromised when people I meet express admiration for the tough way I'm travelling. Throughout the journey people I meet keep telling me I'm so modest about it all, but this is not the whole truth. I am actually rather proud of what I'm doing. On the trip so far I've yet to meet anyone travelling with anything approaching the discomfort and hard work of my trip – even the long-distance cyclists don't have to work this hard, and walking these huge distances does create a sense of having earned my right to be here.

My days at Nkhata Bay are quiet and restful, but I'm not at all happy here. I begin to realize how stressful backpacking venues can be when you're travelling alone – sometimes it feels like they revolve around everything I came to Africa to get away from, and I have to ask myself if I really want to be here at all. You never know if you'll meet someone wonderful at one of these places; but sometimes I wonder if I was staying in one place for a while, having a relationship with someone nice, would I bother spending my evenings in such places? More likely I'd be at home in bed, either with the nice person or with a good book, or preferably both, ideally with some oat porridge on the boil in the background.

But here I am, three-quarters of the way across Africa, eight months since I set out from the Skeleton Coast. I still have to question my motivation in crossing Africa on foot. If I succeed I'll have done something few people have done, and not everyone could do. I might consider this trip one of the highlights of my life – I bloody well hope so, after all this backbreaking work. I remind myself I'm not here to have a good time, I'm here to try to do something out of the ordinary, to walk across Africa, and whether that involves having a good time or not is almost irrelevant.

Stanley claimed he 'was not sent into the world to be happy, nor to search for happiness'.[13] While I think this is a daft philosophy for any intelligent person to carry around with them, I'm beginning to understand what he meant – and at times on this journey I'm coming dangerously close to his way of thinking. But at least Stanley found the whole issue clear-cut. He was always acutely aware of the marked contrast between his responses to England and Africa: 'One brings me an inordinate amount of secret pain, the other sapped my strength but left my mind expanded and was purifying.'[14]

I need to get back on the road as quickly as possible, before it all gets even more pompous. Livingstone's words sum up my situation: 'Nothing is so much to be dreaded as inactivity ... to have gone mooning about, in listless idleness, would have ensured fever in its worst form, and probably with fatal results.'[15] While I can't really picture the great doctor 'mooning about', it's a powerful image. I've spent over a week resting at Kande and Nkhata Bay, and the road to the east coast is a long one, over 1,300 kilometres.

But despite the distance ahead, leaving Nkhata Bay comes as a huge relief to me on every level.

14. Kombwe Lagoon
(Malawi: Nkhata Bay to Kombwe Lagoon)

On the Upper Shire Valley, a man, after favouring us with some queer geographical remarks, followed us for several days. The Makololo became very much annoyed with him, for he proclaimed in every village we entered – 'These people have wandered; they do not know where they are going.' In vain did they scold and order him away. As soon as we started, he appeared again in the line of march, with his little bag over his shoulder, containing all his worldly gear, and as ready with his uncalled-for remarks as before. Every effort failed to drive him away, until at length the happy expedient was hit on, of threatening to take him down to the river and wash him; he at once made off, and we saw him no more.

David Livingstone, *Expedition to the Zambesi*

The first stretch out of Nkhata Bay involves a big climb through wooded hills towards the Nyika Plateau. Since passing Nkhotakota I've followed the humid lakeshore north for over 200 kilometres, so I want to walk through the cooler uplands for a change. Unfortunately I still have to get there first. Having smoked heavily and drunk like a fish for the last few weeks, my breathing is hampered and my energy levels frustratingly low. But at least climbing hills with a big pack is just what I need to get back in shape.

This is the hot dry season in Malawi, with the sun's rays more directly overhead than at any other time of the year. I sweat more in this one day than I have ever done before, even back in the Namib Desert – between mid-morning and nightfall I drink nearly nine litres of water without pissing once. Despite my bandanna, sweat drips from the end of my nose, drip, drip, drip; it stings my eyes so I can hardly see, and my clothes are completely sodden. But at least I've got plenty to eat – Livingstone's party became lost here for days while exploring the same hills, and nearly starved to death as a result.

After several days on the road again I start on the path up towards the old mission station of Livingstonia. Away from the lake and on higher ground, the weather now turns pleasantly cool. It's still difficult to find somewhere to camp; eventually I pitch my tent in the dark behind some half-finished building in the middle of a dry and dusty field. 'Hello, sir!' a voice calls softly, right outside my tent. I keep quiet; in any case, a disembodied voice issuing from my tent would sound ridiculous. Fortunately my mystery guest departs without further attempts at conversation.

In the 1960s this part of Malawi was home to a famous diviner called Chikanga ('Little Guineafowl'), whose skill and fame were such that even people from neighbouring countries travelled hundreds of miles to consult him. It was whispered that Chikanga had risen from the dead, and that God had ordered him to stamp out witchcraft in Africa. Chikanga could quickly diagnose the nature of any patient's ailment, and also the identity of the sorcerer who caused the problem; he would then summon the sorcerer to his presence by magical means for a thorough ritual cleansing. Any suspected sorcerers rash enough to ignore this summons found themselves racked with excruciating pains until they obeyed. Whatever the truth behind Chikanga's reputation, his medical practice had a real impact on local agriculture: the neighbouring farmers had to start growing extra food just to feed the rising numbers of pilgrims arriving daily.[1]

Late in the afternoon I stop at a restaurant for the usual *nsima*, here served with *kapenta*, the tiny bitter sardine-like fish sold by the heap at local markets. A conversation ensues with a friendly middle-aged drunkard. 'You are not married?' he demands, his eyebrows disappearing under the brim of his sun-faded pork-pie hat. 'Then you are just a boy!' Most Africans take marriage and family seriously, and consider a single man past his early twenties as someone to be regarded with either sympathy or suspicion.

Working hard for the rest of the day I make good progress. Only a few kilometres short of Livingstonia it starts to rain. After eight months I'd almost forgotten what it's like to be rained on; at first it's pleasant, but after ten minutes the novelty wears off as my gear becomes drenched. I camp beside a gurgling brook that during the night's downpour turns into a fast-flowing stream. I expect in the morning I'll have to get up in a downpour and pack my gear soaking wet – but there's something so enjoyable about being snug in a tent while it pours down outside, whatever you have to face the following day. In the morning I take a steep and slippery shortcut to the top of the plateau. It's still raining heavily, the sky the colour of lead.

The mission station at Livingstonia was founded in the 1890s by the Free Church of Scotland. The small town today has a slightly weird atmosphere, like suddenly walking into a village in Scotland a century ago. The old red-brick buildings convey a strong feeling of past mission-ary endeavour, but the people living here now are black, the white folks having moved on to spiritual pastures new. Even so, I still feel as though I've entered a late-Victorian novel; I half expect some old black guy with frizzy muttonchop whiskers to stomp into town complaining loudly about problems with his flock.

I stop for breakfast at the old and atmospheric Stone House, built by Dr Robert Laws, the founder of the mission station here. Today the building serves as a rest house and the town's museum. The interior itself is like a museum's depiction of a nineteenth-century Scottish house, with heavy wooden Victorian furniture and an unmistakable air of gloom and restraint. Despite this the Stone House is usually popular with backpackers, although today I'm the only white person here. Chewing through an extra thick pancake, I wait for my sodden clothes to dry on me while a succession of besuited black ministers troop past my table, and I consider the sobering implications of the prominent sign: 'No alcohol to be consumed on the premises at any time!' This is completely reasonable; I understand and respect their attitude. But I've arrived cold and soaked, and I'm in no mood for rules and regulations; I'd rather have a party later, even if it's by myself in my own tent.

I leave the town in pelting rain, the paths wet and slippery, the vegetation around me lush and dense. On clear days the views from Livingstonia across the escarpment are staggering, with even the Living-stone Mountains in Tanzania visible on the other side of Lake Malawi. Unfortunately today the mist and heavy downpour have reduced visibil-ity to a hundred metres or so. I've found Livingstonia depressing – although in fairness I don't feel as bad as the hundreds of dead frogs lying on every path around town, as if they've fallen from the skies in some biblical curse.

The road down from Livingstonia is steep, the short cuts between its hairpin bends even steeper; after trying to save walking a few extra hundred metres, I find they're much harder work than sticking to the road and also provide an excellent opportunity to break your ankle, particularly when carrying a heavy pack. A number of Westerners have been beaten up and robbed on this road in recent years, although on the way down I don't see a soul, criminally inclined or otherwise.

As I descend the climate changes astonishingly quickly, from cool and breezy on the plateau to hot and clammy beside the lake. It's like walking down a long natural staircase into the steam room of a sauna. The difference between the climate here and that of the Namib Desert brings it home forcibly to me that I've walked a hell of a long way to get this far. The chilly fog on the Skeleton Coast and the freezing nights near Grootfontein seem a world away from here. It's not the first time on the trip I've felt I'm making real progress, but now there's a conviction that goals are being reached and ideas are becoming reality. Until now that's all they were, just ideas. Grogan's men experienced something similar, although in their case it was due more to their belief in Grogan as a magician, even though in two years of travelling they must have realized he was essentially no different from them. In Malawi Grogan spoke of the snow-capped mountains, volcanoes and huge lakes ahead on his intended route, and even of the wonders of Cairo. During the long journey north his men saw all these things appear, and concluded that he had put them there.[2]

I continue north up the lakeshore while the leaden sky flings down sheets of heavy rain. The Livingstonia side of the Nyika Plateau towers over the lake, dark and brooding with an almost gothic grandeur as the rain thunders down until mid-afternoon.

I make good progress today, over forty-five kilometres. But it's still not easy to find somewhere discreet to camp unobserved. Peering through the bushes in darkness to check out a likely spot, a thorn painfully catches my eyelid. I could have sworn I was stationary when it happened, and there's no breath of wind stirring – it's as if the bush attacked me, taking a swipe when it thought I wasn't looking.

On the road to Karonga I find myself decidedly grumpy with the locals. I get absolutely no peace, and I'm dog-tired; when I stop I need to

213

be alone, otherwise I just can't bloody rest. The need for shade and peace and quiet becomes all-consuming – meeting strangers at such times, however nice and friendly they may be, hardly makes for relaxation. One man pesters me so relentlessly when I'm trying to rest under a tree in the middle of nowhere that I get genuinely angry, jumping to my feet and stomping off swearing; alarmed, he beats a hasty retreat in the opposite direction. As soon as I've moved on I feel extremely guilty – if I saw this fellow again I'd apologize for my behaviour, for which there was no excuse. And later the same day, as evening approaches, a local guy appears and with great natural courtesy stops ten metres or so away from where I'm sitting.

'Are you all right, sir?'

'Yes, I'm fine, thank you.'

'I thought you might need some assistance with food …'

I feel even guiltier about my earlier grumpiness.

At the next village, about forty kilometres before Karonga, the people are so friendly it's embarrassing. While downing a lukewarm Coca-Cola at a local stall I talk to one particularly jolly fellow named Happy, who could hardly be a miserable sod with a name like that – people would laugh.

The insect world has lately intruded more and more on my journey. Giant ants have by now dined so thoroughly on my tent that the groundsheet resembles a string vest; they've also started on my straw hat, and it seems only a matter of time before they start on me. Sometimes I'm amazed just how painful the bite of a tiny insect can be, especially when the insect in question is minute and its proboscis or whatever does the damage is microscopic – it can still feel like a hot needle jabbed into your flesh. Big dragonflies hover above the road like tiny helicopters, and they're *loud*; I wonder what they're saying to each other. The mosquitoes here are remarkably agile, capable of more complicated aerobatic manoeuvres than those further west. Back in Zambia and Caprivi the mosquitoes were comparatively easy to swat, but not these ones. Here, their characteristic high-pitched whine at night sounds more like an attack from tiny Stukas.

By now I've cursed mosquitoes more than any other living thing in my life before. If the little bastards are going to give me malaria, why can't they do it quietly? In fairness, I don't hate all mosquitoes; I don't have a problem with the males as it's only the females that bite, needing the protein from blood to produce eggs. Their humming wings, vibrating at anything up to 500 beats per second, are designed to attract amorous males; inside my tent they also attract a shoe or a rolled-up newspaper. They're particularly fond of biting the tops of my feet, where it's easy for them to tap straight into a vein. Mosquito bites are fiendishly itchy, and scratching them only makes them worse; on your insteps this becomes a real problem when you have to walk big distances each day.

'What is my name?'

Children often approach me without preamble and ask this Rumpel-stiltskin-like question. At other times they shout 'Good morning, teacher!' to me. Often the kids here are good fun; at other times it's *awful*, when they descend like harpies in shrieking pandemonium.

When a complete stranger falls in step right behind me without a word, it feels anything but companionable. It's like working at a desk and someone you've never seen before coming up behind you to stand in silence peering over your shoulder. On the road to Karonga one kid rides his bike a metre or two behind me in complete silence for several kilometres, keeping at exactly the pace I'm going without speaking or smiling, or even changing his expression. He doesn't seem to be enjoying this any more than I am. It's like a human shadow: if I stop, he stops; if I smile or speak to him, he looks back blankly. If I walk back a few paces behind him, he waits until I start again then falls in behind me once more. I nearly offer him money to go away. It's like Chinese water torture; before long it becomes so maddening I consider taking the wheels off his bike or just ramming a fallen branch through his spokes. But finally he departs, still without having spoken a single word or smiled once.

Sleeping in dry riverbeds is generally very unwise, but the night before I reach Karonga I take the risk: the prospect of a quiet secluded place to camp for once is just too tempting. I drift off to sleep remembering that enough people have drowned in flash floods through doing the same thing; all it takes is a particularly heavy rainstorm a few kilometres upstream. But the danger if any on this occasion comes from a different source. I'm woken by the meaty thump of an axe biting into living wood right outside my tent. A local man is busy chopping down a tree, which looks about ready to topple over directly on to my tent; judging by the slightly wild look of the fellow, this might even have been his intention. I make myself scarce.

On the outskirts of Karonga I sit outside a little shop, eating a slurp as I watch the world go by. A cow stands patiently on the opposite side of the road, minding its own business; a local guy approaches, and for no apparent reason gives the cow a hefty kick as he passes, then turns and grins at me. What am I supposed to do, applaud politely? The cow's response is to give the man an incredibly *human* look – intelligent, dignified and full of pathos. It's as though it's saying: 'Look, I may only be a cow, but it's still not fair for you to kick me just because you feel like it.' For a few moments I toy with the idea of crossing the road and giving the guy a similar kick in the arse. But then he might turn out to be the local madman; you never know with these local squabbles. And if we started rolling around on the ground brawling, the cow might enter the fray on the guy's side and give me a good trampling for interfering – such things happen in domestic arguments.

Karonga itself is dusty and dull, quiet to the point of being soporific. The combination of heat, glaring sunlight and dust seems oddly oppressive – it's like Nkhotakota again, and even though it's a town and therefore comfortable I feel no urge to linger here. The only splash of colour is the market, where stalls sell big clusters of brightly coloured plastic carrier bags. Lake Malawi is the fourth deepest in the world, lying in an enormous trough formed by the Great Rift Valley; but the lake is so shallow here that I have to wade out some distance before I can swim. I'm worried I'll cut my foot on a sharp stone and be laid up here for weeks, but I'll take the risk – there's no way I'm not going to swim while I've got the chance, particularly as this will be my last sight of Lake Malawi (the lake is nearly 600 kilometres long but I'm very close to its northern end). If things go according to plan the next big expanse of water I see will be the Indian Ocean.

Back on the road again, a couple of kilometres north out of Karonga I pass the Kombwe Lagoon, heavily reeded and already dazzling in the mid-morning sun. The fertile region and its inhabitants greatly impressed the early explorers of Lake Malawi; Joseph Thomson, arriving in

1878, felt he'd 'fallen upon some enchanted place ... a perfect Arcadia about which idyllic poets have sung'.[3] But the lagoon was also the scene of a gruesome massacre, a Victorian My Lai that sparked off a little-remembered war between the Arab slavers and the British.

The local Nkonde tribe had been ill prepared for this calamity. Far removed from the wholescale violence so common further down the lakeshore, they had enjoyed years of peace and plenty. By the time of Thomson's visit they had for years avoided attack from both the Angoni and the Yao slavers; but in the 1880s the Nkonde faced an enemy even crueller than the Angoni, with the arrival of the evil slave trader Mlozi.

Mlozi's slaving gangs had made him a fortune elsewhere in slaves and ivory, but he realized he would always be thwarted by any European presence at the northern end of the lake. He decided therefore to demonstrate his growing power by massacring the Nkonde. On 27 October 1887, Mlozi's Arabs arrived at the Kombwe Lagoon and opened fire on the villagers gathered here; they then set fire to the surrounding reeds. Many who escaped the bullets were burnt to death, while others were devoured by crocodiles drawn to the slaughter. The Nkonde's chief witch doctor was unfortunate enough to fall into Mlozi's hands alive: tied to a raft laden with pieces of bloody goat meat, he was pushed out into the lake, and Mlozi watched with delight as the man was torn to pieces by crocodiles.

Mlozi's Arabs then besieged the European fortress at Karonga; the defenders were forced to abandon the fort, leaving enormous spoils for the slavers. After Mlozi's initial successes, what had now become a full-blown war with the British took a new turn only with the arrival at the lake of Captain Frederick Lugard, later to become one of the colonial statesmen of East Africa.

At this early stage of his career, however, Lugard was half-crazed with grief, having recently discovered his intended bride in the arms of a rival suitor. A heroic death in some forgotten corner of the African interior would be the perfect balm to his woes, and dry and dusty Karonga – depressing at the best of times – seemed purpose-made. But aside from his patently suicidal tendencies, or even partly because of them, Lugard was to prove a highly courageous and able commander. His first priority was to make rapid improvements in his men's training and morale. To his frustration Lugard found most of his native levies incapable of firing a rifle with one eye closed, and it was difficult to convince them that the bullet's velocity did not depend on how hard you pulled the trigger. Whenever Lugard gave the order to lie down under cover, his troops immediately fell asleep; he also found it almost impossible to persuade his men that the object of the war was not capturing nubile women.

Despite these obstacles, things soon improved sufficiently under Lugard's command for him to proceed with his attack on Mlozi's fort at Mpande. Unfortunately Lugard's own kamikaze brand of courage far outstripped that of his men. Leading the charge up to the stockade walls – four metres high, interlaced with thorns and mounted with severed heads – Lugard suddenly realized he was completely alone. A lesser or more rational commander might well have decided at this point that he'd done his bit, and retreated as best he could to make some alternative plan. Instead, Lugard proceeded to scale the stockade alone, his mad solo assault ending only when an Arab marksman shot him at point blank range. This single musket ball entered and exited Lugard's right elbow, chest and left wrist in no fewer than six different places, but failed to finish him off. Ten hours later, having nearly bled to death, Lugard crawled into Fort Karonga more dead than alive. His ghastly appearance was made even more startling by a bright red tam-o'-shanter he was wearing; this, he explained, was a gift from a friendly native he met during his excruciating crawl to safety.

Lugard's life hung in the balance for weeks. During this time he was completely paralysed, suffering agonies from his wounds and from malaria, as well as from the residual pangs of unrequited love. To make things worse, during the attack on Fort Karonga he had carried in his breast pocket a few treasured love letters from his unfaithful lover; the Arab's bullet had exploded these into his body, so even months later the unfortunate Lugard was still picking tiny shreds of writing paper from his arm. His perilous state of health eventually forced Lugard to return home, leaving the war in the hands of others; but he had won great respect and affection from his troops.

Mlozi was finally defeated when the proconsul Harry Johnson took command of the forces against him. Johnson hanged Mlozi before his captured fortress; vicious and devious during his lifetime, Mlozi nonetheless met his own fate with courage and dignity.[4]

15. To Go With Ghosts
(Tanzania: Malawi Border to Mbuyuni)

The sight of a white man always infuses a tremor into their dark
bosoms ... they appeared immensely relieved when I had fairly
passed, without having sprung upon them.

David Livingstone, *Missionary Travels*

I've been in Malawi for nearly two months when I reach the Tanzanian
border. Here I nearly get arrested for having spent the last three weeks
in Malawi illegally. I explain to the border officials that this is not entirely
my fault: thirty days earlier I'd reported to a police station to extend my
visitor's status. The senior policeman there – who had lots of medals and
stripes, a big impressive teak desk, and even a framed photo of himself
shaking hands with the president – neglected to tell me that the exten-
sion he gave me was worthless.

I feel more philosophical than alarmed. In theory it doesn't matter if
I get deported from Malawi, providing of course I'm forcibly expelled in
the direction of Tanzania. Getting fined, jailed or repatriated would
prove more problematic. Fortunately I manage to convince the officials
I'm a kindred spirit by feigning a keen interest in football, and they
pardon me.

At the border I cross the narrow River Songwe, gliding past sluggishly,
the colour of caramel pudding. On the Tanzanian side, dozens of guys
compete fruitlessly to give me a ride on the back of their pushbikes,
ignoring the size and obvious weight of my rucksack. These cycle couriers
seem to have ousted normal taxis from the market. They certainly earn
their money; the uphill climb from the border is hard enough work on
foot, with the heat bouncing off the tarmac, the distant trees and bushes
shimmering. The hill itself prevents any cooling breeze from reaching
me, which makes it even more pleasurable to reach the top and breathe
normally again.

As usual when I enter a new country, I notice subtle changes from the one I've just left. Tanzanian coins feel surprisingly heavy in my pocket – such things are immediately noticeable when you walk everywhere. Local agriculture looks highly organized, with mile after mile of well-ordered tea plantations stretching into the distance. Everything seems lush and verdant, although the houses are uninspiring mud-brick affairs, completely uniform and depressing, and far less attractive than the nicely painted huts of Zambia and Malawi. Tanzanian ants seem fiercer than their counterparts further west, and display a keen interest in biting me as well as my tent. And some of them are *big*, with the physiques of insect bodybuilders. Several species of spider here are very able jumpers, too; in fact, virtually every creepy-crawly I've seen this side of the border appears to be an athlete of some kind. One of the few slothful varieties I encounter is a giant centipede, best part of a foot long, which takes up temporary residence in my hat.

The nights grow cooler as I move north into the highlands, and by dawn each day my tent is sopping wet from condensation. Travelling here is far more comfortable than in the humid heat by Lake Malawi, but it still brings its discomforts: months on the road have left my rucksack impregnated by litres of sweat, and merely carrying it for half an hour now makes my shirt stink. Repeated soakings from the heavens aren't helping either. I start using a nylon rain cover for my rucksack, which to the locals only adds to my odd appearance: in uncertain light it looks as if I'm wearing a big black cape like Batman.

Yet there's something wonderful about the sound and smell of fresh rain on a hot dusty road in Africa. Every afternoon now the air is charged with electricity and the sky darkens; then the rain descends in a soothing hiss, as warm as blood. I can live with spending the rest of the afternoon sodden and stinking.

Travelling like this, I'm missing out on many of the natural functions of life, like making a pot of tea, or lying for hours in the bath sulking. Most of all I long for some decent books. Although I was never especially keen back in England, I start experiencing strange yearnings for baked beans. This is just as well, as my money is vanishing so quickly I'll be living on the bloody things again when I get home. And I'm still craving oat porridge, although I can't understand why I don't yearn for something more exclusive. Obviously by now I'm satisfied by very little.

Even though I still have to cross the largest country in East Africa on foot, for the first time on the journey I start to get a sense of the end gradually coming into sight and becoming a realizable goal. I allow myself the luxury of admitting to myself that the strain of living like this is finally beginning to tell, like someone swimming a huge distance before drowning in sight of the shore. I need some peace soon. Walking every day until I can walk no further, I'll reach Zanzibar a physical wreck – I'm limping along with my lungs full of tar, with a bad knee, a bad back, even a bad haircut. Above all I'm fed up with worrying all the time if my feet will remain in a fit state to carry on – worrying about feet, for God's sake … But on a trip like this feet become crucial, whatever their intrinsic interest back at home. It's unfair that in so many cultures feet are viewed as a 'low' part of the body, and anyone who's fond of them is regarded as slightly kinky. But anyone who has studied feet scientifically knows they're structural wonders – or at least mine were before I started all this walking.

And new physical problems are arising almost daily. I'm getting problems from a painful trapped nerve in my shoulder, where my rucksack strap has been pinching it, and I can't straighten my arm above shoulder level – soon I'll be limping along like Richard III. By now my back is covered with eczema, the result of a perpetually sodden shirt and rucksack pressed against it day after day in this heat. In one place my pack has rubbed a painful hole in my skin through the eczema; carrying my rucksack was unpleasant before, but now it's purgatory. This eczema must also be partly due to eating bad food for so long – I never had this problem at home. I'm expecting my teeth and hair to start falling out before long, and I've got more or less permanent acid indigestion from eating so much junk. Week after week I've lived on lukewarm Coca-Cola, stale buns and doughnuts, slurps, green bananas, powdered milk and far too many cigarettes. With all the rubbishy food and sugary soft drinks I've been consuming, I'll see the east coast through a hypoglycaemic haze.

But I'll reach the east coast on foot if it's literally the last thing I do. I'm not going to be stopped now, and I'll get there under my own steam – even if my legs give way and I have to scoot along on my arse. And once I've reached the ocean I will have walked across Africa. It may be of little significance to anyone except me, but it will still be a fact, and it can't be

221

undone – even if I drop dead on the beach at Bagamoyo and get devoured by a pack of malodorous beach dogs.

Most of the people I meet are friendly; a woman at a village market gives me a free bunch of *ndizi*,* which I find touching. Generosity from people who are flat broke themselves always does it for me. Unfortunately my contact with some of the locals is sometimes more problematic. Children may scream at me all day in a spirit of fun, but when it's growing dark an element of fear enters their voices. This can be intimidating, as there's usually far more to worry about when someone's afraid of you. And it's not just the children. The night before I reach Mbeya is truly terrible, with a mad woman chasing after me, screeching like a banshee: '*Mzungu! MZUNGU!*' ('White guy! White guy!'). Her shrieks bring people tumbling out of their huts. I do everything I can to avoid her, even breaking into a run, which is far from easy with a big pack. This demented harpy pursues me relentlessly for several kilometres, screaming fit to wake the dead; all the time I'm expecting one of her neighbours to run out and bury a panga in my head. Eventually I'm so stressed I'm only slightly less crazy than she is; I start roaring at her like a sergeant major, at which point she vanishes.

If I was tired before, I'm completely exhausted now. And by now the darkness is so absolute I can't see two metres in front of me. But I must find some place to pitch my tent soon; I can't go on much longer. All I need is a tiny amount of space behind a bush – it's not much to ask, I'm not doing anyone any harm. I plod on for another hour or so to avoid any possible hue and cry from my last encounter with the mad woman. I stop beside a small stream, which I can't even see – I only know it's there by its gurgling. Maybe I can risk pitching my tent right where I am, surrounded by maize plants around the path – I definitely can't just lie down beside the road, as the mosquitoes would make sleep impossible as well as giving me malaria. Through the maize stalks I can see chinks of lamplight from a cluster of huts a few hundred metres away, but if I'm lucky I'll get away with it until dawn.

I've just started unloading my gear in the dark when a group of four middle-aged women appears; they walk right up to me before they notice

*Small eating bananas, named after the West Indies, from where they were originally introduced.

a white stranger sitting on the ground at their feet. I get up and say hello in Swahili, trying to look as friendly and unthreatening as possible. Understandably, they run off in terror.

Shit, shit, and then more shit.

If I'm still here in five minutes there's every chance they'll be back with their husbands. Or more likely they'll send their husbands to investigate, all carrying machetes. There's still time to get my head kicked in or much, much worse. I gather my belongings in record time and make yet another undignified exit. This is my least favourite thing in the whole world right now, skulking around in darkness when I'm dead beat and hurrying away like a thief in the night.

I walk for another soul-destroying hour in the dark. By this stage I can barely put one foot in front of the other, but eventually I find somewhere to camp in peace. Even so, this particular evening really shook me up. It's my own fault entirely – what I'm doing is far from sensible, and the stress is phenomenal. Of course, it must be strange to find a white man sitting in the bushes near your village after dark. But these ladies did seem particularly agitated. I'm convinced they mistook me for a ghost, however outrageous it sounds. Many Africans never venture from their huts after dark, for fear of encountering a ghost. Like their European counterparts, African ghosts are white and come out at night. They also like eating people, and possess a giant thumbnail to slice human flesh and saw through bones. They also carry strong associations with madness, and Africans unfortunate enough to meet a ghost are likely to be followed for the rest of their lives; they appear to talk to themselves, while in fact they are talking to the unseen ghost. 'He goes with ghosts' is a common Swahili euphemism for insanity.[1]

Even if people at night realize I'm no ghost, there's still the language problem. English is not widely spoken outside the big towns, and I'm worried some terrible misunderstanding will occur in the dark, leaving me with no means of explaining myself.

By day the main problem is the children. Wherever the kids shriek at me, the first shriek always sounds exactly the same, eerily so, as though the same child has followed me across the continent with the sole purpose of inciting other kids to howl like demons when I pass their village. Some of the kids here could hardly scream more frantically if their diapers caught fire. But so far no one has stoned me, apart from

223

one kid half-heartedly throwing a single rock at me in the dark as I passed his village. But that could have happened anywhere, and didn't cause any major upsets.

White people travelling in Africa, particularly backpackers, often use the word *mzungu* in their conversation, possibly to give the impression they know the ropes. I feel like pleading with them never to use that word when I'm within earshot – I've had it shrieked at me from so many thousands of throats that I never wish to hear it ever again. Even when a white person uses the word I still break out in a clammy sweat, almost a Pavlovian response. I know the word doesn't have any intrinsically negative connotations, unless used in a very disparaging context, in which case any word would be offensive. Even so, an African might feel uncomfortable walking across England with every single kid along the way howling 'black guy!' as he passes. At its worst, one can feel almost like hunted prey, or a runaway slave.

But there's some justice in all this. The word *mzungu* comes from the days of the great expeditions, from the Kiswahili verb *kuzunguka*, used to describe the European explorers: 'to wander around aimlessly'. And after all, I don't have any business being here, apart from self-indulgence.

Pop stars might receive or occasionally even deserve attention like this. To any celebrity it must always be a kind of flattery, a response to something they've done. The attention is flattering to me too, if I'm honest, but at the same time it's so unwanted, so dependent on the idea that white people are somehow special. I find myself longing for the coldness and isolation of Europe, with everything insular and anonymous once more. In my defence, at these times I'm exhausted, sometimes on the verge of heatstroke, dripping with sweat, living in a fair amount of hardship, walking thousands of kilometres with little respite and little money. The irony is that the screaming attention of the kids is hardly typical of this part of Africa – Tanzanian adults as a rule are dignified, almost reserved in their greetings, and local etiquette favours elaborate, leisurely preambles to conversation rather than Western directness, especially towards strangers.

But apart from the screaming I usually get on well with African kids. Inevitably, they assume I've appeared solely to entertain them, and act towards me in the way they might behave towards some exotic but harmless creepy-crawly, giving me the verbal equivalent of a prod to see

224

if I'll do something interesting. It's no different back in England when children see a tramp – or at least it wasn't until the last two decades or so, before so many people started sleeping rough in every city. When I was a child tramps were always strangely compelling figures, somehow outside the law, unpredictable, unconstrained by normal values or boundaries. It seemed to me that these itinerant outlaws might do anything, from the magical to the plain disgusting; the fact that they were actively disliked by one's parents only added to their appeal.

And now I am that tramp. Has it come to this?

For many people here, especially the children, this is the only time they've ever seen a white man actually walking past their village, with no sign of a waiting vehicle to whisk him to the next town a hundred kilometres down the road. I can hardly blame the local kids if they think I'm something more than I really am, or if they want to make me so. Even so, I enjoy being stared at by crowds as much as the average road accident victim enjoys their celebrity status as they lie in the road waiting for the ambulance. I can understand why some animals in game parks develop genuine neuroses, with tourists gawking at them all the time. Yet being stared at and mobbed isn't so bad as getting shot full of poisoned arrows, which might well have happened if I'd made this trip a couple of centuries ago.

And no matter how bad I feel towards the end of the journey, in all honesty, how can I complain that life is so hard for me these days? In every town I encounter cadaverous beggars scrabbling in the dust, dragging wasted limbs, wasted lives. Tanzania (like Malawi) is one of the world's very poorest countries, and many people here live in utter poverty. There's little hope for immediate progress here, with such a high proportion of the country's workers having to scratch a living through subsistence farming.

Few Westerners visit this southwestern corner of Tanzania, apart from those speeding past en route to Lake Malawi or the more popular east coast. This part of the country is characterized by lush green hillsides and valleys, with forests thriving on its rich volcanic soil. Apart from the banana plants and tea bushes in plantations stretching into the distance, I could almost be in the Black Forest, or lost in the hills of Transylvania – even the cowbells sound authentically alpine. The climate here is cool and wonderfully refreshing after the sweltering weeks I spent beside Lake Malawi. It's also the wettest region in the whole country, with an annual rainfall of almost three metres; the big waterfalls and crater lakes are not here by coincidence. The long wet season is due to start any time now, but if I get a move on east I might avoid the worst of the downpour here.

The town of Mbeya turns out to be ten kilometres further than my map indicated. For once, instead of swearing I become philosophical: when I get there I'll be ten kilometres nearer my final destination. Near the central bus station a young local tries to pick my pocket, but he's no expert. Again, I'm arriving in a town at the end of the month, when the pickpockets are working overtime to relieve people of their monthly wage-packets. Having so far avoided being involved in this redistribution of wealth, Mbeya fills me with vague paranoia I'll get robbed; illegal guns are common in this part of the country, many of them ancient flintlocks or home-made pistols.

With a population of about 40,000, Mbeya is the biggest town in southern Tanzania. Though it's surrounded by volcanic hills and mountains to the north and south, the town itself has a distinctly Westernized feel to it – it's less run-down than the other big places I've passed recently, and you can find more or less anything you want in its shops, which makes a welcome change. I stay here for a couple of days at the *Moravian Youth Hostel*. Here I half-heartedly chat up a couple of attractive Danish girls staying in the next room, and get absolutely nowhere – but at least they're polite before retiring to bed at seven. Later I feel sorry for an emaciated kitten wandering round the place, and give it a tiny piece of tinned tuna fish. It enjoys this so much it starts a dreadful caterwauling in the hope of more, which lasts the entire night.

Mbeya's electricity supply is at best erratic; throughout the evening the lights grow dimmer and brighter by degrees, as though the whole system is powered by an old man on a bike. In many Tanzanian towns and cities, power cuts have a disastrous effect on businesses and industrial output. At any African hotel or guesthouse, it's wise to keep a torch or matches and candle handy, for all the times you find yourself in pitch-blackness without warning. I ask the proprietor for a candle; the tiny one he produces would look fine on a birthday cake. After all this time out in the bush living by my own devices, these power cuts depress me. I wouldn't mind if the town was completely without electricity – you could get used to that, but it's unsettling to have power one minute and darkness the next. A relaxing read is impossible, with my birthday-cake candle making the room flicker like an old movie. And as soon as the electricity returns after a power cut, the public address systems from the mosques start again, calling Muslims to prayer.

By day, Mbeya's services include those of the most incompetent shoe mender in the world, an old fellow who anywhere else wouldn't make it as a village idiot. I sit beside him for over an hour while he makes a complete balls-up of the most straightforward job. Replacing soles must surely be a simple job for a professional, but instead of using glue like any sensible shoe repairer this guy tries to hammer huge nails through the existing soles of my sandals. Due to great age and infirmity he lacks the strength to hold the hammer, let alone knock the nails with sufficient force – and even if he succeeded they'd obviously stick straight into my feet. After more than an hour of this foolishness we're no further on – in fact I'm worse off than when he started as my sandals now lie in several pieces. The fact that this guy had no other customers should have aroused my suspicions; his busier colleagues nearby have plenty of work. I pay him anyway, just to get away before he does any more damage – I feel sorry for him, even if he is a grumpy old gnome. I haven't the heart just to stomp off without giving him anything; after all, he must find it hard to support himself in his chosen trade.

I find someone else to resole what's left of my sandals. This second guy does a good job, and it's the last time I need my shoes repaired in Africa. He even nails some metal strips on the heels, which work well, although for the next few days I sound like a horse trotting down the newly-surfaced road to Dar es Salaam and the coast.

I'm looking forward to many things when I finish this journey. It will be marvellous to be able to put food straight into my mouth without checking each mouthful for anything moving in it, or in a few cases if the food itself is still moving. But when I'm back in England and no longer walking, I'll surely miss being able to eat with such appetite. Most of the simple cooked meals I've had in Africa have been perfectly acceptable, although one or two would have made a stray dog vomit. Back in Zambia, that horrible long stretch between Sesheke and Livingstone without food did me a lot of good. Since then I've been pleased just to have some food on my plate, any food will do. Every meal set before me fills me with eager anticipation. It's no great disaster if my maize porridge arrives stone-cold, grey and dingy-looking, or if it's reheated and gets flopped in my bowl steaming like old underwear drying on a radiator.

Most people in Tanzania live on rice (*wali*), chapatis, plantain (*batoke*) and of course maize porridge (here called *ugali*). Maize is grown everywhere, often roasted whole and sold at roadside stalls; also common are *mandazi* (a fried doughnut without the jam or the hole in the middle). Every cafe and restaurant serves chicken soup, which is more like lukewarm greasy stock with a piece of floating fowl thrown in than European-style chicken soup. The most common meat in this part of Africa is still goat mutton, although beef is also available. Most restaurants serve you with a glass of *chai*, ultra-sweet milky tea with all its ingredients brewed together in the kettle.

In a cheap restaurant by Mbeya bus station my *ugali* is accompanied by a rubbery greyish substance the waiter insists is chicken, despite the noticeable absence of rats on the premises. In many parts of the country 'chicken' is usually strange poultry-like organs that require a suspicious amount of chewing. A free-range chicken in Africa is a different beast from its European counterpart; the latter is still a reasonably succulent piece of meat, but the chickens here have to forage for their own food, so their tenderness is directly proportional to their foraging skills. Like the stray dogs who live on car demolition sites, during their brief lives they become tough and streetwise; by the time they reach your table their flesh is athletic and full of scar tissue, the legacy of savage chicken turf wars.

In Tanzania the women seem more colourfully dressed than those back in Malawi, usually wearing brightly patterned *kangas*. In the towns you'll see lots of men – hardly ever women – sitting outside shops working old museum-piece Singer sewing machines, operated by a foot pedal. Many locals pull huge barrows around town, often with a couple of men pushing as well. When they're heavily laden – as they usually are – the guys pulling are hidden from those pushing, so they have to communicate by means of boisterous yells. Having no brakes, they reach tremendous speeds downhill in towns; a rubber skid and careful steering are all that keep these barrow boys from disaster in a thousand emergency stops.

I stock up on a few provisions for the road, including a bottle of Tanzanian 'Chemi-Cola', which admittedly tastes no more artificial than the normal variety. I also invest in a bar of 'Madonna Antiseptic Medicated Soap', the wrapper depicting the singer looking simultaneously coquettish and well-scrubbed.

Leaving Mbeya I pass dozens of goats grazing beside the road on short tethers; Tanzanian goats must be less trustworthy than those back in Zambia and Malawi, where they were free to browse in more of an open-prison arrangement. With or without tethers goats are voracious eaters, literally stripping the ground of vegetation, which in many places is causing serious soil erosion. Tanzanian donkeys are light-coloured and attractive, bigger and in much better condition than those I saw in Namibia. I may be imagining it, but these ones seem happier. There is something so calm about a donkey, even in the face of adversity. I wonder how Tsondab is faring these days.

Around this time my second tick takes up residence in such an awkward and embarrassing place that burning it off with a cigarette is totally out of the question. It's no simple matter to dig this one out with a needle and mirror, contorting myself behind a bush on a quiet stretch of road. Tics possess an uncanny ability to attach themselves to the most inaccessible parts of the host animal's body, before summoning their friends to good feeding sites by means of special pheromones. 'Don't even think about it,' I warn this one as I finally dislodge the little bastard.

The first night out of Mbeya a big flesh-coloured creepy-crawly races into my tent, intent on some strange business of its own. When I clobber it with a trekking pole the horrible creature runs out again even faster than it came in. I'm not sure if it was a spider or a scorpion or something entirely different, but at least it's gone, and that's the main thing. The amber-coloured ants here also move at amazing speed when frightened; as a general rule I try to make any visit to my tent as frightening as possible.

Several days east of Mbeya I pass through a stretch of countryside where there are no people to be found for love or money. After yearning for it so long I finally have peace and solitude, but no bloody water. The

229

landscape here is completely different from the green and fertile tea plantations back towards Malawi. The vegetation is so sparse and scrubby it's almost like being in Namibia again. The trees are devoid of leaves, the ground below parched. Everything looks desolate and depressing; in spite of the heat it's almost wintry. It reminds me of the desolate landscapes from one of those fairy stories from childhood, where the entire countryside is blighted by some evil sorcerer.

Depressing or not, water is the priority. I get excited when I see a river ahead, but drawing near I find it has dried up completely. In twenty kilometres I find only one small group of four huts. I beg a cup of water from a family, and give the young father a packet of biscuits – I assume he'll share them with his family, who stand anxiously in the doorway behind him, peering wide-eyed over his shoulder as they watch this transaction. Instead, the man just walks off with the biscuits, eating the lot himself two at a time without a backward glance.

More public-spirited is the driver of a Tanzanian Guinness lorry parked in the middle of nowhere, the only stationary vehicle I pass in days. He's standing talking to three local guys. I can't imagine where the latter come from – there's no sign of any village nearby, no smoke, no children, nothing. I ask the driver for water, but he has none. I walk on, but he chases after me:

'I'm sorry mister, I forgot I have Guinness – will that do instead?'

I've answered more difficult questions than this. He gives me a couple of bottles, refusing to take any money, and I drink one immediately; it tastes vaguely like treacle. I gaze longingly at the second, wishing I had a whole crate of them. But the local guys are still sitting beside the road, staring gloomily into space. I can hardly drink both bottles in front of them when they have nothing, so I hand it to them and they're delighted. They can probably afford to drink Guinness once a year, if that.

The following day I stop at a restaurant in Igawa and chat to the owner, who tells me that the lions in the Mikumi game park ahead sometimes eat truck drivers who've broken down. I also hear that man-eating lions are making their presence felt in other parts of Tanzania, terrorizing villages in the coastal districts just south of Dar es Salaam, less than fifty kilometres from the city centre. Seventeen people have been killed so far this year; in response the villagers have killed nineteen lions, so at least the humans are slightly ahead. The government has awarded money to the families of those killed, but now the survivors of lion attacks are also claiming compensation, so far without success. Yet the survivors' claims seem perfectly reasonable to me, as many of them have been permanently disabled and are now unable to work.

Lions aren't the only potential threat from wildlife dead ahead. A pregnant Indian woman died recently in the Mikumi Park when her family car hit a baby elephant, and the mother elephant promptly attacked the car. The family managed to escape, but the pregnant woman was trapped inside; the elephant trampled the car so thoroughly it looked as if it had been in a scrapyard compressor.

While much of East Africa ties in with most foreigners' image of the 'real Africa', to me the landscape east of Igawa looks more like the Scottish Highlands. There's no heather, and the trees aren't exactly the same, but the resemblance is still striking – there's the same kind of desolate beauty, and towards evening the countryside here even shares something of the melancholy allure of Scotland. Maybe I'm just tired, or even homesick. Once again, I can't see any people. At one point I stop for ten minutes to admire the view and for no other reason, one of the first normal things I've done for months. Just by this one action I start to feel that this really is the home stretch.

By now I'm always trying to think up clever ways of avoiding walking even a few unnecessary kilometres without cheating. Unfortunately there aren't any. I've become so accustomed to big distances in Africa that any attempts to calculate comparable distances back in England leave me feeling rather pleased with myself. At one point I'm congratulating myself on having only a comparatively short distance still to walk, then I remember it's still the distance from London to Glasgow – Tanzania is around half the size of Western Europe.

Local buses still display rousing slogans, such as: 'Lost time never found!' The driver of this particular bus has obviously taken this message to heart – if sheer speed and recklessness were the sole requirements, African drivers would sweep all opposition before them in the Monte Carlo Rally. Tanzanian bus drivers have the annoying habit of sounding their horns whenever they pass me. And they're *loud*, the type of horn more usually associated with ocean-going liners; when they blast out right behind me I usually leap several feet in the air, even with a heavy rucksack.

Stopping briefly at a roadside stall in Iyayi, I buy a piece of cooked liver, vaguely rancid with green bits in it. But I'm hungry, so I tell myself maybe it's supposed to look like this. A crippled youth grovels in the dirt nearby, obviously crazy as well as disabled; every so often he stops to drool and vomit on the ground, his hunted eyes rolling in their sockets. He's in such a state I find it unsettling just to look at him. Wondering if I'm doing the right thing, I offer him some change. He seems terrified of me, so I give the money to a sympathetic-looking woman standing nearby to pass on to him when he calms down. Back at home it's easy enough to feel pity for beggars in the street. But despite the cold winters back at home, for sheer unpleasantness the lives of most English beggars don't compare to those of their African counterparts.

As I pass a village school just east of Iyayi, a small crowd of teenage boys follows me.

'Why are you walking, sir?'

Why? I try to explain in a nutshell, but it's impossible – there's no simple answer in local terms. They don't believe me anyway when I tell them I've walked here from the Namibian coast, and remain convinced that anyone walking a long distance must be doing so as some form of punishment. They're understandably curious to know what I did to deserve it.

'I was a very naughty boy,' I tell them. 'Smoking, drinking, swearing, fighting, womanizing … you name it.'

'But mister! It's impossible to walk that far in eight months,' one declares, the others nodding their assent. There isn't much I can say to that.

'How is the Queen of England?' several kids want to know.

'What are you going to do when you leave Africa, sir?' another asks.

'Teach English, I think.'

'Then sir, you must come now and teach us at our school for a few days!'

I decline politely. Teachers here are very badly paid when they're paid at all, and the schools are painfully under-resourced; often there are no desks, or even paper to write on.

232

Despite the poverty in Tanzania, I still encounter kindness at every turn. At one village a man from the local church gives me a packet of candles, refusing to accept any money. I feel a bit of a fraud, and hope he doesn't assume I plan to use them for worship.

Around 200 kilometres east of Mbeya I reach the small town of Makambako. I'm chilled to the bone; this is one of the coldest places in Tanzania, and I spend most of the rainy day utterly miserable, shivering in a guesthouse bed. I venture out briefly and wander around town. Outside the restaurant next door several dozen depressed chickens are crowded into a tiny cage, watching gloomily as one after another of their number goes into the pot right before their eyes – and I thought I had problems. But at least the cold keeps the insects at bay; it's the first night in ages that I haven't gone to sleep surrounded by things with wings.

A more relaxing experience by far is the larger town of Iringa, 190 kilometres northeast of Makambako. The trek to reach it takes me only three and a half days – by my own standards at least I've set such a killing pace to get here that I feel entitled to a rest, and I'm completely knackered.

The capital of the Southern Highlands, Iringa is set appropriately enough on a big plateau with panoramic views over the surrounding countryside and the Little River Ruaha below. At first the town looks like a slightly shabby German market town filled with black Africans; its crumbling colonial buildings stand alongside modern African houses and shops, while its lively market is packed with woven baskets and colourful *kanga* wraps. The locals have warned me that Iringa is a cold place, at least by African standards – its highland altitude (1,635 metres) and heavy rainfall keep it cool. But while I'm here I find it pleasantly warm, and the skies are clear.

Iringa's name comes from the local word for fort. Owing to the town's superb location as a strong defensive point it was developed by the Germans, who were finally driven out by the British during the First World War. Before this the area was no stranger to bloodshed. The hill called *Ilundamatwe* ('the collection of skulls') was once covered with the heads of warriors slain by the Hehe, the most powerful fighting tribe in German East Africa; another hill called *Tagamenda* ('throw cloths') was strewn with the clothes of dead warriors for their relatives to identify.

In the closing years of the nineteenth century, Iringa District was the scene of the Hehe's bitter and bloody rebellion against German rule. The Hehe greatly impressed the Germans with their intelligence, their dignified appearance and above all their prowess in battle. After fighting them for over seven years the Germans came to view the Hehe as the *Herrenvolk* of East Africa, and to this day the tribal classification 'Hehe' still conveys great prestige. The name derives from their fierce war cries; the warriors would charge into battle yelling: *'Hee, hee, hee, Vatavangu Twihoma Ehee!'* ('Hee, hee, hee, we are fighting the enemy, ehee!')

During the conflict with Germany the Hehe found an intelligent and inspiring paramount chief in Mkwawa ('The Conqueror of Many Lands'), still regarded as a local hero. Although violent at times, Mkwawa often demonstrated great fair-mindedness. On one occasion he started abusing one of his wives, seizing her roughly, which so upset the head slave that he struck the chief in the face. Everyone present expected Mkwawa to have the slave put to a slow and agonizing death. Instead Mkwawa admitted he'd been in the wrong and pardoned the slave for hitting him.

In August 1891 the Hehe won fame in a battle with the Germans on the River Ruhaha, forty kilometres from Iringa. In this battle the Hehe annihilated the expedition sent to pacify them; only two out of twelve Germans and 15 out of 150 native askari escaped with their lives. The Hehe losses were so great, however, that Mkwawa forbade the traditional mourning ceremonies, in a desperate attempt to hide their true extent from his people. The following summer the Hehe lured the German garrison of Kilosa to their deaths. Pretending to be peaceful traders, the Hehe drew the garrison outside the fortress, where more warriors rose from concealment, quickly killing all the defenders.

In 1894 the Germans finally captured Mkwawa's capital at Kalenga, some fifteen kilometres west of Iringa. The fighting was particularly savage; at one point a mighty explosion in the powder store blew its roof right across the river. His capital destroyed, Mkwawa managed to escape and waged a highly effective guerrilla war against the Germans, who had no idea even what he looked like. Despite a huge price on Mkwawa's head, the Hehe showed extraordinary loyalty towards their chief. Whenever Mkwawa's men were surprised by a German patrol, they threw themselves on the German guns, sacrificing their lives so he could escape.

By this time the Hehe's rebellion had cost more bloodshed than any other part of German East Africa. Eventually Mkwawa could not resist returning for one last visit to the remains of his old capital. Trapped by German askaris near Iringa, Mkwawa realized that capture was inevitable. Following tradition, he first shot his favourite page, so that the boy could continue serving him in the afterlife, then turned his gun on himself.*

Although peace returned to the area, the Hehe's defeat at the hands of the Germans did nothing to diminish their love of fighting. During the First World War, many Hehe and Angoni warriors served as German askaris. At one point an entire unit was captured by the British. Since fighting of any kind was preferable to sitting out the war in a POW camp, they joined the British forces – although to confuse everyone further they still had to be given their orders in German.[2]

I rest at Iringa for a couple of days, during which time I experience my first bath since leaving Victoria Falls months earlier. Showers can't compare to a bath, and 2,200 kilometres is a long way to walk for a bath. My hands are so unused to being submerged that within minutes they become absurdly wrinkled. I find myself taking four or five baths a day until I leave Iringa – as soon as I get out of the bath I find myself without conscious decision getting straight back in again.

Despite their obvious attraction I can feel these creature comforts undermining my resolve to keep moving. I decide that this will have to be the last nice place I stay until I reach the east coast. By now I'm fantasizing about many things from back home, none of them things commonly associated with longing. I'm constantly thinking of English food, English supermarkets, oat porridge (I still can't get this one out of my head), dark chocolate hobnobs, watching crap on TV or some cosy Christmas picture like *It's a Wonderful Life*. And above all, absolutely no walking – if necessary I'll hire someone to push me around in a bath chair.

*The Germans sent Mkwawa's head to Germany, although in 1954 it was finally returned to the Hehe, who gave him a burial befitting a powerful chief. The skull with its bullet hole can still be seen at the small museum at Kalenga. Mkwawa's spirit might be slightly mollified also to learn that he now has his own website, www.mkwawa.com.

I leave Iringa, heading for Kilosa, around 240 kilometres to the north-east. Beside the road a boy holds an indignant hen by its feet, hoping some passing motorist will stop and buy it on impulse. I feel sorry for the poor creature, hanging upside down in the sun – there must be better ways to spend your final hours on this earth. So often in Africa there's a real indifference to animals suffering, although in reality it's not much different from Europe or anywhere else. Back at home you have to go out of your way to see animals slaughtered or dismembered, and it's easy for the most voracious meat eaters to disassociate themselves from the story behind their dinner. And here the people live with enough hardship, let alone the animals. In this district, thousands of school children have been driven into child labour, usually on sisal and sugar cane plantations. Often the work is hard and dangerous, but many parents lack the money for school fees.

That night I wake to find a tiny light moving around in my tent, up and down my shirt. The darkness in my tent is so absolute and I'm so tired that for a few moments I'm completely disorientated; I've no idea where I am, whether I'm lying in my tent or sitting outside or standing on my head in the middle of the road. I don't know if it's a tiny light close to me or a big light in the distance. I think I'm hallucinating, but it turns out to be a small insect with extraordinarily luminous eyes, so bright they appear as a single light.

East of Iringa the flies are terrible; every few minutes I pull them out of my hair like handfuls of raisins. Whenever I stop and sit down my head is surrounded by a seething cloud of insects. The vicious thorn bushes here pose another problem; they seem to possess some devilish will of their own, and whenever I get stuck every move I make serves only to entangle me further. Sometimes this creates the bizarre sensation of being attacked by animate thorn bushes, like something out of a fairy tale illustrated by Arthur Rackham. On one such occasion a giant thorn sticks deep into my forearm. Within minutes, a painful swelling the size of a duck egg rises as if by magic, and my whole arm aches abominably for the rest of the day. I'm convinced I'll get tetanus; even if I don't, the thorn has undoubtedly flooded my entire bloodstream with virulent toxins, and I'll die of something equally unpleasant.

Often I come across dead dogs quietly decomposing in the middle of the road. Some of these road-accident victims (the more recent statistics) are still in reasonable condition, while others have been here so long they've started to liquefy. The fresh ones smell awful, but the more putrid specimens smell fantastically bad – the stench is so foul that it actually leaves a vile taste in my mouth as I pass. On a practical level this brings further drawbacks to walking in the dark: if there's a deceased dog resting in peace on the road at night there's every chance I'll step in it, then climb into my tent for the night with my foot covered in goo from a liquefied dog. There are worse things in life than putting your foot in a putrefying dog, but the list is not extensive. In some parts of Africa dead dogs are hung at village gateposts to ward off evil spirits – I suspect they work, too.

Passing Mbuyuni, I leave the main road and set off down the path to Kilosa. Here there's no traffic, and no people either, though plenty of olive baboons, which cause a great deal of damage to crops. Later I talk to an Irish guy who works on local projects here, trying to raise money back at home to help the Tanzanian farmers. One of his first steps is buying nets to trap the baboons, although this is proving a difficult project to sell back in Ireland – the only slogan they have come up with so far is: '40 Euros will kill a family of baboons'. While they're waiting for the funds, in the absence of nets the local farmers resort to a cruel but effective way of dealing with baboons. Whenever they catch one alive they flay the skin off its face, then release it. When the other baboons see their unfortunate colleague they take fright, and flee the area for good.

I cross a dry and dusty plain filled with grey baobab trees standing watch in silence like a petrified forest of ancient sentries. They're quite freaky: in some nightmare they might pull up their roots and march like a regiment of triffids. Baobab trees have incredible powers of endurance: in times of drought they simply shed their leaves and sit it out patiently. Even if they're knocked down by a storm they will survive if a few roots remain in the soil. They can live for over 4,000 years. I find it hard to imagine anything living that long, especially something standing right in front of me, something I can see and touch. Some of the trees here may well have been alive at the time of Christ, or even before the Pyramids were built. And what of the baby baobab trees of today, the youngsters born since the French Revolution – what will happen during their lives?

The fruit of a baobab, the calabash, is used throughout Africa as a vessel for liquids, and the tree produces cream of tartar. It's sometimes called the 'monkey-bread tree', as monkeys often make their homes in its branches. In African mythology the baobab is often inhabited by spirits, who feel understandably secure living in the tree that never dies. In some parts of East Africa a baobab can only be cut down after its resident ghosts have been given two weeks' written notice to quit; this allows the spirits time to find another home, instead of moving into human habitations and upsetting honest folk.[3]

With the sudden approach of twilight the distant mountains fade to a long smudge of blue smoke, and the baobab trees start to assume new and sinister shapes. The absence of people here should mean a peaceful night for me, but I pitch my tent to the sound of a troop of baboons fighting. The noise is extraordinary, the screams almost human; the baboon doing most of the screeching sounds half-demented. I wonder if it's safe to sleep near a bunch of pissed-off baboons: the adults are vicious fighters, and despite their modest size they're extremely powerful creatures.

But eventually the baboons settle down for the night, and so do I. In the rapidly fading light the legions of baobabs still wait in frozen immobility, each as stark as a gibbet. Every tree is completely individual – this is no team effort. They're positively creepy in the twilight, their grey waxy trunks the bodies of squat trolls, their branches hurled skywards to be frozen for centuries. The moon rises and hangs in the sky like a ghostly white disc. Eventually I drift off to sleep, dreaming about baobabs multiplying around me, their gaunt skeletal hands rising from the ground as if sleeping giants stir beneath the earth, reaching out to claw at the fleeing baboons.

16. The Boundless Ocean
(Tanzania: Mbuyuni to Bagamoyo)

My companions looked upon the boundless ocean with awe. On describing their feelings afterwards, they remarked that 'we marched along with our father, believing that what the ancients had always told us was true, that the world has no end; but all at once the world said to us, "I am finished; there is no more of me!"' They had always imagined the world was one extended plain without limit.

David Livingstone, on reaching the Atlantic coast,
Missionary Travels

After all this time on the road I'm still surprised at how physically exhausting stress can be, and not just the stress of having to push yourself every single day. I notice this particularly when my stress levels rise unexpectedly on the way to Kilosa, when I lose my way and run out of water.

It's unnerving just how much thirst undermines your resolve. I can't remember the last time back in England I was genuinely thirsty, which presumably means I never was – real thirst is not something you forget in a hurry. Surveys done on stressful experiences back at home tend to focus on familiar unpleasant events, such as the death of a partner, redundancy, divorce or moving house. If anyone felt the need to compile such a list in Africa they'd have to include thirst and hunger, and to put them at the top of the list. Almost as bad as the thirst itself is the stress of having no idea where the next drink is coming from. Or, in this case, if I'll have to give up and walk back fifty kilometres the way I've come in order to find water (it's about the same distance on to Kilosa, if I carry on). Walking another fifty kilometres in this heat without water won't kill me, but it will be a memorable experience. I still have my compass, but a sense of overall direction doesn't help me choose a route between the hills towering around me. There's no one to ask, nor indeed any signs of human life.

People have died of thirst in Africa with abundant water only hours away, sometimes even when they had a compass, local bearers and the stars to guide them. One such case was Frederick Selous's young friend Robert French, who in 1879 joined the famous hunter on an expedition through Caprivi. Accompanied by his gunbearer and water carrier, French became lost in the bush. He immediately started to lead his companions back to where he thought Selous's camp lay, overriding their protests that they were heading in the wrong direction. After their water ran out, the two natives pleaded with French to cut across to the Chobe River and follow it back to camp, yet still he refused to be guided. After two days of hopeless wandering, the unfortunate white man started coughing blood and collapsed. He scratched on the stock of his rifle: 'I cannot go any further, when I die peace with all.' He died a few hours later, a victim of his own idea of superior European judgement. As soon as French was dead, his companions – who had shown immense loyalty in risking their own lives to stay with him as long as they did – made straight for the Chobe, following it back to the safety of Selous's camp. For the rest of his life, Selous blamed himself for his friend's death.[1]

Right now I'd be delighted to accept advice from anyone as to which path to take, if only there was someone to ask. My tongue is stuck fast to the roof of my mouth as though with envelope gum. Back at home thirst was never more than mild discomfort, hardly a major worry – more of an abstract issue, something you might read about in adventure stories, or even joke about: a man goes into a pub really thirsty ... But not to me right now. The thirst itself seems to induce almost a mild form of shock, which must be more to do with anxiety than any short-term physical effects of dehydration. Merely worrying about thirst seems to make you a lot thirstier, just as hypochondriacs find that as soon as they start worrying about some part of their body it starts to hurt. I'm fully aware that this is nothing compared to what some people have experienced; but my admiration for people who have faced the real thing with courage and resolve has suddenly grown out of all proportion. Meanwhile my stress levels are rising like mercury in a thermometer dipped in hot water.

Towards evening, without having seen a soul all day, I hear the indescribably lovely sound of trickling water. Almost in a frenzy I locate the source, a tiny sluggish stream, barely moving in the heat. I'd imagined that if I was sufficiently thirsty literally any water would taste good, but I've managed to find an exception. The stagnant water here reminds me of a picture I once saw in a children's book of a primordial swamp – thick with swarming insects, with huge red and green dragonflies hovering ponderously over its surface. If the insects further west resembled miniature helicopters, these guys are the genuine Lancaster bombers of the insect world. And it smells as if a dead cow is floating ten metres upstream.

But I don't have a great deal of choice in the matter. Without a second to lose I start pumping this foul broth through my water filter. Even after filtering the water retains a curious horror all of its own, with an extraordinarily unpleasant alkaline texture, like super-concentrated Alka-Seltzer. My first few gulps cause a completely involuntary gagging reflex, and I have to force it down before it shoots straight out of my mouth again.

'No one knows the value of water till he is deprived of it,' wrote Livingstone. 'I have drunk water swarming with insects ... thick with mud, putrid with rhinoceros' urine and buffalo dung, and no stinted draughts either, and yet I felt no inconvenience from it.'[2] He's welcome to this pool – in any case, throughout his travels Livingstone had enough ongoing problems with his bowels to make his claims highly questionable.

Eventually I stumble across a tiny village in the hills, where I beg some drinkable water. Completely worn out by now, I sleep just outside of the village, hidden from the path in a cleft in the rockface. The rather pathetic thought enters my head that I must surely be the first white person ever to sleep in this exact spot. Now I really am scraping the barrel – this must be a reaction to an extremely difficult day.

Even without the problems of thirst, crossing the hills drains me utterly. Reaching the village of Kisanga the following morning, I simply can't go any further; I *must* rest for a day. The only place to stay is a horrible squalid guesthouse with a sinister pair of crutches resting in one corner of my room. By midday the sun beating down on the tin roof has turned the room into an oven. Deafening music blares from the next building all day and for most of the night too, with several cockerels singing along. Despite having supposedly given up, I smoke a few cigarettes, reasoning that nothing could make me feel worse, and there's always the remote chance that smoking might make me feel slightly better. It doesn't; I still feel as though I've been beaten up by a gang of thugs wielding baseball bats.

On the positive side, it's a relief to reach a large village where there's at least some choice in what I can buy. The roadside stalls between villages usually stock huge piles of onions and little else; here the markets are filled with mountains of tiny sardines gleaming like mounds of silver paper in the sun. When you buy a paper bag of peanuts or something similar in a Tanzanian market, you'll often receive a free sample in your bag of whatever else that particular trader sells: a few tiny fish-heads, a rusty bolt, or sometimes just a piece of old twig. But by now I've grown used to not putting things straight into my mouth without first checking. Some of the market stalls sell pieces of sugar cane; unlike the huge lengths sold inland, these are only about a foot long, like sticks of Blackpool rock. They're pleasant enough to chew on, but not particularly satisfying, and with little real food value. Some market sellers try to charge you over the going rate; if you know the real price and challenge them, the trader will often say: 'Yes, but if you come back again I'll give you a better price.' Explaining to them that you won't be coming back under those terms cuts little ice.

Leaving Kisanga, another tough day follows, over fifty kilometres of it. The path winds tortuously through woods and fields. By late afternoon I reach the village of Uleya, where a friendly local teacher called Mr Matogold Kinda invites me into his home for some bananas and tea. I get some water from his village pump. 'It is best to boil the water from village pumps,' he tells me, 'to avoid *inconveniences*.' I've learnt a great deal about those by now, but I don't wish to go into detail with my host.

I camp on marshy ground just outside the village, the mosquitoes outside my tent howling in a miniature blitzkrieg. Tonight they clearly want my blood badly, and I have to keep my tent door tightly fastened. Sweat trickles down my chest, and any movement is exhausting – but lying here in a state of sweltering torpor is still preferable to being eaten alive by the mosquitoes outside.

The following day the afternoon heat is even fiercer than usual. I'm getting nearer the coast now, and the cool upland weather is rapidly giving way to a hot and humid tropical climate. I try soaking my shirt in a river to cool down, which proves remarkably effective in the short term.

But after only minutes next to my rucksack, my wet shirt starts chafing badly. So I now have to choose between nappy rash or heat stroke. As a compromise, I soak my baseball cap in a stream, and this works surprisingly well for five minutes or so. On paper five minutes may not sound like much; in reality five minutes of moderate comfort here is a vast improvement on nothing at all.

As I'm getting closer to the equator the sun is now almost directly overhead, which makes it much more difficult to find shade. Whenever I stop for a break now getting into the shade assumes real urgency: it can't wait a moment longer, it's like scrambling out of a river full of crocodiles or getting to a toilet when you're absolutely bursting. But now I have to find a tree or large bush with overhanging boughs, which usually proves difficult at short notice. It's horrible to stop to rest under some pathetic bit of shade, only to find after ten minutes that the sun has moved slightly, leaving me with the choice of either getting up and carrying on exhausted or staying put and sweltering.

For months now I've carried my sleeping bag strapped on top of my rucksack. This provides some portable shade; the benefits far outweigh the slight disadvantage of having my gear piled so high. Experts on the subject of efficient loading of rucksacks advise you not to carry anything higher than head height. Not for the first time on this trip these experts can mind their own business: I'll settle for shade any day. The sun by now is such a problem I might soon have to revert to covering the back of my neck with a handkerchief, as I did on those first days back on the Skeleton Coast, on the other side of the continent.

'You look like Prince Charles!' announces a middle-aged man called Matthew, sitting outside a local store. I thought I'd left such comparisons behind me in England; however far you travel, you can never truly escape yourself. Matthew then changes his mind: 'No ... you're more like Mr Bean ...' He seems suspiciously au fait with English celebrities.

I reach the outskirts of Kilosa completely exhausted. To hell with not smoking; I buy a cigarette at the first store I find. Unfortunately my arrival coincides with the school lunch break; within minutes I'm surrounded by a huge crowd of schoolchildren and equally curious adults, although for once none of them seems especially friendly. 'I hate all this attention,' I confide to the man who owns the store. 'I don't deserve it – I have a white skin, but that counts for nothing.' The guy translates this remark for the benefit of the crowd, and they all laugh; the tension eases instantly and the situation immediately becomes more good-humoured.

Like so many places in this part of Africa, Kilosa has something of a violent past. In 1905 it was the most northerly town in German East Africa drawn into the Maji Maji Rebellion. This bloody and highly determined revolt against all foreign rule consumed a large proportion of what is now Tanzania. It took its name from *Maji-maji*, sacred water carried around in maize stalks which it was thought would turn German bullets to water and make slain African warriors rise from the dead after seven days to continue fighting the Europeans.

The German threat was perceived as so great that for the first time in the country's history centuries-old inter-tribal rivalries were set aside and enemies became allies. Despite this new-found unity, as with the Herero revolt taking place simultaneously in Namibia, the Germans' over-whelming technological superiority and discipline enabled them to crush the rebellion utterly. Over 120,000 men, women and children died either in battle or in the wholesale hangings and famine that followed, and the entire southern region was devastated.

After the revolt the Germans did make a lot of improvements in their colonial rule here – hence some of the Hehe and Ngoni actually fought on the German side in the First World War. And many historians feel that the early tribal unity displayed by formerly bitter enemies paved the way for modern Tanzania's extraordinarily non-tribal attitudes today – rare in a continent where tribal rivalries still account for so much bloodshed and suffering.

After resting in Kilosa for a couple of days, I follow the railway track past Kimamba, a rainbow dead ahead of me for most of the afternoon, the baboons still shrieking from every direction. The path here is narrow, and often I have to negotiate around local guys cycling in the opposite direction laden with stupendous loads of firewood. Sometimes old men who can't afford a bike carry more or less the same loads on foot, which looks even more bizarre – all I can see is the wood, as though a woodpile has sprouted a pair of spindly legs and taken off.

I've reached the stage where a slow and numbing fatigue lends a strange desperation to every thought and action. The expression 'If I don't sit down I'll fall down' may once have been an exaggeration born of self-pity; by now, at the end of a typical day it's a fair comment. And the mental strain of travelling like this is worsening – after walking so far under the African sun I wonder if my brain still functions quite as it should.

I'd hardly be the first traveller in Africa to lose the plot completely. Sekwebu, one of Livingstone's most trusted companions on his traversa, suddenly went insane on reaching the east coast at Quelimane; though a strong swimmer, he deliberately drowned himself by pulling himself hand under hand along the anchor chain of the very ship waiting to take Livingstone back to England. Another tragic descent into madness right at the end of an epic journey was that of Safeni, coxswain of the *Lady Alice* on Stanley's first African crossing. Only two weeks away from their final destination on the west coast, many of Stanley's companions were literally dying of sickness and starvation, and without warning Safeni went insane. 'We have reached the sea!' he cried. 'We are home! We shall no more be tormented by empty stomachs and accursed savages!' Placing his beloved pet parrot on his shoulder, Safeni dashed off into the forest. A search party, its members themselves almost incapacitated by hunger, was unable to find him, and Safeni was never seen again.[3]

Two days after leaving Kilosa I reach the farming town of Morogoro, set at the foot of the blue Uluguru Mountains; in the cool early morning their peaks are still swathed in mist. During the First World War the Geman garrison of Morogoro finally retreated to these mountains after fierce fighting with the British forces – though not before they blew up their big ammunition dump. It's the last big town before the east coast, so I stop here to rest for a couple of days. I'm shocked when I see my reflection in a bathroom mirror: completely haggard, with sunken cheeks and dark rings under my eyes.

Only four days to the end now.

I'm tempted to start composing postcards to people back in England, but decide against it. It may prove a classic case of counting one's chickens before they've hatched. I finish when I finish, and not a moment before. The journey is over only when I dip my big toe in the lukewarm Indian Ocean.

I couldn't bear to be stopped now through illness. I've been getting increasingly paranoid about malaria, as there's a far greater risk of catching it during the rainy season. I'm also hearing lurid rumours that cholera has just broken out in Dar es Salaam, exactly where I'm heading. No one is yet sure of the extent, although one local man I talk to insists that people in the capital are going down like skittles.

Just four more days, that's all I ask – I don't much care what I catch after that, even Ebola. Right now the idea of being looked after by sympathetic nurses doesn't seem so bad after all. But I can't get the thought out of my head that soon I won't have to walk any further. Nothing matters after this. Reaching the coast is as far ahead as I can see – I deliberately don't want to think beyond the end of the journey. It's almost like being in love, when nothing exists beyond the one you love, when you have no plans except those involving them. It also makes me think of a long-term prisoner yearning for his release – but when the great day approaches anticipation is replaced largely by fear.

It seems absurd for me to try to convince myself that everything will be wonderful when I finish this journey – before I left England I persuaded myself that everything would be better when I got to Africa. I'm glad I have so many things to sort out when I return to England, even if most of them are problems. When I reach the east coast I'll certainly be able to rest – but I know with certainty that there's more *peace* while the journey continues, with a clear goal still ahead of me.

Meanwhile, the nearer I get to this goal the more difficult the final stretch becomes. The remaining 150 kilometres to the east coast suddenly feels a very long way. As a young child I once heard a story about a giant who offended an evil magician, who promptly put a spell on him; as the giant tried to return to his home, he found the more he walked towards his house the further away it seemed. As a child I found this such a terrifying image that I don't even remember the end of the story, having blotted it from memory completely. And now it's happening to me: the nearer I get to the east coast, the more difficult it is to carry on. I was not expecting to have to make some last supreme effort to even reach the coast before I collapsed, but this is what seems to be happening. It's as if I'm drowning within sight of the shore, and I've just realized why: my raison d'être for the entire last year is shortly to vanish forever.

Anything is possible at roadsides in Africa, with so many ancient vehicles hurtling past in a blur of scrap metal. Drunken driving is extremely common, especially in the afternoons and evenings and towards the end of the month with the arrival of pay day. African roads are the most dangerous in the world, with appalling fatality rates and many more people maimed in accidents. Just out of Morogoro I stop beside the road to fix my rucksack, facing the direction in which I've come. A bus races up behind me; as it passes, a young guy leans right out of the door and whacks my arse with a large stick.

'Come back here, you *FUCKER!*' I shout rather impotently after him as the bus speeds away, without much real hope that he'll return and do battle like a gentleman. After he's gone I have to admit that this was rather funny. But I'd recognize that laugh again anywhere …

Heading east of Morogoro, smoky clouds hang low over the hills, and the noise from insects and birds is terrific. Huge mango trees line the road, stretching their enormous dark branches into a powder-blue sky, offering the most tempting shade I've experienced in months. The woods behind them seem dense and primeval; from the road they resemble the emerald-green forest I once associated with Tarzan, although this is only a façade and they're not so large. They're actually shrinking at an alarming rate – deforestation has become a serious problem here, with around 4,000 square kilometres of Tanzania's woodland disappearing every year. The main cause is wholesale charcoal-burning, to meet the population's insatiable demands for cheap cooking fuel; it takes ten tonnes of raw wood to produce a single tonne of charcoal.

Environmental impact aside, the widespread use here of fuel wood and cow dung for cooking can bring sinister results. Regular use of these fuels often causes red, bloodshot eyes, which are sometimes taken as proof that a person is a witch. Hundreds of people, usually old women, are still murdered each year on suspicion of witchcraft, held responsible for deaths in the community and bewitching children. The killers often cut the left side of the head, shoulder and thigh; in some areas, the murders show such uniformity that the police suspect they're being carried out by a syndicate. Many Tanzanians – even those too embarrassed to admit it – still consult witch doctors; football players in particular often attribute poor form to the bad magic induced by a rival team's witchdoctor.

At one village restaurant I buy a sizeable measure of the local variety of Chibuku, here known as *mpata*. I share it with a middle-aged local man, who bears a strong resemblance to Chuck Berry. While we drink he clutches to his breast a small bag of tiny cassava branches he's cut down for transplanting. 'My friend, do you know the secret of successful cassava planting?' he suddenly demands, producing a cassava twig from his bag and waving it under my nose. I confess my ignorance and pour him some more *mpata*. 'Then, young man, I will tell you,' he continues. 'You must plant the cassava branches *the right way up*.'

I start encountering more and more Masai people, arguably the most visually striking of all the tribes in East Africa. They're usually extremely tidy and colourful in their dress, wearing their amazingly colourful beads and bright red togas on an everyday basis rather than merely dressing up for tourists. (Admittedly they've grown wise to their photogenic qualities, and usually ask for money if any foreigner wishes to take their picture.) Traditionally they believe the whole world's cattle belong to them; over the years they've had to make certain adjustments to this philosophy. Several historians believe the tribe is descended from the lost legion of Mark Antony, and there's even some evidence to support this curious theory. Their battle tactics are reminiscent of the Roman armies, and the traditional Masai stabbing sword bears some resemblance to the Roman *gladius*. Although the most ludicrously circumstantial of evidence, I can't help noticing a lot of Masai men wear white sandals with a broad strip of beads around their ankles, which makes their footwear look for all the world like Roman *caligulae*. The short Masai robe wouldn't look out of place in a gladiator movie, either. To me this all sounds a bit too H. Rider Haggard for plausibility, although without doubt the Masai have always had a warlike reputation – even the hard-bitten Stanley always gave them a wide berth, far out of proportion to the actual threat they posed to his heavily armed expeditions. Not so the peaceful Joseph Thomson, who no doubt wished he'd followed Stanley's example when Masai warriors forced him take his boots off and wiggle his toes, before pinching him repeatedly while trying to take his trousers down. Fortunately Thomson was less ready with his elephant gun than Stanley, and managed to avoid bloodshed by resorting to

Western magic, frothing Eno's fruit salts into a glass of water and whipping out his false teeth to general applause.

As I get nearer the coast the temperature and humidity soar. There's been no breeze at all for several days now – certainly no sign of the famous trade winds that brought the Arabs to the East African coast in the first place. The heat would be bearable with a breath of wind to accompany it, but without any breeze I'm constantly drenched in sweat. By now my shirt is so stinky I try washing it in a muddy pond beside the road; but despite the oppressive heat it simply won't dry in this humidity, and after hanging on a bush under the sun for nearly an hour it's just as wet when I put it on again. The only relief from the heat comes for an hour or two every afternoon when the heavens open in a torrential downpour.

The noise of frogs, birds and insects after heavy tropical rain is deafening, a surreal pulsating sound like something produced on a giant natural synthesizer. The frog chorus in particular is orchestral in scope, as though each frog has a different instrument and a different opinion, which is almost certainly the case; and the volume is extraordinary, almost Wagnerian. Livingstone recorded how once he was captivated by a tiny tree frog, a couple of centimetres long, which began 'a tune as loud as that of many birds, and very sweet; it was surprising to hear so much music out of so small a musician'.[4]

More sinister are the enormous science fiction snails lurking everywhere, brought out by the heavy rainfall. They look more like sea creatures than land snails, their shells the size of mangoes. Walking in twilight I try hard to avoid stepping on one of these monsters; they look as if they might attack me, even in their death throes. I've walked too far to succumb to giant snail attack at the eleventh hour – and I don't want the bloody things chasing me down the road either. I feel better disposed towards the thousands of fireflies beside the road at night; I'm completely alone, so it feels like a magic show solely for my benefit. Watching them weave and dance in the air before me, it's easy to see how people once believed in fairies and woodland sprites.

I squelch through a sodden field to pitch my tent, sinking with each step, my feet huge with mud. Inside my tent I collapse into a dull and dreamless sleep, while the frog chorus outside builds into a deep and thunderous pulse.

The heat on the penultimate day is terrible. By noon, cooling down assumes far greater urgency than ever before. I try everything short of stopping, from pouring stream water over my head to soaking my baseball cap in a stinking pond. Every time I rinse my face in a stream or puddle my eyes become alarmingly gummy; I'm worried the water is full of bilharzia, or some equally horrible fluke or microscopic life form. But I'd rather worry about some unpleasant infection or parasite in several weeks' time than collapse with heatstroke this minute.

To take my mind off the heat I try hard to imagine icy country roads back in England at this time of year, winter fields with frosty grass crunching underfoot like breakfast cereal, crisp cold air making my cheeks glow and searing my lungs. But the images I conjure have no substance, and soon I realize I'm well on the way to heatstroke. I stop for a few minutes beside a stream and close my eyes. The whole sky suddenly turns black, and the sun comes crashing down on my head. Completely dizzy and disorientated, I nearly fall headfirst into the stream – which would at least have cooled me down.

While I'm pouring hatfuls of water over the back of my neck, an army truck stops. A soldier sticks his head out of the driver's window to ask if I need help – seeing my olive green rucksack he obviously assumes I'm a colleague. I tell him I'm walking to the coast.

'And what connection do you have with Bagamoyo, my friend? You are in radio contact with the coast?'

Presumably everyone in his line of work relies on radio contact. I tell him that when I reach Bagamoyo it will be the first anyone knows about it. He seems to find this rather *irregular*, and drives off shaking his head.

By evening, I'm determined that the next day absolutely *must* be the last day of walking. So before I stop for the night I have to reach the turn-off to Bagamoyo, which means walking for over an hour and a half after dark. Walking at night here is terrible, worse than at almost any time before on the journey, the only light coming from fireflies or the occasional vehicle hurtling past with blinding headlights. For most of the time it's so dark I literally can't see anything beside the road, which makes avoiding traffic even more hazardous – several times I nearly break my ankle falling into potholes, and I can't see if I'm stepping into a field or on to a footpath or if there's just a big drop. And you never know what might jump out of the bushes at you.

Eventually I reach the large village of Mlandizi. I lurch into the nearest guesthouse, a converted brothel that apparently reverts to its former function around midnight. Perhaps because of this, the guest register is very discreet: many visiting Tanzanian men in transit have cryptically recorded their occupation as 'recluse' or 'peasant'. The cheap rates here have also attracted a large population of cockroaches and flying creatures. By now I should have learnt that spraying a room with insecticide only makes things worse; after a good blast of Doom, legions of furious creepy-crawlies appear. But at least the shower has running water; although the water is barely more than a cold trickle, it feels like the biggest luxury I've experienced in weeks.

The remainder of the evening is punctuated by tiny pops and fizzes as insects fly into the candle flame before spending the rest of the night buzzing and writhing in protracted death throes. So many horrible creatures crawl and fly around the room that all I can do is switch off the light and tell myself it's not happening. Such an attitude has proved disastrous before now – in the most unfortunate creepy-crawly episode from all the great expeditions, John Hanning Speke (the discoverer of the source of the White Nile) found his tent one night invaded by hundreds of black beetles. Because of their sheer numbers he decided to ignore them, until one of the creatures burrowed into his ear and drilled right through his tympanum; unable to persuade the beetle to leave voluntarily he was forced to stab it with a penknife blade, which left him permanently deaf in that ear.

But I'm so exhausted I sleep like a corpse. In the morning I leave a bag of popcorn for the maid busy sweeping all the used condoms out into the corridor, a task to rival that of Hercules cleaning out the Augean stables.

Immediately out of Mlandizi I ask directions from the only person around, a hatchet-faced local. 'I will be your guide,' he announces with a most unpleasant leer. 'There is a hidden left turn at the top of the hill which you must take to get to the sea.' This sounds like pure bullshit: we're still over thirty kilometres from the sea, and it's obvious that any left turn where he says would take me in the wrong direction completely. Also, I trust this fellow as far as I can throw him – he doesn't exactly look like a pillar of the community. I put on speed, leaving him behind. It amuses me that I've had so much practice walking with a heavy pack that I can still walk faster with it than most people I meet. Sure enough, at the top of the hill there's a small left turn, a little path leading straight into the woods, presumably where he intended to relieve me of my possessions. Bastard. But I'm in no mood to go back and give him a thick ear – on the last day of a very long journey I want to reach the ocean as soon as possible.

A few kilometres further east the road passes through woodland and leafy glades, affording a merciful degree of shade after the usual stretches of baking-hot road. Two hours later I rest under a tree outside a small village. Any snakes in the grass can piss off; I'm too tired to move. Within minutes a large and anxious crowd has gathered around me in silence. Thankfully, after some long and awkward moments, they prove friendly enough. 'We were afraid of you,' says one man, obviously the spokesman. 'We thought you might be an enemy, or perhaps that you were sick.'

'I'm nobody's enemy,' I tell him. 'I get on with everyone.' This may not be entirely true, but it results in everyone smiling happily, and the crowd melts away.

Entering the village, I stop for lunch in a tiny restaurant. I've just started on my *ugali* when a middle-aged fool puffs his way in, proclaiming himself the local Justice of the Peace, and demands to see my identification.

'May I ask why you want to see it?'

'Why? Because I am the Justice of the Peace! I have already informed you on this matter.' He seems to feel that not enough is being made of the occasion, and warms to his subject: 'These precautions are for your security! I must make these enquiries so I can tell the people on the road ahead, so they will know who you are.'

He can go and tell it on the mountain for all I care, if he'll leave me in peace while he's doing it. I'll be in Bagamoyo by nightfall, so he'll have to move fast if he wants to tell anyone en route I'm coming. God knows whom he plans to tell anyway – the only people who'd be interested in my progress would be the very people who'd like to rob me. I'm tired and want to be left alone, and if he doesn't leave me in peace to get on with my porridge there's a good chance he'll soon be wearing it.

'Perhaps we can discuss these security precautions later?' I ask politely.

'But I am a very busy man!' he cries. 'I am far too busy to discuss anything later!'

Fucking clot. The only way to get rid of him without him throwing his teddy in the corner is to do what he asks and show him my passport. After scrutinizing it for at least ten minutes, going through every page – even studying the blank ones from several angles – he finally makes his grand exit.

'That guy asked you a lot of questions, hey?' This new, friendlier speaker is a councillor of some kind – everyone at this tiny village seems to have an important-sounding job.

'Yes, he's crazy,' I answer wearily.

'You know, he calls himself a Justice of the Peace ... but really he's just a fool!'

I can't stop myself laughing out loud at this. At the same time I feel sorry for the guy who's just left, for the fact that he has to act like such a clown to try to gain some self-respect. But I move on quickly, in case he decides to dignify us with his presence once more. No doubt to this day he still bestrides the village like a colossus.

Night is falling when I reach the outskirts of Bagamoyo.

The town was once one of the most important in East Africa, with vast riches generated from slaves and ivory. Bagamoyo was where many of the great African journeys began or ended; it was from here that Stanley began his first traversa and ended his second. It was from here that Livingstone's body left Africa, bound for England and his state funeral in Westminster Abbey* More significantly, it was from here that hundreds of thousands of slaves left the African mainland forever, en route to Zanzibar and the East; its name means: 'Lay down your heart'.

Despite its historical importance, Bagamoyo today is little more than a scruffy, run-down fishing settlement, its buildings crumbling, the unpaved sandy streets in almost total darkness. Although it's where the journey ends, there's nothing here today to excite imagination, no streets paved with gold, no welcoming committee. I want a minimum of fuss on

*See p. 266.

arriving here – for once I don't mind in the least that I'm arriving at an African town under the cover of night and completely alone.

When I started out across Africa I imagined I wouldn't want cheering crowds at the end of it. It crossed my mind that perhaps I felt that way because I was at the start of the journey and I hadn't achieved anything yet – I might well change my views on this completely by the time I'd walked across a continent. But now I'm about to end the journey I'm even more certain that I don't want cheering crowds, or any journalist quizzing me about how I feel, in terms that would make good newspaper copy. Enough people seem to think you should end a long journey by running around the beach screaming, carrying on like someone who has just passed an audition for *The X Factor*. But instead, the moment feels more private than that.

I've toyed with the idea of going straight down to the ocean without delay, but suddenly I find I'm in no hurry after all. I'll walk the last hundred metres in the morning.

The town is extraordinarily quiet tonight. In the darkness I'll have to be careful where I'm walking, and to make sure I avoid the palm trees. After crossing a continent on foot I don't want to get killed now by a falling coconut – enough people die this way each year.

I check into a lodge close enough to the beach to hear the waves and smell the salt in the air but not so close as to see the ocean. I'm exhausted, but for one of the first times on the journey I can't get to sleep for ages. After the lack of comforts on the journey, the fan in my room is so powerful that I feel like I'm reclining on the deck of a speedboat. I'm almost afraid of sleeping, as though I'll never wake again. I can't expire now, so close to the end. But the ocean will wait until daylight. It's not going anywhere, and neither am I until morning.

The thought that the next day this whole long and arduous journey will be finished is almost bewildering. Arriving after dark has only heightened this sense of disorientation. Even though when I turn off the fan I can hear the ocean clearly, I can't quite believe that I'm finally here. And all the hardships of the last year are over, to be replaced by the comforts and ludicrous problems of life back in England again.

Success.

The Indian Ocean at last, having walked almost 5,000 kilometres to get here.

The day is overcast, surprisingly cool for the east coast of Africa. A gentle rain falls as I walk down to the water, more like a soft Irish drizzle than the drenching tropical downpours I've been experiencing inland. I really should take my rucksack down to the sea as I'd originally intended – the bloody thing has come all this way with me. And in spite of all the nasty things I've thought and said about it, my rucksack has done me proud. To leave it behind at this final moment of the journey feels like some small betrayal. But I'm too tired for sentiment; it can stay in my room and to hell with it. A large part of me never wants to go near another backpack as long as I live. Often on the journey I'd promised myself that when I reached the Indian Ocean I'd swap my rucksack for a crate of ale or something equally symbolic; if this proved unworkable I'd give it a Viking funeral by setting the bastard alight and pushing it out to sea. But I've no thought of doing this now. We've been through some trying times together, in sickness and in health. As a Victorian lady once remarked of the Bible, 'What a pity it couldn't end in a marriage.'

The ocean is as warm as milk. I'd forgotten you're far more buoyant in salt water than fresh, which is just as well: I'm so exhausted I haven't the strength to swim properly, and might otherwise have drowned. I sit wallowing with the sea up to my neck, like a half-starved dugong with nowhere to go.

I'm glad I'm not famous. There's no one to welcome me, yet I'm happy.

This is where I've wanted to be for so long.

17. A Man Unfit for Society
(Tanzania: Zanzibar)

Cheerfulness vanishes, and the whole mental horizon is overcast with black clouds of gloom and sadness. The liveliest joke cannot provoke even the semblance of a smile ... the few utterances are made in the piping voice of a wailing infant. At such times a man feels very much like a fool, if he does not act like one. Nothing is right, nothing pleases the fever-stricken victim. He is peevish, prone to find fault and to contradict, and think himself insulted, and is exactly what an Irish naval surgeon before a court-martial defined a drunken man to be: 'a man unfit for society'.

David Livingstone on malaria,
Expedition to the Zambesi

I check in at a cheap hotel in Zanzibar's Stone Town. I've been looking forward to spending a week or two here recuperating before the inevitable return to England, doing some normal tourist sightseeing for once – exploring its labyrinthine alleyways and Arab bazaars, fingering trinkets (or whatever one is supposed to do in Arab bazaars). But as it turns out I'm to see virtually nothing of these things. I'm very tired, and coming down with a heavy cold; I can't actually remember much between arriving at the east coast on foot at Bagamoyo several days ago and taking the ferry here. But I'm counting myself extremely fortunate, having walked across Africa without catching malaria, which was always going to be the biggest single threat to completing the whole journey. This is much better luck than all the odds suggested. True, I'm as thin as a rake, I've had giardiasis ever since crossing Caprivi, and my feet are still wrecked; otherwise, the sudden onset of a heavy cold seems a small price to pay for walking across a continent.

I decide to get an early night as this heavy cold is getting slightly worse, and there's no rush now for anything – I'm happy to potter around like an elderly person.

I wake up late the following morning dizzy and disorientated, with a headache so intense I'm convinced my skull has collided with a wrecking ball. A dozen Chibuku hangovers have crystallized into one ghastly sensation, until I remember I've been sober as a judge for the last week. The symptoms then start to change: one minute I'm frozen, the next racked with furious heat, while a burning icicle bores through my brain; my joints ache appallingly, and my lower spine feels ready to snap. I've barely the strength to lurch to the bathroom; before I throw up I notice my tongue is so thickly coated I could grow magic mushrooms on it. And for tropical Africa this sense of freezing cold is *unreal* – my teeth start chattering like one of those clockwork sets of joke dentures popular when I was a child.

I don't need three guesses as to what all this means. I drag myself to reception to ask if there's a doctor nearby. 'There is a clinic around the corner,' says the young Arab at the desk. Seeing the state I'm in – my teeth are still going at it like castanets – he looks concerned and adds politely: 'Do you think you can find it?'

I'm so spaced out I'd have trouble finding my own arse with both hands. But eventually I totter to the clinic, where a blood test confirms malaria.

After dosing myself with larium I feel progressively worse for the rest of the day, more and more out of it. Small problems cascade into monstrous doubt; mundane things blossom into horrors before slithering back together in a gradual connection of the senses. Self-pity out of nowhere has turned into an overwhelming force, and at one point I nearly start crying merely because my trousers are worn out and full of holes. Malaria has worked some strange inverse alchemy in which everything has turned to shit.

I can't face leaving my room, and I can't face staying here either. The pattern on the threadbare curtains blends into a kaleidoscopic swirl; twee clusters of bright pink roses turn into grinning piglets, gargoyles, Medusa heads, great smirking slavering hogs, while the walls ripple in silence with infinite menace. By evening I'm the sole passenger on a giant carousel, riding through the night sky like the Flying Dutchman, while discordant fairground music fills the air with raucous energy, accompanied relentlessly by great metallic clangs from some demented blacksmith's forge.

The ride finally over, throbbing pain still pulses through my head; I press my knuckles hard against my eyes and a million stars burn bright as phosphorus. All distinction between night and day breaks down; the darkness outside is filled with unearthly brightness, while lights in the narrow street outside finally reveal themselves *for what they really are*, malevolent staring eyes. Then a strange daylight breaks with fright-wigged witches floating dreamily across skies the colour of honey and blancmange into an endless African dawn.

I don't know how much of this is the malaria and how much the larium. Both can cause psychotic episodes, sometimes extreme, yet this knowledge makes it no less frightening – malaria has killed more people than any other disease in human history. I wish I wasn't alone and as weak as a kitten. With my eyes closed I've no idea if I'm lying in a guesthouse bed or still walking with a pack on my back – I don't know if I'm in Zanzibar or back in Windhoek Airport, if I'm about to leave Africa or just arriving. I've literally forgotten who I am and what I'm doing in this place, although some vague recollection of having just walked almost 5,000 kilometres to get here nags persistently, with a donkey, a couple of mules and a few strange characters involved at some distant stage a long time ago.

After a week of feeling *dreadful*, so wired on larium I don't know if I'm Arthur or Martha, I feel slightly better, or at least more rational. But ending the journey is accompanied instead by a deep, inexplicable melancholy, more profound than the effects of the malaria or larium. And it's not just because I have to return now to England. Many of the Victorian explorers experienced a similar thing, way beyond physical exhaustion or illness. Stanley recorded ending his greatest journeys in despair: 'When a man returns home and finds for the moment nothing to struggle against, the vast resolve, which has sustained him through a long and difficult enterprise, dies away, burning as it sinks in the heart.'[1] People back at home seem to think it almost mandatory that a huge journey like this should end in euphoria; but somehow the reality feels very different, and far removed from the ending of a novel or a Holly-wood movie.

On the flight back to London I overhear a group of four young backpackers in the next aisle discussing their travels. They've just 'done'

Tanzania and Kenya, and they're only sorry they didn't 'do' Malawi as well. Listening to them, rather than feeling smug, to my surprise I find myself wishing I felt as they did, that I could compartmentalize my own journey so easily – somehow I'd be happier now if I could say I'd 'done' Africa, or indeed anywhere else. But most of all I wish I was just setting out again, with all the uncertainties and hardships to come, but at the same time with the clearest goal ahead. Life was so much simpler on a linear journey, and I can't see anything so exciting waiting for me back in London. Yes, I can finally rest now, but I can't derive any pleasure from the fact that this journey is *finally over.*

But maybe that's still the malaria talking.

During the flight I find myself wondering whether anything will have changed back in England. I realize I'm in no hurry to find out, because I strongly suspect not. But looking back over the journey, I know in advance some things will never be quite the same again, the most obvious of these being:

Food Back at home, unless I develop an eating disorder I'll never again be able to eat with such *appetite.* Compared to walking forty or fifty kilometres a day with a heavy pack, I can think of nothing I could possibly do in London that would burn off so many calories each day with no thought of the consequences. For most of the journey across Africa I ate like a pig, at least whenever I could, and I still reached the east coast emaciated, with my trousers falling down, three and half stone lighter than when I started – and I wasn't exactly a tub of lard when I set out.

Sleep I'll never be able to sleep so *soundly* again as I did in Africa, when at the end of each day I was dead beat. Instead I'm more likely to spend sleepless nights worrying about trivial crap again, things I'd forgotten out in the African bush. Back in London, if I'd known with certainty there was a large spider in my bedroom I'd never have been able to get to sleep anyway – obviously this changed quickly in Africa, but I'm sure I'll soon be back to the way I was before …

Distance I'll have to take on my old perceptions of distance again – the idea that London to Cardiff is a bloody long way rather than the distance

259

I have to walk in the next five days. Everything in Africa is on such a large scale compared to England, but in Africa I had no problem with being an ant-sized speck on the map – this was far outweighed by the extra room to breathe, spiritually as well as literally. Back in England it will be a disaster again if I miss the bus and have to walk four miles home in the rain.

Time I'm returning to the usual obsession with time, letting my life be ruled by clocks and by other people's ideas of how I should spend my waking hours. On reaching the east coast at Bagamoyo I checked my watch against a clock for the first time in several months: my watch had been at least an hour wrong ever since I left Malawi (which is on Central African Time) and I hadn't even noticed.

Hospitality No surprises here, but London doesn't compare well. I'll also miss that strange phenomenon on the road where you can sometimes share far greater confidences with a comparative stranger than with friends of long standing back at home.

But it's not all bad news:

Personal hygiene I couldn't continue as I was out in the bush – things were not good.

Books After so long on the road I'll once again be spoilt for choice in reading matter. I'll be able to keep every book I read in one piece, rather than saving weight by periodically ripping out pages one at a time and then using them for a purpose which the author wouldn't expect from even the harshest critic.

On the flight home I start anticipating the inevitable question: 'So why did you do it?' 'Because it's there' won't wash as an honest response. When the going got very tough I often wished I could define my motivation to walk across Africa as easily as Grogan did, and with such a tangible goal: he wanted to get the girl. But, like Grogan's adventure, in many ways the whole journey was an extremely self-indulgent episode, literally an escape. Many people – including myself when I can afford to

260

– like to travel abroad partly to indulge themselves in treats and comforts and comparative luxury. Instead I indulged myself in hardships, although this is not the same thing as masochism. The hardships actually proved a liberating experience, and all the clichés about the rewards of toil (which back at home I sensibly dismissed as bullshit) seemed curiously to have come true in Africa. No matter how hard things got on the journey, after all the backbreaking work I'd put in I always felt a sense of having somehow *earned the right to be there*. Pompous, certainly, but at the same time something I've never felt before or since, when I've been sitting on a tourist bus, or stuck at home twiddling my thumbs, or boozing it up in some bar in Chiang Mai.

In essence, the journey was nothing more than a simple desire for adventure, or at least the kind of adventure that seemed in short supply back in Wimbledon. The scale of Africa seemed to afford more opportunities for this than the quiet London suburbs. Having said that, enough people travelling in exotic places these days simply do the same thing everywhere they visit; but by crossing a continent on foot you must experience at least *something* adventurous, a radical change from the life you left behind to do it. I've often thought, 'Can't adventure speak for itself?' I imagine that every time a mountaineer climbs a difficult peak the one question they emphatically won't hear from fellow mountaineers is: '*Why* did you do it?'

Curiously, the very difficulties, obstacles and scale of a long and arduous journey can make the whole thing easier and more straightforward than a minor undertaking. Doing something on a grand scale simply has to bring out far more commitment and determination in yourself, as you have no choice. If you can't find those things within yourself then you literally won't be able to do it – there's nothing like lack of options to bolster one's dedication to the task in hand. Back at home it seemed far too easy to go through life without ever having to draw on that level of commitment to *anything*. And it was so bloody difficult for me to get to Africa in the first place – if I'd been able to go out there at the drop of a hat with no worries about money or anything else, I suspect I might well have quit just as easily when the going got tough.

Travelling entirely on foot brought me in some ways closer to the local people; and because I wasn't going out of my way to take in scenic routes or visit tourist sights, I often passed through places where most Westerners wouldn't even bother stopping; for all the grandeur of sights like Victoria Falls, often the most interesting places were those with no obvious attraction to any visitor, and where the locals were even kinder and more hospitable than usual in Africa. On the other hand, perhaps my biggest regret is that owing to the rigours, discipline and ground rules of the whole journey, in some ways I was there to do a job, being completely focused on getting from A to B before I collapsed.

And ultimately, no matter how 'un-touristic' my approach, I was still always there as a European, with a Westerner's perspectives and prejudices about what I saw and experienced. I'm hardly the first person to swap the frustrations and predictability of life in England for the dubious idea that one will somehow be *more oneself* in an adventurous, challenging situation in a distant land. But in moments of self-doubt since returning I've wondered if every journey like this must always involve some subconscious degree of 'using' Africa or the Himalayas or wherever as a vast, exotic playground in which to act out some dodgy, rather juvenile Western fantasies of action and adventure, a self-imposed initiation rite to prove that one is somehow *special*.

It's easy in hindsight (and from the comfort of home) to assign these motives to historical figures like the Victorian explorers, but is there also something of this in one's own motives, however unconscious? If so, this is hardly a more evolved viewpoint than that of a young child reading trashy Tarzan comics in hospital and wishing he were somewhere far away. In Africa I certainly met enough Westerners travelling who were actively searching for some liberating experience far removed from the daily grind back at home. But perhaps it's really no more complicated than someone innocently enjoying a holiday abroad – especially holidays involving 'adventure sports' or 'going on safari'. I'm still pondering that one. At least on the journey itself any doubts on this score were offset by the fact that virtually all the Africans I met, black and white, seemed genuinely delighted with the idea of what I was doing.

Whatever the truth of the matter, I felt I'd gained a great deal of experience by travelling exactly as I did. But it also meant missing out on many things too, sometimes ignoring interesting things because of the physical demands of the journey: walking forty or fifty kilometres in a day is not so difficult if you're fit and determined, it's carrying a bloody great pack in the African heat that is so exhausting. The sheer focus required to travel like this can blinker your vision; although I was moving slowly on foot, in order to cover huge distances while the meagre funds lasted I was almost constantly *moving*, with little time to pause and absorb things as much as I would have liked to. Travelling alone on foot for huge distances and sleeping rough can actually be much less stressful than 'normal' travel – for example, no transport connections or accommodation arrangements to make – but the downside is the gruelling physical work month after month.

Since returning to England I've wondered if one day I should make a similar journey in Africa again, following the same route but this time taking transport and doing it in comparative comfort, without the need to push myself forwards relentlessly each day. By doing so I could experience a lot I missed out on first time round because I was exhausted or ill, or just bloody-minded and had another twenty kilometres to walk that day before I could lie down and *sleep*. For much of the time I was in Africa I was absolutely knackered, too dead beat to solve any problem more complex than where to find food or pitch my tent unobserved for the night. But the biggest and most personal reason not to do it again would be this: if I ever repeated this journey in comfort it would somehow always be a ghostly poor relation, and I would never feel so alive as I did that first time.

But one can analyse these things *ad infinitum*. There is something about walking across Africa alien to the idea of ending the journey with a 'What's it all about, Alfie?' moment or a Shakespeare-style soliloquy. Overall I'm very happy with the way it all went. The journey was what it was, no more and no less, and it was enough. There is still great pleasure in doing something difficult and audacious; and so much of the journey was enjoyable and worth experiencing, even the balls-ups. The trip was important to me, and I'm still proud of having done it.

I'm glad I wrote it down as it happened.

Afterword: The Explorers

> To talk of Africa having been 'opened up' by the passing through it
> of [the explorers] is to talk of a large pumpkin being opened up by
> the passing through it of a fine needle.
>
> Alexander Mackay, Victorian missionary

While Africa certainly isn't any different in the slightest for my having
crossed it on foot, the tangible results of even the great expeditions were
often debatable, or in many cases largely negative. Men like Livingstone
and Stanley were not the first individuals to cross Africa overland, but
for better or worse they did succeed in bringing Africa into Western
perception more than anyone had done before them. But even when
regarded simply as pathfinders, they will always be associated to some
degree with the imperialism that followed them in what became the
colonial 'Scramble for Africa' – even altrusitic men like Livingstone who
had no intention of seeing large portions of Africa carved up for
European exploitation.

Graham Greene thought Africa would always be the dark unexplored
continent of the Victorian atlas, but few Africans today would share that
view – and to me it makes as much sense as claiming that England is still
the land of Ancient Britons and Boadicea. But I think it's a mistake to
assume that there was never even a grain of truth in the European myth
of the 'Dark Continent' – not so much in terms of the historical impact
the explorers had on Africa, but in the effect their extraordinary adven-
tures in Africa had on *them*.

Grogan remarked that had it not been for his African trek he would
have remained an aimless young man wandering around Piccadilly
worrying about his tie. He certainly got the girl, and later he went on to
become one of the principal figures in Kenyan politics.

Less happy was Stanley's experience. His two epic trans-African expeditions proved him to be the greatest explorer of his age, and literally no
other individual in the whole Victorian era rose so high from such

humble origins. But a knighthood and all the lionizing he received still paled beside the crippling loneliness that had driven the former workhouse boy to such extreme endeavours in the first place – the crushing rejections of Stanley's appalling childhood had wounded him beyond redemption. After his 1887–89 traversa the prematurely aged Stanley never returned to Africa, and to this day he has been regarded as a highly controversial figure.

But the most poignant end of all the explorers was that of Livingstone. He spent his final years in a doomed quest to find the source of the Nile, convinced from classical sources that the river sprang from the mythical Four Fountains of Herodotus located somewhere deep in the unexplored African wilderness. Wandering hopelessly off-course, had he lived he would have faced yet another crushing disappointment. Desperately ill, he was by this stage accompanied by only a handful of native companions who felt somehow unable to abandon this lonely, driven man. In April 1873 his wanderings finally ground to a halt in a remote Zambian village. As he lay dying of dysentery, unable to walk and in agony from a massive blood clot in his stomach, Livingstone retained his sense of humour to the end, remarking wryly in his journal: 'It is not all pleasure this exploration.'

Livingstone died without knowing his last great dream was another empty chimera. Chuma and Susi, his two most loyal companions in his final years, buried his heart under a tree and then in one of the most remarkable journeys in African history carried the old explorer's body 2,000 kilometres through hostile country to the east coast. For all Livingstone's failings this remains a fitting tribute to the respect he'd won from Africans. Unfortunately, on arriving at Bagamoyo with Livingstone's body Chuma and Susi 'were so far frowned out of notice that not so much as a passage to the island was offered them when their burden was borne away'.[1] From here Livingstone's corpse was taken to Zanzibar, then back to England; his state funeral in Westminster Abbey was regarded by the vast crowd present as the event of the decade – a 'Diana Moment' in the national psyche. Rightly or wrongly, Chuma and Susi's final act of loyalty did more than anything to cement Livingstone's reputation for many years as an almost saintly figure in African history.

Through many bitter disappointments in his life Livingstone learnt the hard way of his shortcomings as an explorer. But lost in the African interior he was never to learn of his greatest triumph – largely as a result of his work, the month before he died the Zanzibar slave trade was finally abolished.

Notes

1. Darkest Wimbledon

1. Tim Jeal, *Stanley*, London 2007, p. 217.
2. Charles Miller, *The Lunatic Express*, New York 1971, p.158.

2. The Skeleton Coast

1. David Livingstone, *Expedition to the Zambesi*, London 1865, p. 427.
2. *Namibia Insight Guide*, London 1996, p. 26.
3. Ibid., pp. 82-3 .
4. David Livingstone, *Missionary Travels*, London 1857, p. 590.
5. Peter Forbath, *The River Congo*, London 1978, pp. 44-55.
6. Frank McLynn, *Hearts of Darkness*, London 1992, p. 6.
7. Bartle Bull, *Safari: A Chronicle of Adventure*, London 1988, p. 277; *Namibia Insight Guide*, p. 122; and Jan Knappert, *African Mythology*, London 1990, p. 113.
8. McLynn, *Hearts of Darkness*, p. 136.

3. Into the Desert

1. Frank McLynn, *Hearts of Darkness*, London 1992, p. 141.
2. Bartle Bull, *Safari: A Chronicle of Adventure*, London 1988, p. 31.
3. McLynn, *Hearts of Darkness*, p. 43.

4. Where You Get Stuck

1. See Francis Galton, *The Narrative of an Explorer in Tropical South Africa*, London 1853.
2. Frank McLynn, *Hearts of Darkness*, London 1992, p. 133.
3. Edward Paice, *Lost Lion of Empire*, London 2001, p. 116.

6. The Waterberg Plateau

1. David Livingstone, *Private Journals, 1851–1853*, ed. by Isaac Schapera, 2 vols, London 1963, p. 169; see also David Livingstone, *Missionary Travels*, London 1857, p. 192.
2. H. Witbooi letter to Kamaherero, 30th May 1890, quoted in Nangolo Mbumba and Norbert H. Noisser, *Namibia in History*, London 1988, p. 141.
3. See Mbumba and Noisser, *Namibia in History*.
4. Quoted in Mbumba and Noisser, *Namibia in History*.
5. See Thomas Packenham, *The Scramble for Africa*, London 1991, pp.610-11.
6. See I. Goldblatt, *A History of South-West Africa from the Beginning of the Nineteenth Century*, Cape Town 1971.
7. For the history of the Herero and Nama revolts, see Goldblatt, *A History of South-West Africa*; Mbumba and Noisser, *Namibia in History*; and Packenham, *The Scramble for Africa*.

7. Squashed Snakes and Cold Ditches

1. Nick Santcross, Gordon Baker and Sebastian Ballard, *Namibia*, Bath 2001, pp. 349–50.
2. Hahn's diary quoted in I. Goldblatt, *A History of South-West Africa from the Beginning of the Nineteenth Century*, Cape Town 1971.
3. David Livingstone, *Private Journals, 1851–1853*, ed. by Isaac Schapera, 2 vols, London 1963, p.169.
4. David Livingstone, *Missionary Travels*, London 1857, p.187.
5. Tim Jeal, *Livingstone*, London 1973, p. 146.

8. Lion Country

1. See Kenneth M. Cameron, *Into Africa: The Story of the East African Safari*, London 1990.
2. David Livingstone, *Expedition to the Zambesi*, London 1865, pp. 159–60.
3. Bartle Bull, *Safari: A Chronicle of Adventure*, London 1988, p.77.
4. Jan Knappert, *African Mythology*, London 1990, p. 142.
5. David Livingstone, *Expedition to the Zambesi*, p. 123.
6. Bull, *Safari*, p. 188; see also Cameron, *Into Africa*
7. Quoted in Frank McLynn, *Hearts of Darkness*, London 1992, p. 281.
8. Bull, *Safari*, p. 25.
9. David Livingstone, *The Last Journals of David Livingstone*, Westport, CT, 1970, vol. 2, pp. 206–8; and *Missionary Travels*, London 1857, p. 232 .
10. Bull, *Safari*, p. 115 .
11. Livingstone, *Missionary Travels*, p. 171.
12. Ibid., p. 143.
13. Francis Galton, *The Art of Travel*, London 1872, p. 21.
14. See Leda Farrant, *The Legendary Grogan*, London 1981.
15. Quoted in McLynn, *Hearts of Darkness*, p. 137.
16. Galton, *The Art of Travel*, London 1872, p. 15.

9. Tales from the Zambezi

1. See Michael Main, *Zambezi: Journal of a River*, Johannesburg 1990.
2. Livingstone's journal entry for 4 August 1851.
3. Letter, DL to Charles Livingstone, quoted in Tim Jeal, *Livingstone*, London 1973, p. 100.
4. David Livingstone, *Missionary Travels*, London 1857, pp. 352–3.
5. Ibid., p. 254.
6. See Mary Kingsley, *Travels in West Africa*, London 1897.
7. Livingstone, *Missionary Travels*, pp. 276 and 551.

10. Hunger March

1. David Livingstone, *Expedition to the Zambesi*, London 1865, p. 408.
2. See Jan and Fiona Teede, *The Zambezi: River of the Gods*, London 1990.
3. Ibid.
4. David Livingstone, *Missionary Travels*, London 1857, p. 523.
5. Ibid., p. 591; and *Expedition to the Zambesi*, p. 193.
6. Frank McLynn, *Hearts of Darkness*, London 1992, p. 229.
7. Livingstone, *Missionary Travels*, pp. 195 and 296.
8. Charles Miller, *The Lunatic Express*, New York 1971, p. 55.

9. David Livingstone, *The Last Journals of David Livingstone*, Westport, CT 1970, vol. 2, pp. 117–18.
10. Livingstone, *Expedition to the Zambesi*, p. 201.
1. See Francis Galton, *The Narrative of an Explorer in Tropical South Africa*, London 1853.
12. Livingstone, *Missionary Travels*, p. 499.
13. Ibid., p. 540–1; and *Expedition to the Zambesi*, pp. 214–5.

11. The Joys of Chibuku

1. Francis Galton, *The Art of Travel*, London 1872, p. 19.
2. Jan Knappert, *African Mythology*, London 1990, p. 91.
3. David Livingstone, *Expedition to the Zambesi*, London 1865, p 179.
4. David Livingstone, *Missionary Travels*, London 1857, p. 452.
5. Knappert, *African Mythology*, p. 77.

12. Crossing the Luangwa

1. David Livingstone, *Missionary Travels*, London 1857, pp. 230–1.
2. Jan Knappert, *African Mythology*, London 1990, p. 175.
3. David Livingstone, *Expedition to the Zambesi*, London 1865, pp. 129–30.
4. Ibid., p. 246.
5. Livingstone, *Missionary Travels*, p. 288.
6. Francis Galton, *The Art of Travel*, London 1872, p. 130.
7. Livingstone, *Missionary Travels*, p. 131.
8. Ibid., p. 585.
9. David Livingstone, *Livingstone's African Journal, 1853–1856*, vol. 2, London 1963, p. 374.
10. Ibid., p. 373.
11. Letter from DL to his parents, 30.9.53 in David Livingstone, *Family Letters 1841–1856*, 2 vols, London 1959, vol. 2, p. 228.
12. Livingstone, *Expedition to the Zambesi*, pp. 151–2.
13. Knappert, *African Mythology*, p. 121.
14. Livingstone, *Missionary Travels*, p. 430.
15. Frank McLynn, *Hearts of Darkness*, London 1992, p. 298.
16. Livingstone, *Expedition to the Zambesi*, p. 136.
17. Livingstone, *Missionary Travels*, pp. 551–2.
18. Ibid., pp. 246 and 601.
19. Livingstone, *Expedition to the Zambesi*, p. 94.
20. Oliver Ransford, *Livingstone's Lake*, London 1966, p. 111.
21. Livingstone, *Missionary Travels*, pp. 275 and 289.
22. Ibid., p. 368.

13. The Lake of Stars

1. David Livingstone, *Missionary Travels*, London 1857, p. 255.
2. Livingstone, *Missionary Travels*, Ibid p. 411.
3. David Livingstone, *Expedition to the Zambesi*, London 1865, p. 111.
4. Livingstone, *Missionary Travels*, p. 132.
5. Livingstone, *Expedition to the Zambesi*, pp. 66.
6. Livingstone, *Expedition to the Zambesi*, p. 138.
7. Quoted in Oliver Ransford, *Livingstone's Lake*, London 1966, p. 110.

8. For the history of Lake Malawi from the pygmy age to Livingstone's arrival, see Ransford, *Livingstone's Lake*, pp. 11–63.
9. Quoted in Ransford, *Livingstone's Lake*, p. 112.
10. David Livingstone, *The Last Journals of David Livingstone*, Westport, CT 1970, vol. 2, p. 212.
11. Quoted in Ransford, *Livingstone's Lake*, p. 160.
12. New York Herald, 24 Dec 1874, quoted in Frank McLynn, *Stanley: The Making of an African Explorer*, London 1989, pp. 240–41.
13. H.M. Stanley, *The Autobiography of Sir Henry Morton Stanley*, Santa Barbara, CA 2001, p. 9.
14. Quoted in Beau Riffenburgh, *The Myth Of The Explorer*, London 1993.
15. Livingstone, *Expedition to the Zambesi*, p. 258.

14. Kombwe Lagoon

1. Jan Knappert, *African Mythology*, London 1990, p. 55.
2. See Leda Farrant, *The Legendary Grogan*, London 1981.
3. Quoted in Oliver Ransford, *Livingstone's Lake*, London 1966, p. 151.
4. For a full account of the massacre at Kombwe and Mlozi's war with the British, see Oliver Ransford, *Livingstone's Lake*, London 1966, pp. 151–205; and Charles Miller, *The Lunatic Express*, New York 1971, pp. 202–06.

15. To Go With Ghosts

1. Jan Knappert, *African Mythology*, London 1990, p. 96.
2. For a full account of the Hehe revolt, See Andrew Roberts, ed., *Tanzania Before 1900*, Nairobi 1968; and Judith Listowel, *The Making of Tanganyika*, London 1965.
3. Knappert, *African Mythology*, p. 36.

16. The Boundless Ocean

1. See Michael Main, *Zambezi: Journal of a River*, Johannesburg 1990.
2. *Livingstone's Private Journals, 1851–1853*, ed. by Isaac Schapera, London 1960, entry for June 12 1851.
3. See H.M. Stanley, *Through the Dark Continent*, vol. 2, London 1878, p. 335.
4. David Livingstone, *The Last Journals of David Livingstone*, Westport, CT 1970, vol. 2, p. 42.

17. A Man Unfit for Society

1. Quoted in Christopher Hibbert, *Africa Explored*, London 1982.

Afterword

1. David Livingstone, *The Last Journals of David Livingstone*, Westport, CT 1970, vol. 2, p. 344.

Bibliography

Primary Sources

Galton, Francis, *The Narrative of an Explorer in Tropical South Africa* (John Murray, 1853).
—*The Art of Travel* (John Murray, 1872).
Grogan, Ewart, *From The Cape to Cairo* (Thomas Nelson, 1900).
Livingstone, David, *Family Letters 1841–1856*, 2 vols (Chatto & Windus, 1959).
—*Livingstone's Private Journals, 1851–1853*, ed. by Isaac Schapera (Chatto & Windus, 1960).
—*Livingstone's African Journal, 1853–1856*, ed. by Isaac Schapera, 2 vols (Chatto & Windus, 1963).
—*Missionary Travels and Researches in South Africa, etc.* (John Murray, 1857).
—*Narrative of an Expedition to the Zambesi, etc.* (John Murray, 1865).
—*The Last Journals of David Livingstone in Central Africa, etc.* ed. by H. Waller (Greenwood Press, 1970; originally published by John Murray, 1874).
Stanley, Henry Morton, *How I Found Livingstone in Central Africa* (Sampson Low, Marston and Company, 1872).
—*Through the Dark Continent*, 2 vols (Sampson Low, Marston and Company, 1878).
—*In Darkest Africa*, 2 vols (Sampson Low, Marston and Company, 1890).
—*The Autobiography of Sir Henry Morton Stanley* (The Narrative Press, 2001; first published by Sampson Low, Marston and Company, 1909).

Secondary Sources

Bierman, John, *Dark Safari: The Life behind the Legend of Henry Morton Stanley* (Alfred A. Knopf, Inc., 1990).
Bull, Bartle, *Safari: A Chronicle of Adventure* (Viking, 1988).
Cameron, Kenneth M., *Into Africa: The Story of the East African Safari* (Constable & Company Ltd, 1990).
Farrant, Leda, *The Legendary Grogan* (Hamish Hamilton, 1981).
Forbath, Peter, *The River Congo* (Secker and Warburg, 1978).
Goldblatt, I., *A History of South-West Africa from the Beginning of the Nineteenth Century* (Juta and Company, 1971).
Gruesser, John Cullen, *White on Black: Contemporary Literature about Africa* (University of Illinois Press, 1992).
Hall, Richard, *Stanley: An Adventurer Explored* (William Collins Sons & Co Ltd, 1974).
—*Zambia* (Frederick A. Praeger, 1965).
Hibbert, Christopher, *Africa Explored* (Allen Lane, 1982).
Jeal, Tim, *Livingstone* (William Heinemann, 1973).
—*Stanley* (Faber and Faber, 2007).
Kingsley, Mary, *Travels in West Africa* (Macmillan, 1897).

Bibliography

Knappert, Jan, *African Mythology* (Diamond Books, 1990).
—*Myths and Legends of the Swahili* (Heinemann Educational Books, 1970).
Listowel, Judith, *The Making of Tanganyika* (Chatto & Windus, 1965).
—*The Other Livingstone* (Julian Friedmann Publishers Ltd, 1974).
Else, David, *et al.*, *Africa on a Shoestring* (Lonely Planet Publications Pty Ltd, 2004).
Main, Michael, *Zambezi: Journal of a River* (Southern Book Publishers Pty Ltd, 1990).
Mbumba, Nangolo and Noisser, Norbert H., *Namibia in History* (Zed Books Ltd, 1988).
Macnair, James, *Livingstone the Liberator: A Study of a Dynamic Personality* (Collins, 1940).
McLynn, Frank, *Hearts of Darkness* (Hutchinson, 1992).
—*Stanley: The Making of an African Explorer* (Constable and Company Limited, 1989).
—*Stanley: Sorcerer's Apprentice* (Constable and Company Limited, 1991).
Miller, Charles, *The Lunatic Express* (Macmillan, 1971).
Namibia Insight Guide (APA Publications Ltd, 1996).
Omer-Cooper, J.D., *History of Southern Africa* (James Currey, 1987).
Packenham, Thomas, *The Scramble for Africa* (Weidenfeld & Nicolson, 1991).
Paice, Edward, *Lost Lion of Empire* (HarperCollins, 2001).
Ransford, Oliver, *David Livingstone: The Dark Interior* (John Murray, 1978).
—*Livingstone's Lake* (John Murray, 1966).
Riffenburgh, Beau, *The Myth of the Explorer* (Belhaven Press, 1993).
Roberts, Andrew, *A History of Zambia* (Heinemann, 1976).
Roberts, Andrew (ed.), *Tanzania Before 1900* (East African Publishing House, 1968).
Room, Adrian, *African Placenames: Origins and Meanings etc.* (McFarland & Company, 1994)
Santcross, Nick, Baker, Gordon and Ballard, Sebastian, *Namibia* (Footprint Handbooks, 2001).
Severin, Timothy, *The African Adventure* (Hamish Hamilton, 1973).
Stevenson, Robert Louis, *Travels with a Donkey* (Kegan Paul & Co., 1879).
Teede, Jan and Fiona, *The Zambezi – River of the Gods* (Andre Deutsch, 1990).

TRAVERSA
TRANS-AFRICA WALK

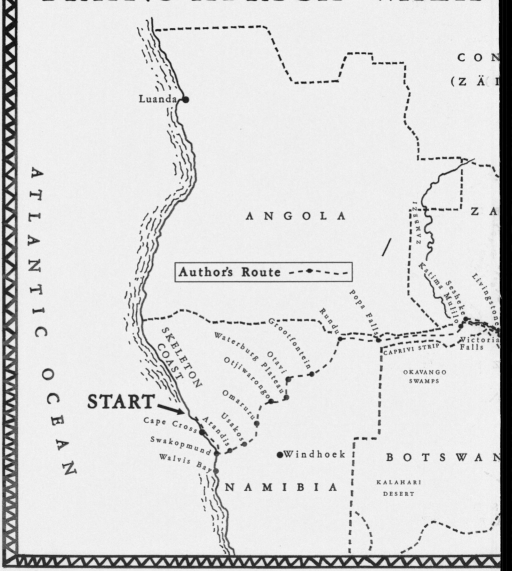

CON
(ZÄ

Luanda

ANGOLA

ZA

ZAMBEZI

Katima Mulilo

Livingstone

Author's Route ···•··

SKELETON COAST

Waterburg Plateau

Popa Falls

Rundu

Grootfontein

Otavi

Otjiwarongo

Seshek

Victoria
Falls

CAPRIVI STRIP

OKAVANGO
SWAMPS

START

Omaruru

Cape Cross   Arandis

Usakos

Swakopmund

Walvis Bay

Windhoek

BOTSWAN

NAMIBIA

KALAHARI
DESERT

ATLANTIC OCEAN